BOCA ROCOCO

Addison Mizner

BOCA ROCOCO

HOW ADDISON MIZNER

INVENTED FLORIDA'S

GOLD COAST

CAROLINE SEEBOHM

CLARKSON POTTER / PUBLISHERS

NEW YORK

OPENING PAGE: Design for the Ritz-Carlton Hotel, Boca Raton.
(COURTESY OF THE KIM MIZNER HOLLINS FAMILY)

FRONTISPIECE: Portrait of Addison Mizner.
(COURTESY OF THE KIM MIZNER HOLLINS FAMILY)

TITLE PAGE: Sketch for an occasional table.
(COURTESY OF THE KIM MIZNER HOLLINS FAMILY)

Published by Clarkson Potter/Publishers, New York, New York.
Member of the Crown Publishing Group.

Random House, Inc. New York, Toronto, London, Sydney, Auckland
www.randomhouse.com

CLARKSON N. POTTER, POTTER, and colophon are trademarks of
Random House, Inc.
Printed in the United States of America

Design by Marysarah Quinn

Library of Congress Cataloging-in-Publication Data
Seebohm, Caroline.
    Boca Rococo : how Addison Mizner invented Florida's gold coast /
by Caroline Seebohm.
        p. cm.
    1. Mizner, Addison, 1872–1933. 2. Architects—Florida—
Biography. 3. Architecture, Modern—20th century—Florida.
I. Title.

NA737.M59 S44 2001
720'.92—dc21

                                                        00-066886

                ISBN 0-609-60515-1

        10 9 8 7 6 5 4 3 2 1

                First Edition

TO THE MEMORY OF

MADENA GALLOWAY NELRICH

AND HER SISTER,

BEATRICE GALLOWAY BARDEL

ACKNOWLEDGMENTS

The inspiration for this book originated with the discovery, revealed to me by my friends Bill and Penny Bardel, of a hitherto unknown archive of Addison Mizner's papers. They were in the possession of Bill's mother, the late Beatrice Bardel, who graciously allowed me to examine the many envelopes and folders of materials that she had been looking after since the death of her sister, Madena Galloway Nelrich, Mizner's last secretary. The Bardel family, including Bill and Penny's son and daughter, Kate and Will, not only helped me sort through the materials and supported me during the writing of the book, but also allowed me to keep the archive in my house, an act of trust any biographer would kill for. Without the Bardels, this book would not have been written, and I am deeply indebted to them all.

The other family critical to the existence of this book is, of course, the Mizner family. The heirs of Kim Mizner Hollins, only child of Addison Mizner's niece, Ysabel, granted me permission to publish anything I wanted from the Madena Galloway Nelrich archive. It was a wonderful gift, and I am deeply grateful for their act of generosity.

It can be tricky when someone else has already written about one's biographical subject, particularly when the published work is good. I admire very much historian Donald W. Curl's architectural biography, *Mizner's Florida: American Resort Architecture,* but I admire Dr. Curl even more for welcoming me so generously to his professional and literary fiefdom. He told me what he knew, pointed me to people, places, and publications I might not otherwise know about, and talked to me informally about Addison Mizner's life and work. I could not have written *Boca Rococo* without Donn's help. His book made my work far easier, and I cannot thank him enough for giving me his time and unstinting support during these years.

Various librarians and curators shared their files, knowledge, and expertise with me. I should like particularly to thank Debi Murray of the Historical Society of Palm Beach County, who, in the midst of many organizational changes in her office, tolerated my frequent visits with patience and enthusiasm, bringing me files and finding elusive documents above and beyond the call of duty. At the Society of the Four Arts in Palm Beach, Joanne Rendon allowed me to study and photograph Addison Mizner's scrapbooks at my leisure. Nila Bent worked the recalcitrant Xerox machine there with impressive skill. Diane Curry at the Oakland Museum of California gave me a full day of her time, carrying the many Mizner files to and from my desk without complaint and often made very useful suggestions. Peggy McCall at the Boca Raton Historical Society provided me with files and space and tireless help. Paul Miller at the Preservation Society of Newport County pointed me to relevant material and pursued leads for me. Janet Parks directed me to the Stanford White holdings at the Avery Architectural and Fine Arts Library of Columbia University, and willingly answered follow-up questions. Anne Odom at Hillwood Museum and Gardens in Washington, D.C., Paul Husbands at the Rare Book, Manuscript and Special Collections Library of Duke University, and A. J. Polkark, Shepherd of the Lambs' Club in New York, kindly looked up information for me. Mark Horowitz, music specialist at the Library of Congress in Washington, D.C., answered my inquiries concerning Irving Berlin's friendship with Addison Mizner. Christina Orr-Cahall, director of the Norton Museum of Art in West Palm Beach and exhibition curator of "The Many Mizners," is one of the most knowledgeable people on Mizner lore, and I am grateful for her help. The public libraries of New York, West Palm Beach, and Benicia were all useful resources.

In California, Judy Nelson at the Solano County Archives and Nancy Morebeck, Margaret Karnath, Harley Wilson, and Ruth Setterquist at the Solano County Genealogical Society opened their files and shared their knowledge with me about the Mizner family's West Coast origins. I owe special thanks to Harry Wassmann, volunteer curator at the Benicia Historical Museum and Cultural Foundation, who not only drove me around Benicia and pointed out all the important landmarks, but also clarified several confusing issues, taking photographs and making notes that proved invaluable.

During my research, I also received help, ideas, and even a bed for the night from various friends, colleagues, advisers, and professionals. They include: Mary Ellin Barrett, Thomas Bollay, Randall Bourscheidt, Morley Clark, Barbara Davidson, Frederick L. Eckel, Edith Eglin, Tony Endino, Stuart Feldman, Ronald Lee Fleming, John Foreman, Kennedy Fraser, Hunter S. Frost, Jane Garmey, Sara and Eugene Gillespie, Phyllis Grissom, Gail Hammer, Gurnee F. Hart, Sally Hollins, Julie Somers Hooi, Joy Jurnovoy, Frederick Krantz, Nathalie Kuchenmeister, Beatriz Lamar, Walter H. Lippincott, Cathleen Cox McFarlane, William McGuire, Nancy Wilson Mendel, Cara Montgomery, Nancy Newhouse, Elizabeth Peters, Arlette Ravet-Rigby, Ann Reynolds, Charles Ryskamp, Diane Sachs, Rose Sachs, Patricia Sullivan, Alexandra Taylor, Phyllis Theroux, Dr. Mary B. Todd, John Weidman, Michael and Elena Wood, Samuel G. White, Thomas H. Wright. (If I have omitted any names, please forgive me.)

I should like to give special thanks to Mimi and Russell Duncan for their overwhelming hospitality when I showed up to stay with them in Palm Beach on my seemingly endless research trips to their hometown.

Finally, I owe a huge debt to the team at Clarkson Potter who shepherded the book through to publication. Gratitude goes first and foremost to my editor, Roy Finamore, who steered me away from stylistic excesses and structural inconsistencies with consummate tact and wisdom. His witty observations and sharp comments made our editorial exchanges much more fun than they usually are. *Mille baci,* Edgar. Roy's assistant, Martin Patmos, dealt with everything, including my laughable technological lapses, with serene efficiency. Marysarah Quinn designed a truly beautiful and elegant book that would have delighted Addison Mizner. Thanks also to the production editor, Jean Lynch, and production manager, Joy Sikorski. A reward should be given to copy editor Janet Biehl, who painstakingly exposed my inaccuracies and corrected my errors. (Those that remain are mine alone.) Publisher Chip Gibson and editorial director Lauren Shakely had faith in the book. I thank them all.

CONTENTS

ADDISON'S NAPKIN

In 1997 I was having dinner in a house on the campus of the Lawrenceville School in New Jersey with my old friends William and Penny Bardel, who both work at the school. As I sat down at the dinner table and opened my fine white damask napkin, I noticed it had a small hole. "Oh, dear," Penny Bardel said, "that must be one of Addison's."

"Addison's?" I asked.

"Yes, Addison Mizner."

I gasped. I knew the name. Addison Mizner was the legendary 1920s architect who had transformed Palm Beach, Florida, from a swampy jungle into a romantic Mediterranean village with the huge, glamorous Spanish-style mansions he built for the rich leisure class who came there for the winter season.

"This is Addison Mizner's napkin?"

The story was soon told. In 1928 a young woman from North Carolina named Madena Galloway came to Palm Beach to find work and after a few months became secretary to the famous architect Addison Mizner. She became deeply attached to him and worked for him until his death in 1933 at the age of sixty-one. Having no responsible family, Mizner made her coexecutor of his will, a thankless task since in spite of his success, he left only debts, which she tried for several years to pay off.

In July 1935 Madena married William Nelrich, an accountant at the Everglades Club. She had been a very popular girl in Palm Beach, but her loyalty to Addison precluded consideration of any other suitor until after the architect's death. (Although Addison was not the marrying kind, Madena was only one of many women who were devoted to him.) When the Mizner estate was finally closed, the couple stayed on for a few years. In 1950 they left Palm Beach, planning to open an antique shop in Pinehurst, North Carolina, with the residue of Addison's Spanish artifacts that Madena had kept (and paid for) in storage. But Nelrich's early death and a hurricane that destroyed many of their belongings put an end to the plan. Moving to Asheboro to be near her sister, Madena died there in 1983.

All those years she carefully kept Addison's possessions and papers in the basement of her house, protected from prying eyes. She never returned to Palm Beach and never discussed her time there with anyone. She would not talk to interviewers pursuing the Mizner story. She refused to be a guest of honor at a memorial ceremony in honor of the architect, some years ago in Boca Raton. The idea of reopening memories that had meant so much to her was clearly too painful.

Bill Bardel had grown up knowing something about this story, and some of Mizner's property that Madena had brought back from Palm Beach had come to the Bardel family. But until Addison's napkin fell into my lap, so to speak, nobody had found a way to make use of these archives. For me, it was a thrill beyond imagining to discover that a treasure trove of material, never seen by anybody except Madena and her family, was sitting in North Carolina, like a sleeping beauty, waiting to be awakened with, if not a kiss, then a cry of revelation.[1]

The files, photographs, scrapbooks, and letters that Madena kept so close by her to the end of her life revealed an Addison Mizner far different from the legend that has been accepted over the years. The stories about him told of an extravagant character, a California frontiersman, a wit and iconoclast who, while knowing almost nothing about architecture, talked his Palm Beach clients into building vastly expensive pink turreted villas, and who became so enveloped in myth that nobody knew anymore what was truth. The tales of his wild ride through America during the explosive years of the early twentieth century inspired at least two theatrical composers—Irving Berlin and Stephen Sondheim—to attempt to write a musical about them.

Addison Mizner's architectural career was blasted by commentators of the time. "An upper-class con man, he went to Florida to get rich in real estate and decided to get rich in architecture instead" was a typical slam in a supposedly respectable history, *America in the Twenties,* by

Geoffrey Perrett.[2] From the endlessly told tale of Addison forgetting to add a staircase to one of his Palm Beach mansions, to the notion that he had never drawn an architectural plan in his life, his life seems to have attracted anecdotes like lint to a sweater.

That he was also a charming, larger-than-life bon vivant makes the stories more convincing. Well over six feet tall, and overweight to the tune of three hundred pounds in his later years, he was an unforgettable sight, greeting passersby along Worth Avenue, usually with a pet monkey on his shoulders. With his brother, Wilson, the shady boulevardier and con artist whose witticisms were daily recorded by the gossip columnists of the day, Addison Mizner bestrode the earth like a colossus, seemingly indestructible—until together the brothers gambled away their position, in true California style, on a distant promise of gold.

Addison lived at a time of uncontrolled growth and energy in the United States, and there is no doubt that he personified the mood of the country with his eagerness to expand his horizons, his willingness to take risks, and his sense that the past could be used to shape the future. Coming from California, he grew up in the wake of men who had pushed ahead, full of hope and expectations, to the last frontier. He was infected by their excitement, their desire for fenceless empires. The unregulated, laissez-faire atmosphere of turn-of-the-century America fed into his free-spirited view of life and work. That after making millions he ended with $2,500 in the bank was somehow perfectly all right. His whole life was a matter of ups and downs, success and failure, optimism and defeat. The extremes by which he was buffeted are not unique but are in my view peculiarly American. Addison's story represents the power and fallibility of the American Dream.

His choice of career could hardly have been more apposite as an emblem of the country and the age. Like art and music, architecture is constantly trying to reinvent itself. The difference is that art and music can be turned off or avoided. Architecture presents itself boldly. Houses, office blocks, residential developments, retirement homes, bricks and mortar, glass and stone rise up in front of us, blocking our sight lines, casting shadows that darken our path. Only through natural disaster, decrepitude, or a landlord's wish to replace the old with the new does a building ever come down.

A good architect responds viscerally to his surroundings. We think of Frank Lloyd Wright as inseparable from his Prairie style, the natural outcome of his midwestern experience. If he had landed in Palm Beach in 1918, perhaps, absorbing the history of southern Florida, its flatness, the palm trees, the sunlight, and the humidity, he might have gone in the direction of his contemporary. Addison Mizner was in love with fourteenth-century Moorish Spain, an architectural style that turned out to be brilliantly appropriate for the region. Palm Beach was, and still remains, the beneficiary of his vision. He laid out its Mediterranean-style courtyards, streets, and gardens with the instincts of a trained town planner. He followed his design path as a historian and an artist, and he gave his rich clients who flocked there an aesthetic standard that was unequaled.

But Mizner was a product of the premodern age; his taste had been formed before the so-called International Style swept the country, and he died in 1933, a few months after Philip Johnson and Henry-Russell Hitchcock introduced this new architecture in a groundbreaking exhibition at the Museum of Modern Art. That is why, after his death, Mizner was such an easy target. Historicism was out—and so was Addison Mizner. The scabrous attacks on his architecture were the popular responses of critics of the period, and the gossip about his character, supported in part by his own published autobiography, in which he projected himself as a carefree adventurer, and other books about the Mizners, diminished his reputation further.

The Madena Galloway Nelrich papers help to redress the balance. Addison's early diaries and notes, preserved in the archive, reveal a sensitive, thoughtful young man who took his responsibilities seriously. His correspondence with his brother Wilson indicates a concern and affection little understood by their contemporaries or biographers. In addition, the huge number of letters Addison wrote to his mother express a devotion hardly in keeping with his image as a shallow trickster and social climber. But most important, thanks to Nelrich's collection of blueprints, watercolors, scrapbooks, and sketches, there is no longer any doubt as to Mizner's authenticity as a fine architect, a good builder, a gifted interior designer, and an artist of space.

There is, of course, another test, and that is to look at his work. His houses have survived hurricanes, floods, and the vagaries of "restoration," "addition," and "makeover" without losing their integrity. Walk into the entertaining room of his own tower apartment on Via Mizner, and you are immediately blessed with what design faddists call feng shui—a sense of serenity and comfort. The ground-floor reception area of the Villa Flora and the library of the Villa Encantada share a quality of spatial rightness that is almost tangible. Mizner's work invited touch—the colorful tiles, the pecky cypress beams, the elegant wrought-ironwork, the courtyard plantings. His work was to a great extent romantic, but it was backed by knowledge. The combination gave his houses lasting value.

Dead now for seventy years, Addison Mizner has outlived the competition and assumed a position in the architectural pantheon that will endure as long as his wrought-iron railings and stone fountains. But his immortality does not rest on his houses alone. Today, in a wonderfully absurd twist, the two words *Addison Mizner* are worth countless dollars to developers of the condominiums, apartments, and gated communities springing up in southern Florida. Mizner Lake Estates, Addison's Reserve, Mizner Park—there is no end to the inventiveness of builders who want to give their developments a little class, a little background, a little glamour. The architect's name, like a luxury brand, gives them all that. Addison Mizner, who died broke, is now worth a fortune. How he would have loved the irony.

BOCA ROCOCO

"WHAT COULD POSSIBLY GO WRONG?"

It was going to be Venice-on-the-Atlantic. A shimmering city, rising from the water, with turrets, domes, minarets, and bell towers. The streets would be lined with pastel stucco mansions, the roofs would glow in terra-cotta tiles, and courtyards, cloisters, and patios would be perfumed by scented flowers and shrubs. Canals and small lakes would intersect this Renaissance paradise, with public gardens, golf courses, playgrounds, and endless vistas of the intracoastal waterway and the majestic ocean. Elaborate irrigation, electricity, and drainage systems would make the infrastructure impregnable. Welcome to Boca Raton, Florida, the ultimate expression of the richest nation in the world: Boca Raton, the first perfectly designed twentieth-century city.

The date was 1925, the central year of the infamous decade that witnessed the greatest stock market boom the United States had ever known, the vortex of a time described by F. Scott Fitzgerald as the Jazz Age, when "New York had all the iridescence of the beginning of the world." People had forgotten the darkness of the First World War; they were tearing off their inhibitions and their dollar bills, building great houses, importing whole rooms from Italy and France, acquiring magnificent paintings from ancient European collections. In a strange irony, while these new millionaires tried to recreate for themselves the Old World that, they believed, epitomized sophistication and style, thousands of European immigrants were arriving on American shores intent on turning their backs on that tired continent, yearning instead to create a new life that, they believed, would surpass everything they had left behind. Boca Raton, iridescent like New York in its illusory beauty, was the culmination of this energy, dissatisfaction, and desire.

The man behind this colossal dream was an architect, adventurer, taste-maker, and conduit of rich people's caprices named Addison Mizner. He was fifty-two years old in 1925 and had already created a stunning vacation colony a few miles to the north of Boca Raton in Palm Beach. His astonishingly wealthy clients eagerly responded to the romantic architecture he offered them—Spanish-style houses with tiled roofs, interior courtyards, and wrought-iron balconies, houses that spoke of medieval grandeur and Mediterranean pleasures, winter palaces that would equal in majesty the vast English castles and French châteaux that the same clients had built for themselves in Boston, Philadelphia, and New York.

Born in California, Addison Mizner had emerged, Gatsby-like, from a mysterious past to become the close friend of social hostesses like Mrs. Hermann Oelrichs and Mrs. Oliver Belmont of New York, and Mrs. Edward Stotesbury of Philadelphia, as well as Broadway luminaries like Irving Berlin and Marie Dressler. His rough language and quick wit worked like a sort of magic on his bemused clients and delighted friends. This charm, combined with his equally impressive erudition, made his sales pitch for Boca Raton irresistible. Having traveled widely in Europe and South America, he understood better than most what made a city work. He had proved his skills as an architect. But perhaps most important, he had the confidence of a true believer. It did not take much persuasion to raise money for the Boca Raton project—people were already hungry to share in the Florida real estate bonanza—but Addison's huge personality and innocent enthusiasm brought doubters to their knees.

In the spring of 1925, when Addison's company, the Mizner Development Corporation, released to the press the first announcements of "the world's most architecturally beautiful playground," the country was ready. Boca Raton was what Americans had been waiting for—a combination of Paris, the City of Light; Rome, the Eternal City; and something more, still undefined, inexpressible. Boca Raton would eclipse Europe's historic citadels and show the world that the United States had finally shaken off its nostalgia for the old classical forms and come up with its own inimitable design for living.

"Boca Raton will be blended into one flawless mosaic of poetic harmony, gracefulness and enduring charm," promised the brochures. "It will contribute to every known comfort and convenience of this modern age." Every street was to measure at least sixty feet wide; each building would be made of stucco or brick; a specially dredged lake would play host to the largest yachts in the world. This was development raised to a high art, a lure to investors of something far more spiritual than bricks and mortar. Addison Mizner offered them nothing less than elevation to the ranks of the greatest patrons in history. If Mizner was Michelangelo, his backers were the popes, the Medici, the ermine-clad aristocrats of aesthetic excellence.

Money poured into Addison's office. From all over, developers, real estate investors, and private individuals rushed to offer their commitment to this thrilling venture. Addison himself became the hero of the hour. His six-foot-three, portly form was seen all over Palm Beach, surrounded by admirers hell-bent on acquiring a piece of this divine pie. His handsome, boyish face, with his mischievous blue eyes, straight nose, and fair hair, was plastered all over the newspapers, inspiring confidence and worshipful admiration. Addison was doing for the New World what the builders of the pyramids and the Taj Mahal had done for the Old. His imaginary city was proof of God's blessings on the American people, the ultimate shrine to prosperity, the expansion of frontiers, and a stock market that would surely go up forever.

The fact that Boca Raton was in a completely unknown part of southern Florida was irrelevant, or that its name—originally spelled Boca Ratones—meant, depressingly, "rat's mouth" or "thieves inlet" in Spanish. That this particular piece of land, inhabited by Seminole Indians and a few farmers, was basically a desert, stubbled with rocks, palmetto, and mosquito-infested ponds also escaped comment. Who cared? Addison and his supporters, standing on that inhospitable stretch of sand between the inland waterway and the ocean, saw, not a desiccated landscape implacably unsuited to development, but a triumphant grid of promenades, squares, and fountains, stretching to the radiant horizon.

Addison felt certain he could fulfill that vision. Had he not already dazzled the richest families in America with houses that outstripped in opulence the great royal palaces of Spain and Italy? He issued a torrent of sketches showing how his dream would convert to reality. He platted the city on an elegant grid, with the Camino Real, twin plazas, Lake Esmeralda, and a Venetian bridge and canals all in place. He sketched the house he would build for himself, a fantastic fourteenth-century

Spanish castle with a drawbridge and a 135-foot-square courtyard; it would be filled with ancient treasures and ultimately turned into a museum. If this was a folly, it was no more so than those monuments to the picturesque that the great eighteenth-century aristocrats had created for themselves in Europe. The lyrical mood at this moment in America required equally virtuosic leaps of the imagination.

If Palm Beach was the culmination of Addison Mizner's architectural career, Boca Raton would move him into a new realm, that of a creator of cities. It would be his own never-never-land, more beautiful even than the "White City" he had seen in 1893 as a youth at the World's Columbian Exposition in Chicago. He visualized a form of urban planning that would take the most romantic of the old and the most technologically advanced of the new, so that Boca Raton would overtake San Francisco, Chicago, and even New York as the most beautiful, workable city in the country. The dream was self-deceiving perhaps, but no more than the dreams of many others swept along by the swollen economic tide and the avidity of real estate entrepreneurs. Addison put his whole heart into the transformation of this alien wilderness. These were the Roaring Twenties, after all. Every dream conveyed the promise of fulfillment. It merely required individuals with enough imagination, talent, and expertise to pull it off. What could possibly go wrong?

The collapse came quickly. In 1926, eight months after the first million-dollar investments had been made, the Boca bacchanal was over, leaving only a ghastly hangover. As in all financial bubbles, a sudden crisis of confidence ripped through his land scheme, and not even Addison's tireless reassurances could restore it. Investors by the thousands panicked and pulled out. Banks folded. Bankruptcies escalated. Many families lost everything. Just as, seventy-five years later, blinded by the same optimism and greed, people invested in Internet companies that had been formed with the irrational hope of eventual profits, so the Boca Raton speculators purchased a possibility that never came close to fruition. The result was a financial disaster even more devastating than the hurricane that swept through southern Florida that fall of 1926, killing hundreds of people and causing millions of dollars in damage.

Addison himself, of course, lost everything in the bust. His destiny, like the fabulous blueprints of his city, crumbled into dust. But his life had always been this way, a matter of highs and lows, of feast and famine, steering a course from the mesa to the arroyo as the weather changed. His western background could hardly have been more inimical to an artistic career, and yet from it he wrested some of the most beautiful and highly prized artifacts in the country. His journey across the United States to the East Coast was complex and diverting, and he met his fate in Florida only after a series of adventures that make the glittering disaster of Boca Raton seem as inevitable as the Jazz Age itself.

PART ONE
CALIFORNIA
BLUEPRINT FOR AN OPTIMIST

ST. MARY OF THE PACIFIC

(Courtesy of the Camel Barn Museum, Benicia, California)

CHAPTER 1

"I AM GETTING TO BE A PERFECT CHILD ABOUT YOU."

TUESDAY, APRIL 28, 1891. SAN FRANCISCO. *I Addison Mizner commence a diary at the age of 18 on the above date. I am at present a student at Mr. Bates School, San Rafael. I am not all to geather a bad schollar but my one and most serious faling is my bad spelling as perhapse you will notice before you have read many lines. For the last weeak I have been off on sick leave staying with my Sister Mrs. Horace B. Chase alias Minie Mizner. I came to the city yesterday and hapened to see the president Harison who is visiting San Francisco. He is the most miserable looking dish-faced thing I ever saw.*

Thus the young Addison Mizner made his first diary entry, demonstrating his typical candor, brio, and atrocious spelling in an elegant slanting hand. After the description of Benjamin Harrison, Mizner reinforced his impression of the president by drawing a nasty little portrait.

He had always made drawings, in his schoolbooks, on scraps of paper, in letters. The sketches are not always first-rate, particularly his renderings of people, who tend to have too-short arms or legs, but they show a mind receptive to visual impressions, perhaps more so than most schoolboys of his age. Addison himself does not seem to have found this compulsion significant. Indeed, he spent much of his life avoiding or abandoning the talent that ultimately made him famous.

As for his spelling, it remained hopeless throughout his life (but inventive: "sewerside" for "suicide," as one example). The reason for this failing was his education, which was decidedly spotty. Addison Cairns Mizner was the seventh of eight children (only one of them female, the above-mentioned Minnie, whose real name was Mary Isabella). This meant that his mother was pregnant or just out of pregnancy for roughly sixteen years of her married life. This marathon might have worn down some women, but not Ella Watson Mizner, who could probably have entered a triathlon even after her childbearing years were over. The size of the family did mean, however, that by the time Addison and his younger brother, Wilson, came along, the parental grip on the Mizner boys had weakened, and their education suffered.

Addison's father was Lansing Bond Mizner, the eldest of three children, who started life in Walnut Grove, Illinois, on December 5, 1825. The name *Mizner,* like its young heir, fell victim to various spellings throughout the nineteenth century. Lansing's grandfather was Lawrence Mizener, who came from Germany and settled in Mendham, New Jersey, in the early 1790s. (Perhaps the best-known American with that name, literary critic and F. Scott Fitzgerald expert Arthur Mizener, was also a descendant of immigrants from Germany.) The name began to lose its first *e* sometime before Lawrence's death in 1795, for in his will the name is spelled both ways seemingly at random. Lawrence's wife, Sarah, who died in Geneva, New York, in 1820, chose not to use the *e,* but it lingered for a while and was finally retired for good in the next generation.[1]

The origins of the name Mizner remain obscure. Much later in his life, Addison was asked by a Palm Beach matron if his name was Jewish. In the anti-Semitic Palm Beach of the 1920s, the suggestion was not pleasing from a career point of view, and while himself having the most eclectic friendships, he denied it. There is no evidence that he was lying. His brother Henry, who became the family genealogist, researched the name in both England and Germany, finding it attached to Protestant families. Not surprisingly, given his interests, Addison had more elevated ambitions for his antecedents, toying with a connection to Meissen, the Dresden porcelain maker, and Juste Meissonier, a leading eighteenth-century French Rococo designer.

The name may have lacked romance, but Addison's American ancestors compensated by becoming prominent members of midwestern society. Lansing's father was Henry Caldwell Mizner, a lawyer in Harrisonville, Illinois, whose two brothers were both generals in the U.S. Army. Henry was born after his father died, and as Henry himself died when Lansing was four, both father and son grew up fatherless.

Lansing's mother was Mary Stevenson Cairns, daughter of Dr. Caldwell Cairns, one of the framers of the Illinois constitution, and niece of Shadrach Bond, the first governor. (The Caldwells were Huguenots who had emigrated to Scotland in 1598.) After Henry's death in 1829, Mary married General James Semple, an Illinois politician. In 1837 Semple was appointed minister to New Granada (now Colombia and Panama), and in 1840 Lansing moved with the rest of the family to Bogotá, where he learned to speak fluent Spanish.

Returning to Illinois in 1843 at the age of eighteen, Lansing started law school at Shurtleff College, in Alton, Illinois, but spent only two years there before volunteering for the Mexican War. At the age of twenty, he was appointed captain and commissary agent for his company. According to his proud son Addison, at the critical battle of Buena Vista in February 1847, Lansing was the only man there who could speak both Spanish and English and thus played a vital role in negotiating the Mexican surrender.[2]

The young war hero then returned to Illinois, but it seems that after his wartime adventures, life back home palled, for when he received a letter from his stepfather's brother, General Robert Baylor Semple, inviting him to come to the pioneering land of California, he jumped at the chance. Semple was already deeply involved in real estate in Benicia, Solano County, thirty miles north of San Francisco, a fledgling coastal city that for a while held out the promise of becoming the capital of burgeoning California. Benicia was named after the wife of Semple's partner, General Mariano Guadalupe Vallejo, who owned much of the land.

Semple was excited by the potential of the region and wrote to Lansing, "Now, my dear boy, if you have finished your studies and can get to this country, with a small library and your knowledge of the Spanish language, and my influence, you can make ten thousand dollars a year in the practice of law."[3] That was a lot of money in those days, and Lansing did not hesitate. Arriving in 1849 by way of New Orleans and Panama, he discovered not only that a large percentage of the male population of Benicia had departed to join the gold rush farther north but that his resourceful stepuncle was working as a printer and a dentist when he was not selling lots in Benicia on the side at eighteen dollars each.[4] When Lansing completed his law studies in California (he was admitted to the bar in 1850), he promptly went into business with Semple. His first entrepreneurial step, after purchasing several pieces of land and building a house, was to organize a mule stage to carry passengers from Benicia to Sacramento.[5]

Lansing Mizner was a handsome, energetic man of imposing height. (All his sons were well over six feet tall.) Boys whose fathers die young assume early responsibilities within the family, and Lansing used this experience to good advantage in the receptive climate of California. His impressive family background of generals, lawyers, diplomats, and politicians gave him entree into high-level state circles, and his fluency in Spanish was a huge advantage in a region where Spanish was the dominant language. He was well liked by his colleagues, and when the Republicans of Solano County recommended that he become lieutenant governor of the state, they described him as "a gentleman of fine talents, splendid address and captivating manners, and . . . one of the most popular public speakers in the State."[6] During the go-getting 1850s in Benicia, Lansing Mizner cut a dashing figure, and sometime in 1853, while promoting railroads and real estate and engaging in a busy law practice, he caught the eye of a young woman called Ella Watson, whose story to that point was already worthy of an adventure novel.

Ella (Elmira) was born in Armstrong County, Pennsylvania, on February 29, 1836, the second daughter of Mary Reynolds and John Smiley Watson. Ella's great-grandfather, Bratton Caldwell, was born in Ireland. (The name Caldwell coincidentally pops up on both sides of Addison Mizner's family.) Caldwell had settled in Lycoming County, Pennsylvania, a Native American territory, in the middle of the eighteenth century, before the Revolutionary War. When Caldwell married Elsie Hughes in her parents' log cabin, they were the first white couple to get married in Lycoming County.

Their daughter, Mary Caldwell, married James Watson (also born in Ireland) in 1783 in Lycoming County. This marriage produced Ella's father, John, who was born there in 1810 and married Mary Reynolds in Kittanning, Armstrong County, in 1833. (Mary was grandniece of the English painter Sir Joshua Reynolds, and Addison later used to enjoy saying, "I josh and I paint.") They had eight children. Three died in infancy, leaving four girls and only one boy. (As in many families at that time—

including that of Lansing's uncle, who also buried three small boys—infant death was all too common.)

In about 1838 the Watsons moved from Pennsylvania to St. Louis, and in January 1853, like many others, they decided to leave St. Louis for California, the promised land. Without the speed and directness of trains, the journey was very long and arduous. The family, consisting of the parents, three daughters (the eldest, Mary, was already married and living in Pennsylvania), and one son traveled to New Orleans, took a boat down the Gulf of Mexico, and then crossed Central America via the San Juan River, finally sailing up to San Juan del Sur on the Pacific coast of Nicaragua. There they boarded the steamship *Independence,* which would take them north to San Francisco. On February 16, in a huge storm, the steamship struck a rock at Margarita Island in Magdalena Bay, off what is now Baja California.

The collision occurred early in the morning, while the passengers were asleep. "At first the passengers were assured by the ship's officers that there was no danger, but suddenly fire broke out from the engine room and spread rapidly over the doomed vessel. Then ensued a panic among the passengers that baffles description." Prefiguring the *Titanic* disaster in 1912, there were not enough lifeboats. Many passengers panicked and jumped into the raging waters in an attempt to get to shore. In a nightmare vision, soon the surface was dotted with the corpses of the unfortunates. According to the records, in less than an hour, 150 of the 402 passengers of the *Independence* had drowned.[7]

Over fifty years later, Addison's brother Henry attended a reunion in Alton, Illinois, of the Mexican War regiment in which their father had served. Inquiring whether any of the veterans remembered Lansing Mizner, he found that a lively eighty-year-old colonel, Andrew Fuller Rodgers, not only remembered his old school friend and compatriot "Lance" but also, astonishingly, was one of the survivors of the wreck of the *Independence.* The old soldier told Henry that it was the most awful scene he had ever witnessed—worse than anything in the Mexican War, the vigilante times, or the Civil War.

By thrusting a leg through a hawser hole, Colonel Rodgers told Henry, he had been able to pass women and children, including Mary Watson and Ella, from the sinking ship to the last waiting lifeboat. When he finally climbed back on deck, he saw a man standing there with a little girl in his arms. Rodgers seized her and threw her into the arms of her mother, who was in the lifeboat just drawing away. The child was Elsie Watson, Ella's youngest sister. The only remaining passengers on the ship, apart from the captain and Rodgers, were one Judge Tarr with his son Horace, and John Watson with his only son, Asa. The fire was engulfing them—they would have to jump ship. Judge Tarr, who could not swim, entreated Rodgers to save his son. John Watson made the same request. Since Tarr asked first, Rodgers took Horace Tarr and struggled through the heavy seas to shore. Exhausted, the brave young man could not find the energy to fight his way back to the ship. Still desperately waiting on deck, John Watson told his son to take off his overcoat and throw it overboard; he did the same. They climbed down the side of the ship with a rope. John told Asa to catch hold of his coat collar, and he would try to swim. But the waves overwhelmed them, and the boy was lost. Judge Tarr also drowned.[8]

Mary Watson later wrote a letter to her brother describing in agonizing detail the shipwreck and the loss of her son. "I was on shore and knew that my husband and child were struggling for life and I could give them no assistance. Oh! How I screamed and begged and prayed for the sailors to take back the boat, but they would not do it."[9]

The survivors had to wait for three days on Margarita Island under grueling conditions before help arrived. Bodies of the victims kept washing ashore and had to be given makeshift burials. Among them was a woman whom Mary Watson had observed on the steamer clutching a bundle of lily bulbs. Refusing to leave them behind, she perished along with her precious burden. On the island there was no food or water. Mary Watson did her best to help the suffering children, who were frantic with thirst: "For my part I neither ate or drank the three days we were on the island." The survivors were rescued by the whaling ship *Meteor,* which finally brought them through the Golden Gate on the morning of March 31. The journey on the whaler was hardly less horrific than the days on the island. One woman died; her body was sewn up in sailcloth and placed on top of the cabin occupied by the women survivors. Elsie Watson came down with scarlet fever. The food consisted of moldy flour and whale oil, which Mary Watson, now the group's leader, was asked by the French cook to approve before it was served to the desperate passengers. Ella's seventeenth birthday was spent aboard the *Meteor*.

Addison grew up on stories about the tragedy, which affected him deeply. In his book collection, found after his death, was a charming copy of James Thomson's and Thomas Gray's poems in a gold-and-gray binding, slightly water-damaged. In it is inscribed "[I]n the pocket of Father's coat when we were wrecked on the *Independence*." John Watson had been reading the poems on board the steamer and had tucked the small volume into a pocket of the coat that he later tossed over the side. The purser had found it among the wreckage and presented it to Ella, and it was passed down through the family to Addison, who treasured it as a poignant memento of that terrible journey.

After this unlucky start, the Watsons did not stay long in California. John Watson died in San Francisco in 1857, aged forty-seven. It is not clear how he died, but for him as for many survivors of tragedies, life had lost its savor. (Another passenger, a Mr. Coots, also lost his son, aged twelve, in the disaster. Mr. Coots died a year or two later.)[10] After John Watson's death, his widow returned to the east with two of her daughters, Isadora and Elsie, and took up residence again in Kittanning. She died there in 1883, at sixty-eight.

Ella, however, already reckoned the beauty of the family, had married before her father's death. Lansing Mizner had met her soon after her arrival in San Francisco, and by the following year was keenly interested in this charming eighteen-year-old and her tragic story. Upon receiving a letter from her just before Thanksgiving in 1854, he wrote that he was so delighted that he "went off into a bachelor's reverie, with letter in one hand and picture in the other." He then evoked a glorious fantasy about their growing old together, and how all through the changing seasons, "she who was the reservoir, the fountain of my thoughts, still maintained her calm and beauteous sway, and with smiles melted winter away."

With a satirist's eye for his own bombastic flights, he then went on: "How high this Babel Tower, this airy castle, might have been built I know not, for just as I was about to take undisputed possession of the edifice I had erected, Tom rushed into the room, and said a man at the door wanted $10 for a load of wood. 'Oh, what a fall was then, my countrymen!' Down came castle and tower, columns, cornice and pilaster, down niche and portico . . . and I beneath the ruins." (Quite apart from

Lansing's stylistic panache, it is interesting to note his familiarity with the language of architecture.)[11]

While Lansing was practicing law and wooing Ella, he was also spending time in Sacramento with one of the most notorious characters in town. Hugh Campbell Murray, like Mizner, was originally from St. Louis and had come west in 1849. He and Mizner had been fellow students at Shurtleff College and were now equally interested in California politics and law. Later Murray did well, becoming, like his friend, a member of the California Supreme Court, but in 1853 he was known mostly for his drunkenness and questionable public behavior. What Ella thought of her suitor's unsuitable companion is not known, but this friendship represented a streak of rebelliousness in Lansing that contrasts with the portrait of him painted by Cyrus Pease in 1853, when Lansing was twenty-eight. As well as emphasizing the strong features and the intensity of one of the reigning princes of Benicia, it also shows him as a paragon of seriousness.

Eleven years older than Ella, Lansing Mizner was highly eligible and could have found a wealthy wife, but his heart was smitten by the young Miss Watson. He wrote to her frequently during his stays in Sacramento, chiding her (in verse) when she did not respond, and expressing his frustration that he could not see her more often. "I am getting to be a perfect child about you, can't stay 3 or 4 days without getting into a stew and neglecting important business."[12] Finally, in early 1856, at the age of twenty, she succumbed to his pressure and agreed to marry him. On May 26 of that year they were married in Grace Church in San Francisco. (Benicia did not yet have an Episcopal church.) The rector who married them was William Ingraham Kip, who became the first Episcopal bishop of California and was to play quite a role in the new Mrs. Mizner's life. The reception was held at Ella's parents' house on Perry Street.

The wedding day was fraught with drama. Less than two weeks earlier, on May 14, James King, the editor of the San Francisco *Evening Bulletin,* had been assassinated, infuriating the citizenry and provoking a revival of the vigilantes, who had briefly held sway in 1851. The days leading up to the Watson-Mizner wedding were extremely tense, with the vigilantes, fully armed, demanding that Governor J. Neely Johnson hand over the murderer to be hanged in public. As Lansing Mizner was by now chief justice of California, he might have been called on to help maintain the rule of law rather than take his vows as husband of Ella Watson.[13] But his presence was not needed, and the wedding took place.

The next year, with her father dead and her mother and sisters returning east, the young bride was left to learn the ways of California and start producing what became known as "the Mizner tribe." Ella Watson Mizner was up to the task.

CHAPTER 2

"THE RESULT WAS NEITHER PRETTY OR MODEST."

In 1850 California had been voted the thirty-first state in the Union, and Benicia looked set to become a key to its future. In 1853 the legislature selected Benicia as the state capital, and a fine neoclassical brick building was erected to celebrate its new status. But visiting politicians found the town wanting in amenities, and a year later Sacramento, more central to the gold-mining towns and more established, got the job.

Still, Lansing Mizner had high ambitions for his town. Topographically, Benicia is in a marvelous position, surrounded by high mountains and offering a good inland waterway, deeper than San Francisco's, which at that time required lighters to lead large ships to the docks. In the early 1850s and 1860s, the Benicia arsenal was an important local political and economic asset, and high-ranking military personnel were a constant feature of the social life of the town.

While Lansing was becoming a very successful lawyer (in 1866 he was admitted to the bar of the U.S. Supreme Court), he dabbled in real estate, pulling off a major land purchase from Manuel Cabeza Vaca in what was called the Vaca Valley. (Mizner's fluent Spanish gave him a great advantage with the local landowners.) Part of his investment was transformed into Vacaville, platted in 1851 and later a busy town with a railroad that ultimately connected to San Francisco. (Vacaville provided a haven for refugees from the city after the earthquake of 1906.) In 1874 Mizner became president and stockholder of the Golden Gate Mining Company, adding to his investment portfolio.

During the Civil War the Benicia arsenal was in Union hands, but this had little effect on Benicia's fortunes. It was after the war that the town began to fall on hard times. With political and economic focus moving to Sacramento and San Francisco, disappointed investors began to leave. In 1890 the town could still boast the barracks, a few canneries, tanneries, shipyards, and a brewery, all of which kept some of the locals employed, but its real estate values, along with its optimism, plummeted.

Elsie Robinson, a West Coast syndicated columnist in the early 1900s, was born in Benicia and later wrote about it with the mixture of love and hate that many American small towns lacking in identity tend to inspire: "Crumbling Mexican adobe, red-tiled, blue-shadowed—splintering pine of ready-made fabricated walls that had 'come around the Horn,' now standing stark on baked earth, their white paint peeling under the blistering sun . . . unfenced acreage of tangled weeds."[1] She described the rocky landscape with the Sierra Nevada mountains in the distance, rowdy saloons, a red-light district, rows of shacks, the smell in the harbor of rotting oranges and fish, and the streets filled with old Spaniards who had once owned the place, pig-tailed Chinese, Portuguese sailors, Gypsies, Mormon missionaries, Indians, and immigrants from Europe like her Irish mother, who bravely planted daffodils in this desert climate to remind her of home.

For Addison, this polyglot town was the center of his childhood world, with his father as king and emperor. Unaware of Benicia's decline, Addison was happy that his father, having abandoned his midwestern roots, had assumed a far more heroic role as one of the elite California pioneers. (Both Addison and Wilson would later take great pride in their West Coast origins.) Addison also watched as his father became an important political figure in the town. (Lansing had been a Democrat, but during the Civil War he became a Republican, and after the war was over, he entered local Republican politics enthusiastically, supporting both Lincoln and Harrison.)

In fact, during Addison's early childhood, Lansing Mizner had only two rivals for the position of Benicia's leading citizen. Captain John Walsh had come to Benicia during the gold rush, and when the town was made a port of entry in 1849, Walsh was named deputy collector of customs. Like many entrepreneurial figures in the region, Walsh had many business interests, including a fleet of ships plying the China trade routes. His local popularity was celebrated at a great dinner in 1873, with a brass band brought from the barracks. Lansing Mizner presented gifts and made a speech, capping an evening of "rational festivity and enjoyment never to be forgotten by any who had the pleasure of partici-pating therein."[2]

The other contender was Daniel N. Hastings, a successful business-man who had succumbed to the millionaire's disease: a mania for build-ing. Architecture was not Benicia's strongest point, but Hastings became obsessed with building a house that would surpass every architectural fantasy hitherto conceived. Ultimately he created the Mar-a-Lago of its day, a forty-room mansion that the locals considered to be the most beautiful house in the county. But its huge cost, its failure to provide the social standing he had hoped for, and several business reverses eventu-ally brought its owner to his knees. Dubbed Hastings's Folly, the house ruined him.[3]

Lansing's architectural ambitions were more modest. In early 1850 three frame houses made by a housing company in Boston had been shipped around Cape Horn and reconstructed in Benicia.[4] When Lan-sing first arrived in town, he built his own house, but after he married Ella, they moved into one of these frame houses. It stood in the center of town, as befitted a man who was deeply involved in local business and politics, on a hill with a creek running through the land. The house was soon too small for his expanding family, and he ended up adding rooms (and then cottages) as the number of children grew. This house remained the Mizner estate until Lansing's death.

Addison had few illusions about his family home. "From the air it must have looked like a telescope, with the smaller end toward the street," he said later. "The porch was entirely covered with vines, and the planting of great trees and shrubs crowded it in on either side. After luncheon, when the front door . . . opened and vomited forth the family, people must have thought it was a subway exit." Not that Addison was interested, then, in architectural follies. As the seventh of eight children, the experience of growing up in those rather cramped living quarters encouraged the tribal feeling that dominated his childhood.

The first Mizner child to appear was Murray McLaughlin, born in San Francisco on March 19, 1857. He was named after Lansing's friend Hugh Murray, who died prematurely of tuberculosis (brought on, some said, by his wild life) six months later. Next came Lansing, born Novem-ber 9, 1858, called Lanny or Lan to distinguish him from his father. The only daughter, Mary Isabella, known as Min or Minnie to the family, was born on July 24, 1860. (She later liked to spell her name Ysabel, although nobody else ever quite got it right.) Edgar Ames arrived on September 2, 1862, in St. Louis; William Garrison on January 26, 1864, and Henry Watson on September 2, 1868, both in San Francisco. The last two were born in Benicia: Addison Cairns on December 12, 1872, and Wilson on May 19, 1876. (Like his brother Lansing, Wilson was not given a middle name, but he added Reynolds when it seemed useful.)

Two years after Addison was born, his eldest brother, Murray, died at the age of seventeen. In the offhand manner that was to characterize most Mizner reactions to family tragedy ("he cooled off" was a favorite expression for "he died"), Addison later said simply that Murray "snapped to the Great Beyond," without elaborating. In fact, Murray, who had been delicate since early childhood, caught what was then called typhoid pneumonia on a hunting trip, which infected his lungs and chest. He was sick for eighteen months and had several operations to remove an abscess on his lung before he succumbed. A tribute to him, published as a paperback booklet decorated with a gold cross, "for the family only," describes him saying toward the end, "I am not afraid."[5]

For his mother, the loss of her firstborn after such a long-drawn-out struggle was a devastating blow. But Ella was made of the same stuff as her mother, who had had to watch her little boy drown in the rough waters of the Pacific. The Mizner grieving process required that all thoughts of Murray be disposed of silently and privately, and there is no mention of Murray in any of Ella's extant letters to her surviving children. Perhaps the only sign of her true feelings was in her attitude toward her last son. Wilson was born when Ella was forty years old, two years after Murray's death, and from the very first, little Wilson was special in her eyes, the one she treasured most, her favorite, Murray's replacement, "Mama's Angel Birdie."

From all accounts, Ella Watson Mizner—always known as "Mama Mizner"—was a strong, lively, humorous woman. "Her placidity was never ruffled for long," said her adoring son Addison, "for behind it was the most divine sense of humor that I have ever known." While Lansing Mizner worked at the law and Republican politics, Ella became involved in the community. One of her priorities was to build the first Episcopal church in Benicia, with the help of the man who had officiated at her wedding, now the bishop of California, William Ingraham Kip. St. Paul's, a handsome "California Gothic" structure, was consecrated by Kip in 1860. Ella was very anxious to appoint a clergyman from back east as the church's rector, but Kip dissuaded her, telling her it was important to get a local man immediately and get the parish going "before the Congregationalists can build." His most compelling argument against getting someone from the East was, as he wrote her, underlining for emphasis, that *"the [parishioners] cannot generally get a clergyman out without paying his passage."*[6]

Bringing up eight headstrong children in the young western town of Benicia tested Mama Mizner to the utmost. Admittedly, she had some help. While Chinese immigrants were regarded with great suspicion in California, middle-class families found them indispensable as domestic servants, and the Mizners regarded their Chinese cook, Ying Lee, as a member of the family. He traveled with them abroad, worked for Minnie Mizner after her father's death, and died with them after thirty-two years of service. In later years, Addison called several of his chow dogs Ying, and Wilson put a character called Ying Lee into one of his plays. Mama Mizner also had a housekeeper, Mary Hamilton, to help with the running of the household. Mary became such a part of the family that when she died, she was buried next to Murray Mizner.

Lansing Mizner had acquired several small ranches with streams and woods, and the children spent their days there hunting, shooting, and fishing. Horses, chickens, cats, turtles, and terrapins were part of the menagerie. The place was a paradise for young children, a landscape where they could run wild, close to nature, in mostly undeveloped land. For fifteen years, Benicia seemed overrun with Mizners. They were everywhere—Lansing and Ella as pillars of the community, their eight children, large, confident, and boisterous, running around in gangs, dominating the small town with their devilish escapades.

All the Mizners were artistic. They loved putting on amateur theatricals and circus shows for their neighbors in a barn they called the "opera house." Once Addison performed as a bareback rider in a mosquito-net skirt, but his most infamous appearance was as Fatima in *Bluebeard*. For the role, he "thought it unnecessary to use anything except the top part of one of Min's ballgowns for a costume." Standing in a barn on a tower made of bales of hay, calling, "Sister Anne, Sister Anne, do you see anyone coming?" he lost his balance and tumbled headfirst into the audience. "The result was neither pretty or modest." After that, Mama Mizner closed the opera house.

Addison's childhood was in many respects idyllic. But with both parents busy and active, and being second to last in the birth order, he had to struggle for attention, and much of his exhibitionist behavior stemmed from competition for Papa Mizner's approval and Mama Mizner's love. The larger the family, the more intense the competition.

Henry was the neatest child, shy, and the least likely to get into trouble. (When Addison, at about five, slid into a fountain, Henry watched, yelling, until Ying Lee and Mary Hamilton ran to the scene and rescued the drowning boy. When Henry was asked why he had not saved his brother, he answered, "I had on my best suit.") Naturally he was a frequent target of the other boys. Henry's room, like those of his siblings, had a small rug by the bed where he said his prayers. (Mama Mizner, her Episcopalian beliefs in place, made sure all the children prayed before they went to bed.) On one occasion, William and Addison decided it would be fun to grab Henry by the legs and scare him as he came into his room to pray. The ruse worked on several occasions, making him scream in fear. Finally, to avoid his attackers, he started jumping straight onto his bed from the door. William and Addison decided it would be a brilliant idea to move the bed. "Although they found William and [Addison] sound asleep in bed," a friend later wrote, "they also found that Henry had broken his collar-bone."[7]

Sibling feuds often descended into violence. With so many large and energetic boys around, fist-fighting was an everyday affair, gradually becoming more institutionalized in the form of boxing, a sport in which the younger Mizners, like many of their contemporaries, developed a passionate interest. One of Benicia's odder claims to fame was as the hometown of the famous "Benicia Boy," John C. Heenan, a legendary boxer who made worldwide news in 1869 when he fought a classic thirty-seven-round match in England against the local champion, Tom Sayres. (The referee finally called it a draw.) The Mizners did not aspire to such heights but became highly proficient with their fists, a skill that later came in useful for both Addison and Wilson.

When arguments grew too violent, Ella Mizner would tell the combatants to take their disputes to the "tank house," a V-shaped iron tank with the lower part clapboarded in—the remains of the bow of a deserted sailing ship. If she wished to summon any of the children, she would ring a bell on top of the tank house: each child had his number of rings and must immediately report to the house.

The Mizner household rules were written up and placed on the dining-room wall. The first was, No tattling. "If I tattled on Wilson for stealing apples out of the convent yard," Addison said, "I got a clubbing that went with that crime, and Wilson went free." Ella and Lansing made other efforts to impose order, but by the time Addison and Wilson came along, discipline was beginning to unravel. Once when Ella went to San Francisco for the day, the two youngest boys decided to clean out the gun room, which meant heaping up a pile of gunpowder in their mother's best punch bowl, putting it in the middle of the floor, and throwing matches at it from a nearby grape arbor. That was the end of the punch bowl, as well as two sets of young eyebrows.

Visitors to the house were given no quarter by the tribe. During a state Republican campaign, a senior politician from the East was sent to help Lansing Mizner get out the vote. The Mizners gave a dinner party in this personage's honor. Addison and Wilson were considered too young to join the party. Curious to see him, the two boys crept out to the guest cottage where the politician was staying and saw him through the shutter powdering his face. The boys were horrified: "No resident of Benicia could get away with that." What was worse, they saw him putting perfume on his handkerchief!

Poor fellow—he didn't stand a chance. While he was at dinner, Addison and Wilson stole into his room and replaced half his powder with sugar, and the perfume with something "the same in color, if not in aroma."

Lansing and Ella Mizner seem to have borne their children's behavior with fortitude and good humor. While the parents were strict (Wilson in particular protested loudly that they were), the boys still seem to have pulled off enough stunts to satisfy most boyhood ambitions. Their parents kept to routines that stabilized the tribe. Mealtimes were the most important family gathering. The dining room was a formal room, with a low ceiling and a large mahogany sideboard, loaded with decanters. Claret was always served with dinner, and as in France, the children were allowed to drink wine. At the dinner table, the Mizner children learned to become quick and fluent conversationalists. "We learned that brevity was the keynote of any discussions or remarks, for you couldn't get in otherwise," Addison recalled later. "These gatherings did more to make or break character and destiny than I can explain."

With Lansing Mizner at the head of the table, his powerful figure and confident manner exuding authority, and Ella Watson Mizner at the other, demanding quicksilver responses and amusing observations from her darling ones, the eight children were constantly being encouraged, corrected, teased, and applauded as they competed for air time. "Pronunciations of words, their derivations, and enunciations were insisted upon by my father, who was considered one of the greatest extemporaneous speakers of the day. He taught us the value of words of one syllable; the colorfulness of similes." Addison learned to get his point in quickly or be left at the starting gate. Indeed, the exchanges could get very rough. On one occasion William was so humiliated that he decided it was safer to keep silent. The damage was lasting, and in adult life he was known as a man of very few words.

Lansing Mizner was interested in history; his extensive library contained a three-volume *Portrait Gallery of Distinguished Persons from Dante to Burke,* and many illustrated volumes of American and European history. Both Mizner parents inculcated in their children a sense of the importance of the age in which they were living. California, they were told, was the greatest American frontier of all, and the beauty and wildness of its landscape were a natural corollary to the material and technological gifts that were being showered upon its inhabitants. When electric lights were first turned on in Benicia, the Mizner children lined up to see the show. When a telephone line finally connected Benicia to San Francisco, Lansing, in a fever of anticipation, was one of the first people to use it. The Mizners were one of the first families to install a flushing toilet in their house, and people came from all over to see how it worked. Lansing and Ella shared a sense of excitement about their adopted home and rarely went back east. They wholeheartedly embraced this place of savage poetry, and they passed their passion on to their children. At the end of his life, tired and burned out in the East, Addison turned for recuperation and strength to his California roots.

Growing up in this rowdy, irreverent family, Addison began to accumulate the verbal and creative habits that later became part of his personality. An added incentive was the sibling competition that dominated his young life. The brothers used to grade each other, saying, "The stronger the body, the weaker the brain." "Edgar, William and I were the strongest," Addison later observed. There were also two kinds of looks in the family: blond, blue-eyed, and fair-skinned (Addison, Edgar, and William), or dark (Lan, Henry, and Wilson).

As in many large families, the children "paired off," so that Edgar and William, the closest in age, spent most of their time together, while Henry and Minnie were inseparable. Lan, the oldest, had already left college and was working with his father by the time Addison was seven years old. Therefore Wilson and Addison "ganged" together, in an accident of birth order that Addison welcomed with guarded enthusiasm.

Ah, Wilson. As a child, Wilson was the naughtiest. Incorrigible, fearless, full of fun, he led Addison, his partner in crime, into scrapes that even Mama Mizner could hardly credit them with. Yet at the dinner table, Wilson was allowed to cut in at any time (no doubt developing his flair for one-liners), for Mama Mizner would always protect him, and in her eyes, he could do no wrong. From the very beginning, she pinned her hopes on her last baby boy—hopes that were not only unrealistic but would one day be transformed into grief.

If Addison was given a useful worldly education around the dinner table, his institutional schooling was another matter. To be sure, Benicia was well supplied with schools, and for a while it was called "The Athens of the Pacific." Among them were St. Catherine's Academy for Young Ladies, St. Mary's Seminary for Young Women, and St. Augustine's Academy for Young Men. (Lansing Mizner was a trustee of both St. Mary's and St. Augustine's.) Also in town were the Benicia Ladies' Academy and a Dominican monastery.*

Since three of these establishments were very close to the Mizner house, not surprisingly, a good many students were to be found after school hanging out with the Mizner boys. Soft-hearted Mama Mizner, ever the hospitable mother-hen, would invite them to meals—to the loud complaints of Ying, who had to feed large numbers of hungry children at very short notice.

Lansing, Edgar, William, and Henry attended St. Augustine's Acad-

---

*So many schools were built in this relatively small town to provide education for the children of the miners crowding into the area in 1849. Reflecting Benicia's decline, by 1889 all these institutions had been closed.

emy, where both Edgar and Henry were singled out as distinguished cadets. Addison and Wilson started out at St. Mary's Seminary. In spite of their familiarity with the local children, it was not easy for Addison to cope with being one of four or five boys in a female institution. "Papa Mizner, being a 'pupil of the old school,' had taught us that we should never talk about ladies. However, I was in a constant blush most of the time," he later confessed. Needless to say, he did not learn very much. He found arithmetic and spelling particularly difficult. He was unpopular and got into fights with the other boys. In his memoir, he passed quickly over these years, but they were evidently unhappy.

Perhaps not all the local kids liked the Mizner boys. Addison's plump, blue-eyed blondness made him seem effeminate and hence an easy target for bullying. (It was no accident he played the female roles in the plays at the barn.) But he was quick to prove his sexual precocity, if we are to believe his memoir's description of his first sexual encounter. It happened with a girl called Mabel, and it took place at the end of June in a deserted barn: "I was eleven, inquisitive, shy, bashful. Mabel was twelve, and the opposite." It is not clear exactly what Mabel got him to do on this occasion, but Addison said, "For days I couldn't make up my mind between shame and a certain pride." Perhaps they were unusually adventurous. Anyway, having succeeded so well, he was eager to try again, observing that if he were to emulate the career of Lord Byron, he would have to accomplish it all before he was fourteen, "or leave a path of deserted mothers in my wake." Nothing ambiguous about that. But after being caught sending a "French picture" to a later crush, the beatings administered to him both at school and at home cured him "like a Virginia ham. I shrank up . . . and hated girls for two or three years." Nothing ambiguous about that either. Certainly, Addison intended his readers to draw the necessary conclusion, however improbable.

When he was eighteen, girls reentered his life in a big way. But by that time the family had split up, Addison had been away from Benicia for two years, and his views of life and love considerably matured.

CHAPTER 3

"I WON'T HAVE IT OFF!"

In May 1888, amid great celebration, Addison's sister, Mary Ysabel Mizner, announced her engagement to Horace Blanchard Chase, a Chicago-born vineyard owner who lived in the Napa Valley. They had met at a party in Napa Soda Springs, where young Californians spent their vacations. Minnie and Horace were to be married in July, just before her twenty-eighth birthday.

Minnie, the only girl child surrounded by seven brothers, enjoyed a favored place in the sibling hierarchy, and since she was born before the first tremors of feminism had spread very far among young women of the educated classes, it is unlikely she felt the constraints of living in a man's world. Higher education was not for Minnie. Although not a world-class beauty, she belonged to a family that was highly regarded in California social circles, and she was a popular debutante. Her name often appeared in the San Francisco gossip columns, and she was courted by many young men. However, she waited until she was twenty-seven to settle on Horace—rather late for girls in those days and a little worrying for her mother. (Perhaps that is why the engagement was brief, only two months.) Addison adored his sister, but even he conceded, "There was a sigh of relief at a definite decision."

But before the wedding came another important event: the Fourth of July. A committed patriot, Lansing Mizner celebrated his country's birthday in a major way, and he encouraged his children to feed the bonfire and participate in the fireworks that took place every year, with countless friends in attendance, at the Mizner house. For Addison and his brothers, it was a wildly exciting family event, and July 4, 1888, was as good a party as ever. Several of the children burned their hands on unexploded Roman candles and rockets and generally terrified the grown-ups with their flame-throwing abilities.

As darkness fell, the final ritual was to leap over the dying embers of the smoldering bonfire. Fifteen-year-old Addison was one of the first to jump, and "with my usual grace, I got my foot in a rut and fell down." Eight or ten other children fell on top of him, and he fainted. He was carried into the house, and "the stupid old army doctor came and said it was a sprain."

Everyone's attention was focused on the wedding ten days later, and Addison's "sprain" was considered a secondary matter. But the ankle grew swollen and purple, he stopped eating, and he began to look very pale and ill. Still, no sprain would prevent him from attending his sister's wedding. "Addie, poor child, was able, with the aid of a plaster cast on his leg, to go to the church for the wedding and take a position in the garden where he could command the situation," his mother said, adding cheerfully, "He fainted when we took him upstairs."[1]

It was a fine occasion, all right. The lead story on the social page of both the *San Francisco Chronicle* and the *Examiner* described Minnie Mizner as possessing "unusual beauty, charming manners and manifold accomplishments." As for the groom, Horace Blanchard Chase was a "gentleman of wealth, well known in Napa Valley." Many San Franciscans traveled by special train to the "pretty little town of Benicia," which was "brought forth from its slumbers" to welcome the visitors.

The bride wore cream silk with a long train; her ushers included two of her brothers, William and Edgar. Their mother wore pearl-gray grosgrain silk, trimmed with a very light pearl silk and point lace—and diamonds. Addison was carried to a pew. St. Paul's Church was decorated with masses of flowers for the ceremony, and the reception was held on the tented, flowered lawns of the bride's family home, where the guests were entertained by a string band from San Francisco. Minnie's list of gifts was impressive. Addison and Wilson gave her gold garter buckles engraved with her initials.[2]

In short, Addison's big sister (she was nearly thirteen years older than he) had married well. Horace Chase had a fair amount of money and was growing wine at Stag's Leap, which was also the name of the house where the young married couple would live. (Today Stag's Leap is a well-known vineyard.) The Chases were a prominent family involved in real estate in Chicago and were very conscious of their social status as one of the oldest prerevolutionary families in the country. Minnie responded well to such pretensions and went merrily into her marriage. Mama

Mizner, ever protective, was less sanguine about the loss of her only daughter. "I feel very much as though we have had a funeral," she lamented, remarking how hard it was for a mother to give a daughter "into any man's keeping."[3]

For Addison, the wedding was the prologue to a nightmarish year. The injury to his ankle turned into a severe case of infection and bone loss. By the end of July, his leg had turned blackish-brown, and doctors from San Francisco were called in. They decided to amputate the leg. Addison was horrified. "I won't have it off," he cried. "I'd rather die than go floating through life on a cork leg." Addison's older brother William, who was at that time studying medicine at Lane's Medical College, saw Addison's leg and said, "Let's take him to Dr. Lane." "That was a long conversation from William," Addison observed, "and impressed the family."

So Addison was taken by train to Dr. Lane, who put the boy on a table and cut open the leg, exposing damaged bone and flesh in a curdled mass of infection. "Green stick fracture. Necrosis has set in." For several weeks, Addison endured the most excruciating pain as the doctors dug and shoved and pushed and squeezed his rotting leg. Finally, he was sent home and told to stay in bed without moving.

He had to lie flat on his back, motionless from the waist down, for about a year. For a teenager, particularly one with great physical strength and energy, such a grim sentence can hardly be imagined. But it forced education on a boy who otherwise would probably never have had one. It was not a conventional course of lessons, of course. Addison simply read a huge number of books that he would never have read in the classroom. He remembered in particular a book about how Charles Dickens had trained his powers of observation and character. "They became games with me that I have played ever since," Addison said later. "I think what I learned from that book has been of more value to me, and more fun, than anything in my life." This time of hibernation turned him into a lifelong reader, and he later accumulated an impressive library. Thanks to this year of sickness, he became a lover of books, but Addison never did learn to spell.

During this time, Addison also developed his visual talents. His brother Henry gave him a paintbox, and the invalid painted pictures of anything and everything he could think of. He developed an ability to produce quick, accurate sketches (a useful tool when he later traveled the world looking at architecture). As well as painting, he also proposed the interesting notion that since his body had to be so stationary, he might as well become a mother-hen and hatch some eggs. He persuaded Ying to give him a dozen eggs, which he placed around his leg. "I waited like an expectant mother. Twenty-one days later I was overjoyed to find I was a parent. I woke in the morning with two little 'dear ones' nestled against my hip."

In spite of this typically lighthearted story, Addison's year of immobility in a household of such vitality was a hardship far greater than he allowed himself to admit. But Mizners did not complain. Direct or personal questions were never asked. Brought up on Anglo-Saxon stoicism, the Mizners understood that adversity was to be endured in silence. A hint as to his true feeling emerged three years later, at school in San Rafael, when he helped his classmates build a gate for a tennis court. After they finished, they lit a bonfire. Addison jumped over it, "to remind me of my accident of three years ago, which is not well yet," he wrote bitterly that night in his diary. Although he did not jump over many more bonfires, his depressing prognosis would never improve, and his leg was to cause him pain, sickness, and inconvenience to the end of his days.

In early January 1889, while Addison was still convalescing, Lansing and Ella paid a visit to Washington, D.C., to visit the newly elected president of the United States, Benjamin Harrison of Indiana (the "miserable looking dish-faced thing," in Addison's memorable phrase). Mizner had campaigned hard for Harrison, and in recompense he had been chosen to carry California's electoral vote to Washington and attend the inauguration. On the eve of the couple's departure, Lansing's friends gave him a dinner at the home of distinguished Benicia resident J. E. Crooks. It was an all-male affair (as was customary), and an excellent meal was served, "washed down with the choicest brands of wines of different kinds. Speeches, toasts, sentiments, responses, served to make the time pass pleasantly until a late hour." Lansing at this point was riding high in his career, and his friends sensed further triumphs were in the offing.[4]

They were not disappointed. He and Ella stayed in the East for two months. After attending the inauguration, they witnessed the parceling out of jobs that came with the new president's installation. Friends of Mizner, pointing to his fluency in Spanish, had urged Harrison to appoint him minister to Mexico, but another candidate, Thomas Ryan, got the post. Instead, Harrison made Mizner minister plenipotentiary to the Central American states (which consisted of Guatemala, Honduras, El Salvador, Nicaragua, and Costa Rica). The appointment was announced on March 30, 1889, and Lansing was immediately expected to take up residence in Guatemala.

Back home, Benicians were elated. That one of their own had been given a major federal post reflected well on the Pacific community, and so naturally another, much greater celebration was in order. On May 11, 1889, on the eve of Lansing's departure for Guatemala, a huge farewell banquet was given at the Masonic Hall, with all of the area's male notables in attendance, including statesmen, businessmen, and judges from Sacramento and San Francisco. (The governor of California, R. W. Waterman, sent his regrets.) After another five-course meal of oysters, caviar, trout, sweetbreads, roast beef, asparagus on toast, roast pheasant, ice cream, and "pyramids of macaroons," more toasts and speeches wishing their local hero godspeed were offered.

Mizner stood up and responded to their good wishes in what the *Benicia New Era* described as "eloquent and emphatic language." He spoke of U.S. government policy toward foreign powers and expressed the pleasure he would find in carrying out his instructions to "use all honorable means in increasing our commercial relations" and in strengthening bonds of amity and friendship with the republics to which he was accredited.

He also referred to his forty years of residence in Benicia, and to "the sadness produced by tearing down the household gods which have been accumulating for these many years," even though his departure was temporary. "He seemed subdued," the reporter noted, "and spoke with deep feeling."[5]

Lansing Mizner was a good American, but he was also a family man. He was confronting not only by far the most important position he had ever held, but also the breakup of the Mizner tribe, which had for so long lived so closely together. The two oldest sons, Lanny (now thirty-one years old) and Edgar (twenty-seven), had not yet left home. Minnie, although married, had not moved far away. In a reversal of the norm, the parents were abandoning the family. It is not surprising, then, that Lansing Mizner was subdued.

When his children learned of Lansing's appointment, in Addison's words, they were flabbergasted. "This meant leaving dear old Benicia. Breaking up the family. Excitement was mingled with tears." Addison was prescient in sensing the profound effect that his father's move would have on the family, and in recalling it over forty years later, he was uncharacteristically emotional. "I sobbed quietly in the corner seat of the train as we left Benicia," Addison confessed. "The entire town turned out to see us off, bringing a band, making speeches." Mama Mizner's thoughts are not recorded. No doubt loyalty to her husband dominated, but she surely shared her son's forebodings.

The logistics of the "home breaking" as Addison brutally described it, were as follows: Lanny, now a practicing lawyer, would stay in Benicia and handle the law and real estate businesses of the Mizner family. William would also stay behind to do his final year of medical internship. Henry was about to start his third year at West Point. Edgar, currently employed in various temporary and uncertain business ventures, was appointed first secretary in the ministry and would work at his father's side in Guatemala City. Addison and Wilson, aged sixteen and twelve, would also go with their parents. Although they had often been left behind when their parents traveled, Mary Hamilton had died in 1888, so Mama Mizner felt obliged to take her two youngest sons with her. The other indispensable member of the family, Ying, also packed up his cooking utensils and said good-bye to Benicia. (A photograph of him taken in Guatemala is affectionately captioned "Señor Don Ying of China.")

"None of us had the haziest idea about Central America," Addison revealed later. "Father had to point it out on the map." Thus did the fractured family start out on their journey to an unknown country. Addison was on crutches, which he found cumbersome and frustrating, but at least he was mobile again. For the first few days, as the steamer took them down the California coast to Mexico, Mama Mizner remained secluded in her cabin (the farewells at the dock had been wrenching), allowing the two young boys free rein. The Mizners had the presidential suite and were treated like royalty. On board was a young portrait painter called Bay Emmett, who taught Addison the use of watercolor and pencil, and he fell madly in love with her.

The route was almost identical to the one Mama Mizner and her family had taken when they left St. Louis thirty-six years earlier. As the ship reached Baja California, Lansing Mizner asked the captain to change course so they could pass the island where the survivors of the *Independence* had spent those terrible days in 1853. Ella Watson Mizner finally appeared on deck and surveyed the remains of the wrecked steamer, which were still visible in the water. "It was a forbidding and awful place," Addison commented.

The next stop could hardly have been more different. The ship docked at Mazatlán, in Mexico, in bright sunlight. "It probably was the greatest day of my life," Addison said later. "For there lying white in the sun was my first Spanish town." For the first time he heard his father speak Spanish, a skill that made him regard his father with a new respect and that he himself was soon to emulate.

After other stops along the Mexican coast, the ship dropped anchor outside San José de Guatemala. The town had no port, and the family had to be winched down to the waiting lighter by derrick and armchair, a frightening experience in the roiling waters. They then took a train through the mountains, where Addison saw monkeys, parrots, macaws, and other flora and fauna of the lush Central American jungle. Finally, hot and exhausted, they reached Guatemala City.

While their parents threw themselves into the duties and rituals of ambassadorship, Addison and Wilson quickly realized that language was the first hurdle to overcome if they were to make friends. They were entered in the Instituto Nacional, "where we learned that boys fought with knives and not with fists. We learned little else except the language." They also took private Spanish lessons, and very soon they were jabbering away in fluent Spanish.

Soon after their arrival in Guatemala, Lansing Mizner had to present his credentials to the four other republics, and he took with him Edgar and Addison. (Wilson presumably was considered too young.) In Nicaragua's capital, Managua, Addison was given a spider monkey, which his father allowed him to keep. He was christened Deuteronomy, which was soon shortened to Deuty. (It was the first of many monkeys Addison called by that name.)

The next stop was Limón, Costa Rica, but the steamer that was supposed to take them failed to appear on time, so Ambassador Mizner, unruffled, hired a thirty-foot dugout to make the trip. After a tough journey without a compass through a steamy night and a blazing hot day, the intrepid travelers arrived in Limón. But customs officials refused to let them land, whereupon an army reception committee was hastily hustled into action. Lansing Mizner hoisted the American flag, and the strange little boat with its distinguished if disheveled passengers approached the landing pier. At that moment, Addison's monkey jumped from the mast onto the top of one of the welcoming generals' plumed hats. There was instant chaos. The soldiers panicked and rushed in every direction, including into the water. The marching band scattered in disarray. Officials shouted orders in vain. Sadly, in the confusion Addison's monkey got hit with a trombone and drowned.

Upon returning to Guatemala City, the Mizners found another kind of drama. In their absence a revolution had been put down, and it turned out that the happy result was due largely to Ella Watson Mizner. Guatemala's beleaguered president, Manuel L. Barillas (who had assumed office in 1885), had the idea of calming his rebellious people by having the American minister's wife appear on a balcony while the national band serenaded her. Mama Mizner thought this a fine idea and decided to reinforce the reassuring picture by traveling through the barricaded city in her open carriage. Confused citizens peered through shutters and saw this sweet little lady, holding up her parasol, serenely trotting through the empty streets. They came to the conclusion that the revolution must be over and peace restored. "By the time she returned home," Addison proudly recorded, "the streets were crowded with people shouting, 'Long live Barillas! Long live the *Presidente*!'"

Addison himself also contributed modestly to Guatemalan history. Like most Latin American dictators, Barillas was constantly being threatened by populist pretenders. One was Juan Rufino Barrios, the nephew of a former president, who was at this time at the height of his popularity with the people. Fearing a coup d'état, Barillas had him arrested and ordered him to be executed. Barrios had an American wife, who rushed to the American Ministry pleading for help. Lansing was away, so Addison was asked to take care of her. She begged Addison to help get her husband out of jail.

Fortunately, Addison by now knew the ways of the palace, and went straight to Barillas and asked for Barrios's release. According to Addison's memoir, the president agreed. Meanwhile (again according to Addison), the president secretly countermanded the order, but by that time Addison and Señora Barrios had reached the prison and gotten Barrios out.

The couple fled to Mexico. Whatever the truth of the rather unlikely story, Addison made a good impression with Señora Barrios, and later she was to return the favor.

Lansing Mizner was deeply interested in pre-Columbian civilizations, and the family (with William, who joined them during the summer) took a trip to Copán, on the border of Honduras, to see the Mayan ruins. Addison was as affected as his father by the beauty and drama of these sacrificial sites, signaling a seriousness that set him apart from his brothers. The ancient architecture "left an indelible picture on my mind of what was once the glory of a great and vanished civilization," he wrote later. "A city that must have housed a half million souls, with all its pomp of royalty, and priesthood."

For Addison, life in Guatemala passed quickly. It was a heady time. The Mizners had a box at the opera, attended bullfights and horse races, and enjoyed a diet of fruits, tortillas, and tropical juices. On Sundays they attended services at the cathedral, where the men were separated from the women, and the Mizner boys made eyes at the beautiful, remote *señoritas*. All the local aristocrats had valets, so Addison and Wilson were assigned Paulino, who was supposed to look after them, carry their books, and generally treat them like grandees. "Poor soul—he was only a few years older than we were, and what a time we gave him," Addison recalled.

The place was exotic, their father was the most important foreigner in the city, and they had an immense amount of freedom. Although Henry did not visit (he had resigned from West Point to take up his true vocation as a clergyman and was studying at the General Episcopal Seminary in New York City), William, Horace, and Minnie all came to stay and enjoy the perks. Minnie took a large number of photographs and placed them in an album, including one of Addison dressed up in Indian costume.

But Addison was homesick. Although he had absorbed lessons in Central American art, architecture, and gardens that would form the basis of his later creative triumphs, he was at this point still a frustrated teenager, bored and alienated by the provincial culture of this colonial outpost. He was nearly seventeen and already much bigger and taller than most of the local boys. He had abandoned his crutches and now used a cane, which he thought made him quite a dandy. He wanted to return to all his friends back home. After some discussion, his parents agreed to let him return to California to continue (if that's the word) his education. Minnie arranged for him to attend the Bates School in San Rafael in the fall. So in late 1890, after just over a year in Guatemala, Addison left his parents and Wilson behind.

For the first time, he was on his own.

CHAPTER 4

"FATHER IS FADING VERY FAST INDEED."

In Guatemala Addison had met an English naval ensign called Robert Falcon Scott. Scott, at twenty-one, was attached to a British training ship in the Pacific. The two young men became good friends, and when Scott was transferred to Victoria, British Columbia, en route home to England, it was arranged that they should take the long journey by steamer together to San Francisco. Scott was at that time depressed about his life and career as a naval officer, and as Addison was equally uncertain about his new life, they forged a bond.

Like Silicon Valley almost exactly a century later, northern California in the 1890s was overflowing with new millionaires who had been made rich by gold, silver, and an economic boom. San Francisco was the main beneficiary of this flood of money. Less than fifty years earlier, it had been a small mining town without legal or political restraints, a hastily built outpost for disparate gold hunters who surged into the area looking for El Dorado. By the time Addison rode into town, San Francisco had generated a largely self-appointed social elite and a thriving cultural life and was now eager to proclaim itself as important an American city as New York, initiating a rivalry that still shows no signs of abating.

In Evelyn Wells's gossipy social history about San Francisco's "champagne days" of the late nineteenth century, most of the anecdotes highlight the merits of San Francisco's opera house, theaters, night life, and so on, in comparison to New York's. She was at pains to glorify the members of San Francisco's emerging aristocracy, although she conceded that the social stratification taking place was not entirely stable. One of the charming features of San Francisco life, she declared, was that "nobody bothered greatly about anyone else's claims to belong." Nevertheless, the social arbiters in the West were just as ambitious as those in the East, and each coast claimed leadership in the arts and society.[1]

Addison was eager to share in this stimulating society when he arrived in San Francisco in the fall of 1890. Not only was he now free from parental supervision, but perhaps more important, he was also absolved from having to look after Wilson. Precocious at seventeen, Addison found that his two older brothers had paved the way very effectively for him in the city. He made the most of it.

Arriving in San Francisco after the long sea journey, Addison, although new in town, wanted to impress his English friend Scott, so he asked a bellhop at their hotel for names of drinking establishments in the area. In spite of the bellhop's dubious glances at this youthful imbiber, the information was given, and after dinner Addison led Scott to a saloon and insouciantly started to order drinks. Suddenly Addison's sangfroid was dashed. Who should be standing almost next to him but his brother Lansing! Lan, the conscientious lawyer, was horrified to recognize his underage brother. Kicking Addison out, he spent the rest of the evening himself visiting bars with Robert Scott.

Addison felt humiliated, but Scott never referred to it except to say how wise Addison was to have left early and that it was no fun being in those places. Addison appreciated this show of tact, and after Scott returned to his naval base in Portsmouth, England, they remained in touch. "He was the nicest, most thoughtful fellow, I think, I have ever known," Addison said later. They corresponded right up to the time that Robert, now Captain Scott, died attempting to reach the South Pole in March 1912.[2]

In his memoir, Addison tells of his fondness for Scott. What he does not say is that his sister Minnie had also met Scott sometime in 1889— possibly in Guatemala, when Addison first knew him—and had developed a fondness for the young Englishman that escalated into a serious crush. When Scott's address book for that period was examined after his death, a poem was found written in Minnie's tall, almost illegible hand. Marked "Hotel Pleasanton, San Francisco, 20 March, 1890," where she was staying with her husband (they normally spent the winter in town), she had written:

The night has a thousand eyes,
When day is done.
The mind has a thousand eyes.
The heart but one.
Yet the light of a whole life dies,
When love is gone.

Was Scott's depression at this time, described so vividly in his journals, partly the result of falling in love with the married Minnie? Was his kindness to Addison some way of keeping in touch with the Mizner he really cared about? Did he try to see Minnie during that visit in the fall of 1890? Did Addison conspire in any of this? Addison, in his memoir, is silent on the subject. A year after Scott died, his wife, Kathleen, wrote in her diary, "Remember Mrs. Chase 24 years ago. She couldn't believe you'd remained unmarried so long."[3] In 1890, when Minnie penned her love note to Scott, she had been married less than two years.

In San Francisco, Addison was swept up in the Mizner boom ushered in by his brothers. By the early 1890s, Lansing, Edgar, and William (now a practicing physician) were integral members of a high-living group of young blades dominating the anarchic social scene. Lansing, appointed city attorney for Benicia, was known as a club man, coming to San Francisco regularly to attend events at the Cotillion Club and the Pacific Union Club.* Lansing, theatrically inclined since childhood, got involved in entertainments, for instance, as impresario of a play entitled *The Scrap of Paper,* in which his brother Edgar and other friends appeared. Lansing brought the comedy to Benicia, causing huge excitement and more kudos to the Mizner tribe.[4]

By this time, Edgar (having returned from Guatemala), was working as a wine salesman, which meant that he was constantly in the best places with the best people, peddling Mumm's champagne with his partner, the ubiquitous Ned Greenway, to a thirsty clientele. Like his brother, he dabbled in the arts. In 1892 *The Wave,* a weekly journal that covered the activities and happenings of the socially prominent, published an article by Edgar entitled "Triumph of Macelrano," about a

---

*The Cotillion Club had been founded by San Francisco's leading society umpire, Ned Greenway, specifically for the purpose of selecting an exclusive membership, like New York's "400."

passé bullfighter in Guatemala who makes one last kill. (Later *The Wave* published rather more distinguished western writers, such as Frank Norris, Jack London, and Ambrose Bierce.)

Edgar was handsome, 6 feet 2 inches tall, blond, with a heavy mustache, and given to wearing sporty tweeds, with a vest, gold chains, and a rakish bowler hat. The most successful Lothario of the brothers, he had conducted a very public romance with Teresa Fair, the very eligible elder daughter of James Fair, one of the Comstock Lode millionaires. For a few years Edgar remained a front-runner and had the honor of sitting next to Mrs. Fair at the head table for Tessie's debutante dance, but the young heiress proved elusive and in 1890 became engaged to Hermann Oelrichs, a wealthy shipping agent from New York twenty years her senior. Oelrichs was a fun-loving athlete and club man, with reportedly one of the best valets in town. (Gossip had it that Mrs. Fair was very anxious to establish her daughter in New York society and that Oelrichs was happy to assist in this estimable ambition.) The wedding was one of the grandest and most lavish San Francisco had ever seen. (Edgar was an usher.) While Tessie's choice of husband was disappointing for Edgar (and even more so for Mama Mizner), it was not a surprise. People observed that while several San Franciscans had aspired to Tessie's hand, "they were a rather tough lot." Western manners had not yet achieved the refinement of those in the East.

For the ambitious young men of the city, the most important institution in San Francisco was the Bohemian Club, founded in 1872, "when San Francisco was still an outpost, removed by time and distance from the artistic advantages of the larger and older cities of the American East," wrote club member Arnold Genthe. (German-born Genthe, who later became a very highly regarded photographer of theater and dance personalities, started his career as a portrait photographer in San Francisco. His early success hinged on his talent for making society ladies appear slimmer than they were, including Mrs. Lansing Mizner and her daughter, Mrs. Horace B. Chase.)[5] The Bohemian Club was a center for writers and artists, and visiting literary figures, such as Oscar Wilde (who came to San Francisco in 1882), would be invited to lunch or dinner. In short, the club epitomized the energy and iconoclasm of the city's new upper-class youth and raised the sophistication level of the still-provincial city.

Addison started at the Bates School in San Rafael, as previously arranged. After an exile of two years, first bedridden in Benicia and then living in Guatemala, he was delighted to land firmly on two feet (in every sense of the word) right in the middle of the social landscape of San Francisco. Most weekends Addison took the train from San Rafael into the city and reconnected with the friends he had not seen for so long. Scions of well-known San Francisco families—Goad, Martin, Greenfield, Nelson—were part of this crowd.[6]

As with most boys his age, the main topics of discussion were parties and girls. Richard Harding Davis, who was at the start of his hugely successful career as war reporter, travel writer, and storyteller, was one of Addison's acquaintances. (Addison once related to Davis the story of his rescue of Barrios and his wife, which the writer used later in his best-selling novel *Soldier of Fortune*.) Addison observed that Davis was "tolerable fond" of Helen Benedict, another wealthy member of Addison's circle. "But I hear from headquarters," Addison said with satisfaction, "that soup awaits the gent for his time is over." (Addison was right. Although Benedict remained a good friend of the writer, in 1900 she married Thomas Hastings, an architect in the partnership of Carrère & Hastings in New York.) The group members fell in and out of love, went to parties, and collected bad jokes. ("Downing, a boy here at school, wanted to know if a surcingle was an unmarried man.") Addison himself was quickly becoming known for his outspoken language; one of the girls in the group told him he was very vulgar for using the expression "full as a tick." He was making a lively start to his social career.

Life at school was not altogether bad. There was a lot of tennis and swimming and visiting the local hotel, where the boys met girls who were vacationing with their parents. Whenever the headmaster, Mr. Bates, made the mistake of leaving the campus for an evening, Addison's friends would come over to the school and have midnight suppers in his room. Each boy paid a small cash contribution. For $1.15 they could buy 1 apple, 2 apricot pies, 25 crackers, 10 pieces of cheese, 15 lemon cakes, 10 lemon drops, and 10 sugars for the lemonade. When danger in the form of a master approached, the boys hid under Addison's bed, munching cookies.

This freedom from parental constraints did not last long, however. Shortly after Addison left Guatemala, Lansing Mizner made a major political blunder. Up until then, the inexperienced diplomat had conducted himself with rectitude. He helped settle border difficulties between Nicaragua and Costa Rica, and when Guatemala and San Salvador went to war, he negotiated a peace agreement within two months. But in August 1890, a serious incident occurred. General J. Martin Barrundia, a former minister of war for Guatemala, had been exiled to Mexico. From there he attempted to invade Guatemala, but the Mexican government thwarted his effort and forced him to board the merchant ship *Acapulco,* which sailed under the U.S. flag. The Guatemalan authorities decided to arrest Barrundia, but out of courtesy they first informed the American consul-general of their plans. He went along, as did the American minister in Guatemala, Lansing Mizner, who added the proviso that Barrundia must be "protected from any injury or molestation to his person."

Guatemalan soldiers stormed the ship, Barrundia resisted, and in the ensuing shoot-out, Barrundia was killed. Although no diplomatic rules had been broken, back home Americans were appalled at what they saw as foreign aggressors assassinating a political outcast on board a U.S.-registered ship without a fair trial, thus dishonoring the American flag, challenging the sovereignty of a friendly country, insulting millions of American citizens, etc., etc.[7] According to the State Department, Mizner should have recommended that the Guatemalans seize Barrundia "at their own risk" rather than implicating the U.S. government in his protection. To appease public opinion, Mizner was charged with interference and recalled to the United States by old dish-face Harrison. Ella Mizner (and others) staunchly defended Mizner and said he had done the right thing. "Papa has no regrets, but I think will make it lively for the Administration when he returns if he does not think it may be better to pose as a martyr," she declared.

The family returned to California in December 1890. They had been away for only a year and a half. Lansing's disgrace was played down for the younger children, who were led to understand that it was their father's poor health that had led him to return home so unexpectedly. But his humiliation cast a pall over the Christmas celebrations that year. For the first time, the tribe's dynamic patriarch had lost his magic.

At the beginning of 1891, Wilson, now nearly fifteen, joined Addison at Bates. Mama's Angel Birdie immediately picked up with his brother's friends and shared the midnight feasts and started to work his particular kind of destructive spell on his older brother. Although Wilson was caught in several lies and trickery and caused much destructive behavior, gullible Addison still believed that his brother would stay the course. Finally, however, even Addison was compromised by Wilson's rebelliousness. After a short vacation at Stag's Leap, Addison returned to school to be greeted by a group of friends yelling, "Your brother's skipped!" One of the boys had set off a cap outside the dining room, and headmaster Bates, in fury, had seized Wilson by the collar and said that if he, Bates, were not a gentleman, he would beat him soundly. While the angry headmaster handed out general punishments, Wilson calmly picked up his hat and overcoat and left. Shortly afterward Bates, still enraged, told Addison to pack Wilson's trunk and send it home. A few days later, Addison was summoned into the headmaster's office and given a letter from his mother telling him also to pack his bags and leave the school—for good. Mama Mizner had taken Wilson's side against Bates, saying "[Bates] had not been decent at all."

Wilson had lasted only four months, which says something about the extreme nature of his behavior. Although Mama Mizner had once again come to the defense of her youngest son, Addison had paid the price. He had been having a lot of fun at Bates and admitted as much in the diary he had begun to write that spring. Now he had to say good-bye to his classmates. Reluctantly he joined his parents at Auburn, north of Benicia, where they were visiting for a month. He hated it: the town, the hotel, the boredom, and the lack of social life. When the family returned to Benicia at the end of June, Addison spent the rest of the summer with his sister at Stag's Leap.

Stag's Leap was a large rustic stone mansion, with separate guest quarters and extensive gardens with palms, ornamental trees, an olive grove, and spectacular views over the crags above Napa Valley. The Chases were rich enough to entertain on a lavish scale. A newspaper story on the house said, "There is no occasion to spend a dull moment when visiting at Stag's Leap, for aside from the ceaseless entertainment afforded by the exuberant spirits and ready wit of the hostess there are in the grounds a three-hole (practice) golf links, a beautiful tennis court shaded by oaks and a Roman bath."

One might wonder why the Mizner family seemed always to be staying at Stag's Leap. With Lansing, Minnie, William, Edgar, and Henry gone, the house in Benicia no longer held any appeal. For after his return from Guatemala, Lansing Mizner sank into a serious decline. His health had already begun to fail during his ministerial tenure, but back home he became increasingly enfeebled with lung disease. Although he was only in his mid-sixties, and although many people were supportive of his role in the Barrundia affair, he never attempted to vindicate himself. Instead he lost every vestige of his entrepreneurial spirit and abandoned hope of a distinguished old age.

Addison watched in confusion as his powerful, confident father dwindled before his eyes. His mother spent most of her time tending to her wasted husband, encouraging him, trying to find ways to pique his interest and recover his old energy. Today doctors would probably diagnose him as clinically depressed, but in those days, not much could be done. Ella hoped that constant changes of scenery might revive her husband's spirits, so the couple spent most of their time traveling, leaving their two youngest sons to fend for themselves. It was a decision they would later regret.

During the fall and spring of 1892, Addison and Wilson enrolled in various schools but never stayed long. In desperation their parents finally sent Wilson to Santa Clara College, a Roman Catholic school run by priests that was guarded by a high wall and patrolled by bulldogs. Wilson immediately got into trouble. One night he stole a couple of beefsteaks that were meant for the priests' dinner and tied them to the dangling rope of the alarm bell. When the dogs were let loose to patrol for the night, the noise that ensued was enough to wake the dead. "Wilson bears the distinction of being the only person ever expelled from Santa Clara," Addison wrote with sneaking admiration. "Imagine being expelled from a penitentiary." This was the effective end of Wilson's education, and little attempt was ever made again to make him go back to school.

Addison could have emulated Wilson's wild behavior—after all, they had "ganged together" as children. But in adolescence their differing temperaments began to emerge. Addison, showing signs of a tenaciousness and determination that were lacking in his brother, made a serious effort to persevere with his studies. At the beginning of March 1892, at nineteen, he entered Boones' College in Berkeley and attempted once more to fulfill the entrance requirements for the University of California. Since his schooling had been erratic and fragmented, it was extremely difficult for him. Awash in knowledge about art, literature, and Spanish colonial and pre-Columbian cultures, he had never learned the basics needed to pass exams in the United States. In the end he never passed the college entrance examination. As he put it with typical eloquence, "When I got into the vast, rustling scales of learning, I realized, before they told me, that I had not even passed water."

According to Addison's later recollections, at some point during this time he enrolled in the University of Salamanca in Spain. There is no record of his attendance, but then, foreign students there were not listed unless they received a degree.[8] He makes only a glancing reference to Salamanca in his autobiography, and no reference at all in his personal journal, which suggests that he was there only briefly and that the experience made no lasting impression upon him.

During his abortive forays into higher education, Addison, like his brothers, was making a name for himself in San Francisco society. His friends at this time were more social than artistic. He spent one and a half months in the late summer of 1891 with the Delmases (a prominent San Francisco family) at Santa Cruz and had "too much of a time." In 1900 he failed for some reason to receive an invitation to the Mardi Gras ball of the San Francisco Art Association. Believing this the fault of Ned Greenway, "hero of a thousand quadrilles," Addison responded by publicly spitting into Greenway's beer. "Society Stunned," screamed the headline in the *San Francisco Call*.

Addison was adopted as a friend by Peter Martin, the son of Eleanor Martin, a widow who was one of San Francisco's authentic grandes dames. A sister of former Governor John G. Downey, Eleanor was extremely wealthy and an extravagant hostess. (Evelyn Wells, social historian of the period, declared her San Francisco's Mrs. William Astor.) Even Arnold Genthe was impressed by her. "Sitting at the head of the table, beautifully coiffed and gowned, with a collar of pearls and diamonds about her throat, she presented an amazing figure."[9]

Eleanor Martin had four sons: Walter, Peter, Andrew, and an older son from a previous marriage, Downey Harvey. These boys were hugely rich, having fortunes from both sides of the family. Addison became close friends with Peter, a young roué who owned polo ponies and partied a lot. Staying with him in the Martins' grand house on Nob Hill was very much to Addison's liking, in spite of the fact that Eleanor Martin and her widowed sister, Annie, ran the household on a tight rein. In 1894, when Eleanor and Annie's brother, the former governor, died, the two sisters announced that they were going to Los Angeles for several days to sort out his estate. On their departure, Peter, Andrew, and Addison promptly hired two bands and "invited everybody we shouldn't have known." The party was to last indefinitely—but at ten o'clock that night, the two women ("pyramids in crepe," Addison described them) appeared at the front door. There had been a flood, and the train never departed. "The horrors of the next few days will never leave me," Addison recalled. "Night and day we had to be on guard to keep guests from breaking in, for everybody thought it just a 'Mizner-Martin' joke." Shortly afterward, Peter and Andrew Martin were sent east to college.

In late 1892, Addison's parents moved into the Occidental Hotel in San Francisco. His father was now very sick with what was called "dropsy," or fluid on the lungs. "Papa is no better and I think is much worse," Addison confided sadly to his diary. Not even the great Mama Mizner could reconstruct for her husband the life they had abandoned four years earlier, and as they huddled in yet another anonymous hotel room, their children continued to roam, untended. The Mizner dynasty was unraveling.

In August 1893 Addison and the Martins set off by train (newly equipped with Pullman sleeping cars) to visit the World's Columbian Exposition in Chicago. It was a long ride across half the country, but it was enjoyable thanks to E. H. Harriman's just-purchased Union Pacific Railroad, a huge improvement on the dangerous, time-consuming sea journey around Cape Horn. On the train, Addison and the Martins "just owned the place," offending the other passengers and generally having a high old time. The friends parted in Chicago, for Addison was to stay with the Chases, Minnie's in-laws. He had caught an infection on the train and arrived feeling very sick, but he was determined to get to the exposition.

The sight that greeted him was breathtaking.

In celebration of the four hundred years since Columbus's arrival in the New World, exhibits from 44 states, 5 territories, 50 nations, and 37 colonies had been constructed on a vast chunk of real estate in what is now Jackson Park. Shimmering in the late summer light, this "White City," as it came to be called, seemed to have risen like a magical metropolis along the shores of Lake Michigan. In the center was the largest electric fountain in the world, designed by Frederick MacMonnies (a close friend of Stanford White's), that cost $50,000 and depicted Columbia with her henchpersons at the helm of the barge of state.

In a remarkable homage to the principles of the École des Beaux-Arts in Paris, the preeminent architecture school in Europe, almost every major building in the exposition was designed in the neoclassical style, with peristyles, colonnades, arcades, pediments, balustrades, and pilasters. These edifices were laid out along allées and boulevards and fronted by formal gardens like a combination of Versailles, the Louvre, and the Vatican. The most spectacular feature of the fair's architecture was the Court of Honor. "Mirrored in its reflecting pool was a triumph of classicism and of a nation," as Frederick Platt described it.[10] Many distinguished architects took part in this slavish salute to the Beaux-Arts, including Richard Morris Hunt of New York, J. S. Silsbee of Chicago, and Peabody & Stearns of Boston.

Two major buildings deviated from the neoclassical mold. One was the New York State Building of McKim, Mead & White, which, although Italianate in style, implied a lighthearted pastiche in the ornamentation of its facade, with swaths of garlands, niches with statuary, and striped awnings over the windows. The other rebel was A. Page Brown of San Francisco. Brown had started his career in New York with McKim, Mead & White and had redesigned the neoclassical Clio and Whig Halls at Princeton University in 1889 before moving to San Francisco later that year. For the exposition's California State Building, he chose a design in the mission style, with bell towers, tile roofs, arched windows, and a roof garden. The exterior was made of cracked and seamed plaster, a salute to the weathered look of the California missions back home. Brown's building stood out amid the Corinthian columns and Palladian porticos like a hibiscus in a wheatfield.

As many architects were infuriated as delighted by the White City; some, like Louis Sullivan, saw its neoclassical uniformity as precisely the wrong statement to convey to the world about the state of American architecture. The pioneering new architecture of Chicago was still in its infancy, with only a few buildings, such as Burnham & Root's sixteen-story Monadnock Building, showing the promise of the new steel-and-concrete technology that would create the modern skyscraper. For many architects, this, not the White City, was the shape of the country's architectural future.

Addison was overwhelmed by the exposition. He had seen the Spanish colonial cathedrals and palaces in South America and loved them, but he had never been to Europe and was unfamiliar with the glories of Renaissance architecture. He knew at once that the White City was important, not only in terms of architecture but also as a textbook example of urban planning. Even at that age, he was immediately aware of how much the exhibition as a whole was affected by the layout and landscaping in which the buildings were set: "Nothing for a moment could describe the sublime grace of the buildings, [or] the artistic and clever way in which the grounds are laid out." While it is not clear that this architectural pageant moved him toward a career in architecture, it was a crucial experience for the young Mizner.

As usual, the exposition also made social demands. Addison spent time trying to cheer up Richard Harding Davis, who had pursued the unresponsive Helen Benedict from San Francisco to Chicago. The Goads were also visiting the show, which aggravated Addison's fever, for he was very keen on their daughter, Aileen. "And oh, didn't the sweetest angel that ever trod the clouds look beautiful in a dainty pink and white waist and white duck skirt," he raved, adding, with an irony that frequently creeps into the diary entries, "She almost looked glad to see me." One day during the stay in Chicago, he felt so ill he stayed in bed. Aileen came to visit him, and while he pretended to be asleep, she planted a little kiss on his cheek. The next day he was cured: "No doctor in the world could have done the good she did me in that half second."

After Chicago, Addison took the train to St. Louis to visit his Watson relatives. He spent a week there before going on to New York, where, without warning, he called on his brother Henry, now a student at the General Episcopal Seminary in Manhattan. The brothers had not seen each other for eight years. "He is just as nice as he can be," Addison wrote in his diary. In spite of the emotion of the occasion, Addison particularly noticed the beautiful church, houses, and gardens that spanned the block of West Twenty-first Street where the seminary still stands.

Addison had a good time in New York, spending a weekend in Rye, going to parties with Richard Harding Davis and Helen Benedict, and racing through town with Peter Martin, who came up from Georgetown University to see him.[11] One night Addison and Peter had dinner at the Waldorf and attempted to leave without paying. They spent the night in jail, but thanks to some phone calls to Peter's influential friends, they ended up drinking champagne in the police captain's office. After visiting Niagara Falls with Peter, Addison started the long train journey back to the West Coast, stopping off again in St. Louis. He arrived back in San Francisco on December 1, 1893, and rushed straight to Stag's Leap. Telegrams about his father's worsening condition had failed to reach him until the end of his trip, and he did not know if he would arrive in time. He kept a touching record of his father's last days, showing a sensitivity to the feelings and pain of others that belied his youth.

"December 5. Father is fading very fast indeed. He has been fading ever since I came home. Father has suffered so much that it cannot be a pleasure for him to live and it is only very selfish for us to want him to stay with us.

"December 7th. Dr Livingston came up this morning and says that a few days will see the last of our father. William, Edgar, Min, Wilson are all here, Lan is expected any moment. Was there ever such another woman in the world like Mama Mizner. She has not left father's side in two years and now stands up like a brave soldier to see the dearest thing that a woman can lose taken from her without a word of complaint, nothing on the outside to show a broken heart inside."

Lansing Mizner died on December 10, and two days later the family went down to Benicia by special train for the burial service at St. Paul's Church. He was put into the ground in Benicia Cemetery, which had been founded in 1847, two years before Lansing first set foot in the town for which he had once held such high hopes. It was Addison's twenty-first birthday. "Could anything be more doleful," he wrote in his diary, "this 12th of December, 1893."

Christmas that year was a disaster. The Mizners assembled at Stag's Leap in a gloomy mood. But on Christmas Day something divisive happened, an incident that caused Addison to write in his journal, "There will never be any time that I shan't remember every detail." Apparently Minnie said something cruel to Wilson, something that was so upsetting to the two brothers that they went straight upstairs and packed their trunks and left the vineyard—all in less than two hours. Addison's memoir does not reveal what the comment was, but Mama Mizner later referred to it as an "accusation," probably something to do with Wilson's irresponsible behavior and his lack of respectfulness toward his parents. Addison, joined at the hip to his brother on this occasion, took equal offense, and they stormed out together, leaving poor Mama Mizner with even more to mourn. (Wilson never forgave his sister for her angry words and only ever entered her house again under extreme family pressure.)[12]

With the death of Lansing Mizner, the surviving members of the tribe had to come to grips with reality. The shock of losing the once-powerful head of the family was intensified by the discovery that he had left behind very little money. His estate was valued at approximately $25,000, but almost all of it was in roughly seventy-five small lots of real estate (in which he had only a half share) in Solano and Contra Costa Counties, so there was little ready cash. Moreover, Mizner had made these many land investments during the heady days when it seemed Benicia was going to be the next great city of the West. But in 1893, local real estate was rapidly declining in value—Benicia had been just another "bubble." Lansing had also still had in his possession a stock certificate in the Golden Gate Mining Company, of which he had once been a proud director, but it was now worthless.

Ever since his courtship of Ella, Lansing had been conscious of money. "My only regret," he wrote on their wedding anniversary in 1866, "is that for your sake I could not command more of this world's goods, but that I can support you all as well as I do is a source of some pride to me."[13] The decline in his fortunes that preceded his death must have destroyed that pride. For the Mizner children, who had grown up as pampered young citizens and had expectations of an equally comfortable future, the discovery was devastating.

On learning the state of the family finances, Addison, now twenty-one, made his first seriously adult decision. Two months after his father's death, he signed on with the San Francisco architect Willis Polk and took the first steps toward what was to be his life's work.

CHAPTER 5

"AN ARCHITECT OF GREAT TASTE AND LITTLE MONEY."

Addison's decision to take the plunge into architecture, like many of his career choices, seems to have been made as much by impulse as by calculation. Although a social animal, he unquestionably had an artistic bent, much more than did his elder brothers. Little pencil drawings abound all over his books and journals. During his adolescence he had produced paintings good enough for his sister to hang at Stag's Leap. In the summer of 1893 he boasted of having sold six pictures for $150. He also began to purchase art—one of his first acquisitions, costing $7.50, was a work by the then-fashionable French salon painter Adolphe Bouguereau. (His taste later improved.)

He had certainly begun to think of himself as an artist. His parents became alarmed at this tendency (an artist, in their view, being "the lowest form of long-haired, flowing cravat ass extant"), so much so that when William was given an appointment as resident doctor on a ship going to China, they decided that Addison should accompany him, in order to remove him from temptation. The ruse did not work. Addison came back with two chow dogs (a breed he was to be loyal to for the rest of his life) and a wardrobe of silk pajamas, which he wore on the streets of San Francisco to much amusement.

While the artistic life appealed, architecture seems not yet to have been a high priority as a profession. It is true that in the stories that Addison began writing as he turned twenty-one, he provides unusual architectural detail. For instance: "The house in which they were to meet was one of the handsomest for many blocks. It stood back from the street and was surrounded by a terraced lawn. Long granite steps led to a heavily arched Gothic lobby."[1] But at this time, he was interested in writing, not architecture. His diary, which he kept on and off for three years, is filled with short stories, encounters, exchanges, and snippets of dramatic ideas. Frequently he said how he wished he could express what he felt in writing.

It was no accident, however, that Addison sought out Willis Polk. As well as being a professional architect, Polk was a member in good standing of the city's most prominent creative and literary circles. Addison, who was only five years younger, had known him socially before he started working for him. Minnie Chase was also a close friend and often entertained him at Stag's Leap. Addison's friendship with Polk put him in touch with San Francisco's most radical young artists, and their work reflected the city's restlessness and insecurity. Since Polk's bohemian world was precisely the world that Addison found most attractive, choosing to go in to business with this talented and controversial figure was for many reasons a very good idea.

Willis Jefferson Polk was born in 1867 in Jacksonville, Illinois, and grew up in St. Louis. His father was a carpenter, and Willis joined him in an architectural firm in Kansas City. After a stint working in New York for A. Page Brown, the architect who designed the mission-style California State Building at the World's Columbian Exposition, in 1886 Polk moved to San Francisco and opened an office. Three years later he launched the first number of *Architectural News*. It lasted for only three issues but was influential far beyond its meager circulation and put Polk's name firmly on the architectural map.[2] In 1889 Page Brown joined Polk, and the two architects worked on several projects together until Brown's accidental death in 1896 at the age of thirty-seven.

Polk, a brilliant theorist, saw the necessity of rescuing American architecture from the confusing mixture of styles in which it was currently drowning. The country's most influential postrevolutionary architect, H. H. Richardson, had broken away from colonial Georgian architecture and created his own American vernacular (mostly of rough-hewn granite in primitive forms) that he called "Romanesque" and that others called Baroque (or "barbaric" if they disliked it). Following Richardson's initiative, the late nineteenth century saw an explosion of architectural definitions: Eastlake, Queen Anne, Second Empire, Victorian, Gothic. All these styles promoted ornamentation as an aesthetic ideal, with balustrades, brackets, scrolls, gables, cupolas, pediments, latticework, colored glass, turrets, porches, bays, and a variety of asymmetrical encrustations clinging to the facades of houses, resulting in what one commentator described as "an epidemic of bad taste, ending in the Titanic inebriation of the Romanesque."[3]

Meanwhile, McKim, Mead & White, George B. Post, and Louis Sullivan, among others, were attempting to move away from "Titanic inebriation" into simplified idioms. Willis Polk sympathized with their principles. Yet while the World's Columbian Exposition in Chicago signed the death warrant, as one critic said, of lingering Richardsonian Romanesque, Polk and his friends felt that Beaux-Arts classicism should not replace it as the dominant influence in American architecture.[4] (Sullivan commented that the Chicago fair set back American architecture fifty years.)

Polk found an equal mishmash of styles in the West. Indeed, California architecture at that time was an oxymoron. Most early California housing had been constructed according to need and available materials by pioneer gold miners and land speculators. A professional architect would have found scant response unrolling blueprints in front of such clients. Critic Claude Bragdon wrote scathingly about the "veritable chamber of horrors" that was western architecture: "It is said that in the early days it was the custom for the builder, at a certain stage in the construction of a house, to appear upon the scene with a wagon load of miscellaneous jig-saw ornaments, which he would then hold up, one by one, in the presence of its owner, until the latter had selected those that pleased him best."[5] The elaborate fretwork of Carpenter Gothic, which reflected the growing prosperity of towns like San Francisco, evolved from these early structures.

But other vernacular architectural styles existed in the West: Spanish, Mexican, and Pueblo. The missions built in California during the eighteenth century hewed to the Spanish colonial tradition of stucco or plastered walls, bell towers, cloisters, and interior courtyards. Houses had covered porches, curvilinear gables, and wooden shingle roofs. While this architecture became tainted by the imperialism with which it was associated, many buildings survived and were treasured for their elegance and beauty. Page Brown's California State Building at the World's Columbian Exposition demonstrated his commitment to this local aesthetic.

Willis Polk was stimulated by the architectural freedom he found in the West. "California is positive," he wrote, "it is individual, it is great in opportunity, and when the ages have lent it dignity, it will go down in history with Egypt, with Greece, with Rome and with France. It will be the inheritor of all their greatest, but the projection of its own."[6] With this high standard in mind, Polk set out to eradicate the overembellished, Carpenter Gothic styles endemic to San Francisco's residential architecture in the 1880s and 1890s. The city had grown out of its mining-camp image and was now entering the lists as a major U.S. city, and Polk was one of the major promoters of its new destiny. He started to design houses that drew on rustic, shingle, and regional sources. While some called it Colonial Revival, Polk liked the expression "academic eclecticism," and it was very modern. His colleagues and collaborators—Page Brown, Ernest Coxhead, and Bernard Maybeck—were also part of this movement to reposition California architecture for the twentieth century.

For one project, Polk suggested a symmetrical eighteenth-century facade. For two others, he used Flemish gables and Tudor detailing. In 1893 he designed a house with Venetian influences, including a Byzantine-style porch and first-floor balcony. A critic described one of his San Francisco projects as having "something of the associated charm of the Alhambra."[7] One of his most elegant neoclassical designs was the Bourn mansion in Woodside, known as Filoli, built toward the end of his career (1915–17) and now perhaps more famous for its spectacular gardens.

Polk favored eclecticism, but he also respected California vernacular, in particular the mission tradition. He praised mission architecture in *Architectural News* and helped rehabilitate Mission Dolores, the beautiful basilica that escaped destruction by the San Francisco earthquake in 1906 and remains the oldest mission in California. In an effort to recapture the authentic qualities of this architecture, rather than distort it for vulgar effect, he studied tile making and Spanish building techniques. "When a country possesses an architectural tradition of as charming and simple a character as our pastoral missions," he wondered, "is it not a pity to note the growing tendency towards its misuse upon our city streets?"[8]

Polk's sensitive approach and discriminating taste were critical to Addison's evolution as an architect, and they set a standard for him as an apprentice that he never forgot. Addison spent a lot of time in Polk's extensive library. He also learned draftsmanship under his eccentric though brilliant employer. But it was Polk's knowledge of hands-on building—learned from his own father and increased by his extensive study of mission architecture—that was ultimately of the greatest value to Addison. Through Polk, Addison began to look at buildings with an eye not only to their infrastructure but also to their proportions—the height of an arcade, the size of a window, the perspective of an interior courtyard. Through Polk he learned to pay close attention to the materials and colors that had been used in the missions—the rustic cypress ceilings, the texture of stucco, the quality of tile work, the cerulean blue stain (ground minerals mixed with cactus juice) on the walls, the trompe l'oeil decoration. Through Polk, he developed a heightened response to light and landscape and recognized their relevance to architecture. Through Polk, he understood that traditional styles of architecture should be respected and were easily debased in the wrong hands. Through Polk, he learned tile making, carpentry, masonry, and other construction techniques. Addison was later severely criticized for not having gone to architecture school. But Willis Polk was his architecture school, and the lessons Addison received from him were beyond price.

The only problem with the relationship was that there was no money in it. Polk's outspokenness and lack of restraint made him a controversial figure in San Francisco. His radical views were widely disseminated in *The Wave,* for which he frequently wrote. He was an enthusiastic member of the Bohemian Club. He also belonged to a group of young artists and poets known as Les Jeunes, who began publishing a journal, *The Lark,* in 1895. (It lasted until 1897.) *The Lark* promoted experimental writing and printing, for instance using typography on only one side of the page, and printing on bamboo paper bought in Chinatown that was dampened and pressed to lie flat. This innovative journal was mostly put together on Polk's kitchen table. The subeditor, in his element, was Addison Mizner. One trusts that spell-checks were not done on his watch.

But these creative ventures had no commercial potential, and as for architecture, Polk's lack of professional degrees and personal obnoxiousness offended many potential clients. Addison described his friend as "a young architect of great taste and little work," a genius "who was only spoiled by having read Whistler's 'The Gentle Art of Making Enemies.'"

(This refers to a collection, put together by the splendidly provocative artist James McNeill Whistler, of the offensive letters and bad reviews he had received in the London press, including his libel suit against art critic John Ruskin, along with Whistler's equally offensive responses—just the kind of stimulating reading matter Addison loved.)[9]

Thus if Addison had hoped to earn a living wage from Polk's architectural practice, he was disappointed. Although proudly listed in the city directory of 1895 as an architect, he received barely a nickel during his apprenticeship. In recognition of this hardship, Polk invited him to become a partner, and for a while they shared a house together on Russian Hill. In his memoirs Addison summoned up a romantic picture of bohemian life in a garret: "We were very poor, and sometimes lived on beans for days." According to Ashton Stevens, a friend of Addison's, they were so poor, they could not afford a clock. They could afford a Chinese servant, however, and Stevens told the story of how each morning at ten o'clock, and every thirty minutes subsequently, the servant would leave a cup of coffee outside Willis's and Addison's bedroom doors. "Thus by counting cups they knew when it was noon and time to begin the day's work."[10]

Even while he remained penniless with Polk, Addison kept in with the rich *gratin* of San Francisco. He went to horse shows, where his friends the Martins, the Hobarts, and the Goads took boxes. He attended polo parties and entertainments. By November 1894 he was sufficiently well known to be appearing in the cartoons of the *Examiner's* famous resident cartoonist Jimmy Swinnerton, who signed his sketches "Swin." (Swinnerton is credited with helping to found the comic strip.) Swin always drew Addison with a retroussé nose and dandyish clothes, a long lock of blond hair flopping down over his ear. This distinguished him dramatically from the cartoon-drawn Willis Polk, who was shown with architectural drawings sticking out of his pocket, and the other Mizner brothers, who were generally depicted with dark hair, heavy black mustaches, and sideburns. These cartoons of "Addie," as he was affectionately known, remind one of the English aesthetes inspired by Oscar Wilde (and parodied by Gilbert and Sullivan), whose witty plays were then wowing London and whose affair with Lord Alfred Douglas in 1894 erupted into scandal and tragedy.

The cartoons also took note of Addison's rotund stomach, which must have hurt. At this time he was very concerned about his weight, and his family teased him relentlessly about it. His appearance, his poverty, and his lack of a Harvard education all haunted him.

For Addison was in love. He had been in love since 1891, when he fell hard for Aileen Goad, whose family was rich and prominent and whose sister, Genevieve, was a famous beauty known as the "California Venus." Addison had spent much of his time at Bates moping over Aileen, frequently writing to her and sending her flowers (sometimes as many as a hundred roses, which he could ill afford). Now, however, his affections had waned. "I think I have broken myself of the Aileen habit at last," he wrote in the fall of 1893, "although it was quite a struggle. We parted with much ceremony and it did not hurt me as much as it used to when I quarreled with her." He was able to describe Aileen's new beaux without emotion, although he was unimpressed by her choices.

The reason Addison could say good-bye to Aileen so easily was that he had found a replacement, one who kept him in painful suspense for the next two years. Ella Hobart was very rich and "a fascinator." (Did it count that she had the same name as his mother?) It was not just her money that fascinated him. Addison was surrounded by girls who had money, including his best friend Mary Belle Gwin, a beauty described by Arnold Genthe as "petite and piquant, with olive skin and sparkling brown eyes." (Her father, William Gwin, a southerner, at midcentury became the first U.S. senator from the state of California.) Addison air-ily dismissed these wealthy young women, saying of one poor reject, "She cannot press her trousers under my mattress." Ella, on the other hand, was not only rich but remote—she kept Addison at arm's length. Having no money, he sensed, was going to be a serious drawback to his romantic plans for her.

The only way Addison could alleviate his misery was by the standard mode of the romantically afflicted—expressing his feelings in writing. His journal at this time is filled with attempts at short stories, delivered in pencil in his beautiful flowing hand and terrible spelling. The stories carry the same gloomy theme: a poor young man is in love with a rich girl; the rich girl rejects him for a more suitable marriage. In one story, the girl kills herself because her father won't allow her to marry the impoverished suitor. In another, the hero is a painter living in a garret who becomes obsessed with his portrait of the loved one. Addison liked this theme: in a longer story the hero, an opera singer, goes abroad to study, promising his loved one that he will come back as a success and marry her. They passionately correspond, but gradually her letters grow more infrequent, and when he returns, he reads in the newspaper that she has married someone else. In a similar tale, the roles are reversed: the rich girl goes abroad and the hero is left behind. Again, he reads in the newspaper that she has married a duke, at which point he tragically drowns himself.

These stories exhibit only a very modest literary talent, yet the fact that this energetic and social young man kept a diary at all is interesting. For all Addison's adolescent flightiness, he was introspective and self-analytical enough to regularly monitor his feelings, thoughts, and ideas—an endeavor that was not typical for a young male growing up in the anti-intellectual climate of fin-de-siècle California, and one not at all compatible with his later reputation as a shallow exhibitionist. That he kept the journal for three years indicates the concentration and determination that would later lead him to overcome many obstacles and complete seemingly impossible assignments. Conversely, these characteristics could also drive him stubbornly to pursue a disastrous course, culminating in the Boca Raton fiasco. Crazy dreams and good judgment were not always linked in Addison's fertile mind.

Meanwhile, as the seasons in San Francisco bloomed and wilted, our hero pined and scribbled. Ella attended all the social events, and her brother was a friend, but Addison could not prevail. He managed to acquire a photograph of her, which he framed in gold with a bow. He would always pass by her house on his way back from a party, even if it was out of his way, in hope of catching sight of her. This inspired another diary plot-line involving a young man who loiters night after night outside a rich girl's house. He is finally arrested by two policemen, but just as he is about to be taken off to jail, the girl comes out of the house and invites him in.

Poor Addie. He had a bad case of lovesickness, and by his twenty-second birthday he was fully in its grip. "Oh, I wish I had the right to tell her that I loved her, but thank God I have the sense to know I am a pauper and even if I did have the nasty money that everyone loves and I hate, I never could be worthy of her." Anyway, he knew she hated him: "No matter how nice I try to be she wiggles off and talks to Smedberg [a rival] or something as abhorrent."

He began to turn a bitter eye on his rich friends. "I am getting tired of society. I like Bohemia so much more. It's more varied. I have been out every night for the past 5 months and teas and receptions in the afternoon until 8 am. I am so sick of invitations that I spit when I think of them." Yet he turned down an offer to travel around the world as personal secretary to an important businessman, because he could not bear to leave his beloved.

Throughout 1895 Addison remained in the thrall of his obsession, awkwardly tugging at his collar when he saw her, thinking of nothing else when they were apart, wildly trying by some stratagem to win her affections. The lack of money continued to hammer at his self-esteem. He admitted that this was the first time he minded the absence of a family inheritance: "I wish she was poor so that I could have her (if she would) and live in a little cottage (doesn't that sound romantic)." He continued to concoct stories about hopeless causes with transcendent endings, achieved with a healthy dose of wishful thinking.

But writing fiction could not transform reality for the lovelorn author. In April 1895 his diary entry is particularly emotional: "I wake up in the morning. I go to bed at night. The only thought I have is that I love I love. I saw her this evening in fact. It isn't my fault when I don't see her. I wish she could bear me or I wish I was dead or something." This *cri de coeur* is written in an uneven, wobbly hand. Perhaps he was drunk as well as desperate. In December, just before his twenty-third birthday, Addison had a fight with Ella that, judging from his diary, was devastating. "I just hope I can make up now and do something besides think of—well, you know." At the bottom of the page, in an angry scrawl, he wrote, "Miss moneybags has just gone." Except for stories, this was the last entry in the journal.

Thirty-five years later he wrote in his memoir that he was always in love. "I was the prize 'mush' of the world." About Aileen Goad, whom he considered the beauty of San Francisco, he wrote: "I couldn't work or sleep, and was either in the clouds, or in the dumps." One night, when something went wrong between them, he decided to commit suicide. But when he was about to do it, he remembered he had a hole in his drawers. "By the time I had got home I had forgotten about it."

He doth protest too much. Addison's state of mind when he had the final row with Ella was undoubtedly as dark as it had ever been. He was not earning any money with Willis Polk, and he saw little point in staying on with his abrasive and impractical partner. Polk filed for bankruptcy in 1897 and five years later left San Francisco to join Daniel H. Burnham in Chicago. After the 1906 earthquake and fire, Polk returned to San Francisco to help rebuild the city, but he had lost most of his creative energy and died in 1924.

Unexpectedly, at this low point, Addison was offered an extraordinary opportunity—in Guatemala, where he had first discovered architecture. In 1892 Juan Rufino Barrios had finally removed Barillas and became the new dictator of Guatemala. His wife, remembering Addison's rescue of her husband and aware of his architectural ambitions, invited him to design a new palace for her in Guatemala City. Addison was to be architect, superintend the project, buy furniture in France, and receive a retainer of $25,000 in gold.

This was a spectacular coup for Addison, who at this point had yet to build a shed, let alone a palace, and was still only twenty-three. He signed the contracts, which were then dispatched by boat to Guatemala. With the promise of the enormous fee, Addison went on a spending binge. "I didn't know there was that money in the world. I was drunk with excitement. I ordered a tropic trousseau, gave dinners, and sent flowers—all charged, of course." Five weeks later, he rushed down to the dock in San Francisco to receive the first check—only to learn that Barrios had been assassinated the night before the boat had left Guatemala. "So that was that!"[11]

What a catastrophe! An opportunity that would have dramatically changed Addison's life and career was suddenly denied him. What was more, he had already spent the money and was now seriously in debt. What could he do? Being a penniless artist had lost its appeal. He had not yet written anything salable. Architecture seemed a dead end.

But in what was to become the pattern of his reckless, uneven, paradoxically lucky life, whenever he found himself out of cards, without the slightest effort on his part, a major shuffle occurred. His gift—and curse—was unthinkingly to embrace the next hand he was offered and take it up with total commitment. Like a true child of California pioneers, he followed his gambling spirit wherever it took him. On this occasion, it was the members of the Mizner tribe who held out to him the promise of a sensational new deal.

CHAPTER 6

"THE OLD PIONEER BLOOD OF THE TRIBE ROSE IN MY BRAIN."

Like a true Mizner, Addison kept his financial troubles to himself after the Guatemalan fiasco, but his mother found out and was very concerned. "Why did you not tell me something of your affairs?" she asked him. "I might have been able to help you in some way. It is not well to be too reticent about your troubles—especially to your mother."[1] But Mama Mizner was in no condition to help her son. After her husband's death, she had sold the Benicia house and much of the real estate (at deeply depressed prices) and had been living in small rented apartments in San Francisco. These soon became too expensive, and she was forced to move in with her daughter and son-in-law at Stag's Leap. Her presence, unsurprisingly, was not entirely welcome. How often is a mother, particularly one as strong-minded as Ella, welcome when she moves in with the in-laws? Minnie was an outspoken woman, and the atmosphere between her and her mother soon became poisonous. Ella Mizner, on this occasion displaying the sensitivity of a clothespin, seemed hurt and puzzled by Minnie's behavior and told Addison she thought her daughter was behaving very oddly: "I see very little of her. I do not feel as though they are glad to have me." Henry was shocked by his sister's behavior and urged his mother to leave, saying to Addison, "She ought not to suffer the indignity of living there."[2] To her adoring sons, Mama Mizner quite openly expressed her deepest wish—that her boys could make enough money to make a comfortable home for them all.

So far none of them held out the faintest promise of doing so. While Lansing was earning a modest salary as a lawyer, Henry was beginning his Episcopal career as canon at Christ Church Cathedral in St. Louis, with equally modest financial expectations. Edgar's various deals in San

Francisco consistently failed to produce any benefits. William, who spent much of his time treating (without pay) the medical problems of the Chase family, had an unprofitable practice. (Minnie and Horace certainly got their money's worth out of the brothers. William was their doctor-in-residence, and Addison fixed up their attic as house architect, also without pay. When the Chases later made some unpleasant remarks about him to Mama Mizner, Addison retorted that he should have charged them for his work.)

While Lansing Mizner's death had had a damaging effect on all his children, the most affected was the youngest, Wilson, who had been seventeen years old when his father died. Totally neglected by his family, he was let loose on the city of San Francisco. In no time he found his way to the Barbary Coast, a notorious area that included a red-light district, seedy bars, and a population of con men, thieves, gamblers, and discarded entertainers. Here Wilson discovered that he could sing, after a fashion, and the more sentimental the song, the better his audience liked it. According to Evelyn Wells, the foul atmosphere of Pacific Street was purified by "the strong young voice of Wilson Mizner," who played the piano and sang with a voice "like a jolt over the heart."[3]

But he failed to establish himself as a club singer, and his attempts at boxing, gambling, and other unimpressive career choices also came to nothing. Finally he received an unexpected blow: his mother would not lend him any more money. (The story went that when he wired her for a loan, she replied, "I never got the telegram.") He wound up promoting a medicine show in the Northwest, and when that failed, he returned to a drug-infested dive on the Barbary Coast and moved in with a bar singer going by the name of Rena Fargo. Wilson was now all of twenty years old. It was an unorthodox life for a young man, to say the least. But from the age of seventeen onward, Wilson had been without supervision from anybody, even Mama Mizner. His brothers later conceded that his behavior was to some extent an inevitable consequence of this sad abdication of parental responsibility.

While Lansing, now reaching his fortieth birthday, was resigned to a low-level legal career, William, Edgar, Addison, and Wilson were all eager to find some high-flying operation that would make them rich. As though by magic, their prayers were answered, and they found themselves poised to participate in the second major gold rush of the century.

They had missed the first, to their chagrin. Now they were being given a chance to make their killing.

The excitement started on June 15, 1897, when the steamship *Excelsior* arrived in San Francisco from Alaska, carrying passengers breathless with the news that they had collected a million dollars' worth of gold dust from the streams of the Yukon River. Just over a month later, the ship *Portland* steamed into Seattle with the same story. People with long memories recalled the first shiny promise of 1849, a promise that had turned into disappointment when thousands of prospectors, finding no gold, turned to gambling and crime instead. But this strike looked different. Rumors of treasure in the Arctic Northwest, in the Dominion of Canada, had been flying around for some time, and now the pioneers had come back with the evidence. The gold was real, and ready for the taking, in a place as remote as California had been fifty years earlier. Gamblers from all over the country once more dropped everything and started the arduous journey to a cold, inhospitable territory with the dream of striking it rich. On July 28 the *Excelsior* sailed from San Francisco with 350 hopeful prospectors and 800 tons of provisions and supplies. More than ten thousand people gathered at the Mission Street Wharf to see the first party of gold seekers depart. It was America at its most adventurous, its craziest, its most optimistic.[4]

William and Edgar were not on the *Excelsior,* but they had their plans in place and led the brothers' charge. Earlier that year William had made an investment in a prospective gold mine in the northern Sierras and told Addison to go up to Delta, in Shasta County, to check out the situation. (At this point Addison was happy to be given any job, however unappealing.) Meanwhile Edgar had finagled for himself a position as manager of the Alaska Commercial Company in the Yukon. When he arrived in Dawson City, the base camp for the Yukon minefields, and learned that the river was truly awash in gold dust, he telegraphed his brothers to make their way as fast as possible to the promised land. In this situation it was every man for himself, and yet at the same time no man could work a mine alone. Edgar reckoned that blood-brotherhood was the best way to keep his partners honest.

When Edgar sent down the news, Addison was in McCall's Gulch, in Delta, learning about the mining business. He slept with three others in a filthy cabin in a remote canyon, and for three weeks drilled, dynamited, and removed debris in order to open up the hoped-for vein of gold. It was a difficult experience, but Addison was not discouraged. He wrote lyrically about it to his mother: "The scenery is simply beautiful, as we are right in the midst of the mountains, where the foliage is quite like a Hudson fall." After this unpleasant taste of gold mining, he might well have forgone Edgar's summons and returned to San Francisco. But Addison was fired up. "The old pioneer blood of the tribe rose in my brain, and I was panting to go. At least I'd get out of Delta."

In those days, however, it took more than "getting out of Delta" to reach the icefields of the Arctic. There were no planes or helicopters, no cars, no trucks, no high-speed river rafts, to convey men to the isolated outposts of the Alaskan tundra. Not for another fifteen years would Roald Amundsen and Addison's friend Robert Scott attempt their journeys to the South Pole. There were just two ways of getting to the Yukon: by steamer, which plied the journey from Juneau up the Yukon River during the summer when the ice melted, or over the mountains by foot. The overland trip was ferociously difficult. You had to drag by sled the enormous amounts of equipment and provisions needed for the duration of your stay. Dogs and horses were of little use: they could not negotiate the narrow passes. Three thousand horses are said to have died attempting the trip. Addison later told the story of how a team of twelve dogs, carrying a thousand pounds, was crossing a bridge when the cables broke. The dogs fell down into the thin ice and were never seen again. The two men who were "punching" the team were found clinging to the ice, frozen to the waist. They had died in only a few moments.

Surviving the journey was only the beginning. Having arrived at Dawson City physically and mentally exhausted, you had to find out where the promising strikes were, stake your claim, and travel even farther, into even more inhospitable territory, carrying still more provisions, in order to set up camp. Then you would start digging a hole. Hopefully you would dig down deep enough to shake out a few grains of gold dust from the recalcitrant gravel at the bottom of the Yukon River. The worst part of all was that this had to be done in the dead of winter, in subzero temperatures. Gold dust could be retrieved from the gorge or riverbed only when the water was frozen—otherwise the area would flood, making it impossible to extricate the precious metal.

The Mizner brothers were astonishingly ill prepared for this brutal experience. Edgar, tall and heavy, had done little or no hard physical labor in his life. Neither had William. Addison, as tall as his brothers but somewhat more portly, was more accustomed to sporting silk pajamas than the uniform of a miner. Wilson, just past his twenty-first birthday, was a strangely proportioned figure with a large head (Addison called it "bullet-shaped"), a thin body, sunken eyes, and unusually small hands and feet. Although the youngest and theoretically the fittest, his careers at the piano and barstool were not exactly the best training for heavy manual labor.

Yet Wilson was in one sense better prepared than his brothers. He had already traveled to the Yukon with Edgar earlier in the summer, and he quickly read the lay of the land. He went back to San Francisco long enough to pick up his bar-singer companion, Rena Fargo (he told his mother he was returning to "attend to some business"), and together they met Addison on the train for Seattle. Addison was a little startled at the appearance of this small, dark, attractive female with his brother, but Wilson assured him she was only going as far as Seattle. (She and Wilson remained together in Alaska until early 1899.) Addison liked Rena Fargo; she resembled many young singing and card-playing babes who gravitated to the gambling playgrounds of the West in hopes of cashing in.

In Seattle they received a message from William telling them to take the boat to Juneau. Rena went along. They arrived at the beginning of December and put up at the Juneau Hotel, which had already declared itself "headquarters for people going to Yukon or Cook Islet Gold Fields." Juneau was a small town, flush with miners working in the huge Treadwell Mine. There the brothers put together their "outfit"—the equipment needed to survive in the Yukon. This included light knee-length parkas with hoods, made of red-fox fur and lined with soft blanket (costing $35), plus sleeping bags and tents. Each also acquired heavy underclothes, socks, rubber shoes, mackinaw pants, sweaters, and caps, all packed in a canvas bag three by eighteen feet. Their food provisions consisted of 800 pounds of flour, 200 of beans, 100 of rice, 300 of bacon, 50 of coffee and butter, 10 of tea, and 150 of roasted oats. They also bought condensed milk, chocolate, cocoa, sardines, beef extract, canned soup, potatoes, dried onions, and flavorings.

December 12, 1897, was Addison's twenty-fifth birthday. A week later William joined them, and the three brothers left Juneau by boat, arriving in Dyea in time for Christmas Day. The Mizner brothers had decided not to wait for warm weather and the steamer; they wanted to get to Dawson as soon as possible and stake their claim before everyone else arrived. It was a foolhardy decision. The plan was to take the Dyea trail to Sheep Camp, the end of the timberline, and from there travel across Crater Lake, Lake Linderman, Lake Bennett, then over the Chilkoot Pass and the long trek to Dawson City, where the Yukon meets the Klondike and the gold was supposedly waiting.

The main difficulty at this point was dragging their stuff (called caches) up the very difficult mountain trails. Because of the amount and weight of their equipment, it had to be done in laborious shifts, cacheing it at various stages and going back for more. Once the caches were all together at the foot of the pass, they had to be carried once again over the summit.*

The Mizners, as well as having to carry their caches, were also weighed down by paraphernalia for the ice boat that William and Wilson thought would get them across the frozen lakes on the other side of the Chilkoot Pass. It weighed half a ton and turned out to be useless, since the lakes were covered with ice and snow and no boat could move. At Lake Bennett, after several futile efforts to get it through, they ditched it.

On February 2, still at Sheep Camp, Addison was trying to cut some frozen bread when the knife slipped, hacking off much of the index finger of his left hand. William made three stitches in the wound without anesthetic, while Addison fainted a few times. He described this cheerfully in a letter to his mother, adding, "Three men here were shot last night in Skagway [like Dyea, a base camp for the miners]. All three died within a few moments after they were shot. It seems there had been some trouble about the title of a Yukon stove."[5]

The poet Robert Service, who spent several years in the Yukon, wrote vividly about the hardships of the men as they struggled through the Canadian wilderness. One of his most famous poems, "The Trail of Ninety-Eight," describes the grim scene:

*Caches were sacred. If a man was caught stealing someone else's cache, he was immediately brought before a quickly assembled "court" and summarily convicted and sentenced—sometimes to a public flogging, which, according to Addison, caused terrible injuries and often death.

We landed in wind-swept Skagway. We joined the weltering mass,
Clamoring over their outfits, waiting to climb the Pass.
Never will I forget it, here on the mountain face,
Ant-like men with their burdens, clinging in icy space.
Dogged, determined, and dauntless, cruel and callous and cold,
Cursing, blaspheming, reviling, and ever that battle-cry—Gold!

On February 14, after a grueling day of sledding, Addison managed to produce a charming sketch and send it to his mother as a valentine. (Men returning to Dyea would take mail and deliver it to one of the steamers going south.) At Sheep Camp two more men joined them, a friend from San Francisco called Fritz Gamble and his partner, Louis Jonke, whom they dubbed "Och Gott Louie."

It turned out that Addison was the strongest, and carried the most, throughout the harsh journey. Rena's skills did not apply. William and Wilson kept hanging back, supposedly trying to think of easier ways of transporting the equipment. (Wilson also complained of rheumatism.) Their great ideas only forced Addison to work harder, a pattern that was to continue.

They struggled on to Crater Lake, where the thermometer registered forty-five below and fog and wind slowed them down. The trail had almost disappeared, and they constantly stumbled up to their armpits in snow. Addison cooked soups and tea to keep the party's spirits up. They then made their way frustratingly slowly (less than six miles a day) through blizzards and high winds to Linderman Canyon. In spite of their slow progress, they were the first of the parties that had set out from Dyea to arrive at Linderman, and many wanderers who caught up later were grateful to rest at the Mizners' camp. Getting over the Chilkoot Pass, where many prospectors had fallen or turned back, was another terrifying proposition. Luckily, the weather was favorable for the Mizners, and they navigated the summit without too much difficulty.

In April they reached Sixty Mile River, a tributary of the Yukon. The snow had melted, and the brothers decided to build a vessel to get up the river. To do this, they had to "whipsaw" wood. After making a sawhorse, one man sat on top of the log to be cut and pushed the seven-foot-long saw into the wood. The other stood below, trying to push it back. The man on top had to balance himself, while pushing and pulling the saw, with almost superhuman strength. The man below had to cope with piles of sawdust that fell into his eyes and mouth while trying to steer the saw back along the line. "It is a heart and back-breaking job," Addison said. Wilson and Addison nearly came to blows doing it, each changing places constantly. (William declared he had to protect his doctor's hands and so could not participate.) Tempers flared. Finally, when Addison chopped a tree down and it fell in the wrong direction, Wilson hit his brother over the head with a caulking iron.

This was the last straw. Tension had built for months. Addison was exhausted from doing most of the work and bitterly resented Wilson's lack of physical or psychological support. One night Addison and Rena were alone together and got drunk on a punch made of Jamaica ginger and lemon extract. "We cemented our friendship but did not commit incest," Addison asserted later, but the incident did not foster brotherly love. After Addison was felled by Wilson's blow, the two rushed at each other in an explosion of anger. William finally parted them, but Addison and Wilson hardly spoke to each other for the rest of the trip.

The journey down the river was extremely dangerous, with racing rapids and huge ice floes, exacerbated by William's reckless determination to beat the other miners to their destination. As communication among the brothers had for all intents ceased, dealing with obstacles became more and more difficult. For seven miles they were hurled through the river's icy waters past cliffs, over rocks, and into canyons, desperately trying to stay afloat. When they reached Lake Laberge, which was still frozen, they were at the breaking point. "We all hated each other," Addison said. William bought a canoe from some Indians and disappeared. Wilson and Rena followed soon after, making their way to Dawson in a leaky boat called the "Klondike coffin."[6]

Considering the hostility among the brothers, Addison welcomed the desertion by William and Wilson, and having Louis Jonke as his only company for the last part of the journey turned out to be a great relief. Och Gott Louie had been a waiter at the Waldorf-Astoria, and he could also cook, which endeared him to his food-loving companion. (Addison was particularly enthusiastic about Louie's dried apricot pie.) Through the latter half of May 1898, the two men traveled peacefully together down the Yukon River toward Dawson City. They accomplished this without navigation, since there were no maps or charts of any part of the region. On June 3 they sighted Dawson and finally arrived there on June 6—to find rains flooding the streets. Although a long way from San Francisco, it was home. Shortly after they arrived, the first steamer of the season docked at Dawson. Addison was mortified. "Friends I had left behind in San Francisco came down the gangplank in store clothes. They had left four months later than we, and traveled with every comfort—hell!"

For all the problems and scares of the overland journey, Addison had been lucky. There were terrible stories of other people's disasters in the trip over the mountains. A father had to leave his son on the summit, where the boy froze to death. Another man cut his own legs off to save his life. Yet another was returning home with a friend and $1,200 in profits from gold; the friend pushed him down a crevasse, robbed him, and disappeared. The poor man broke his thigh and crawled nine miles on his hands and knees to safety—and despair at the loss of his gold. Perhaps the saddest tale was of the sixty-five-year-old man who had spent two months hauling his outfit to the summit, load by load. On the last day, he brought up his tent and cooking utensils. As he reached the top, he found that someone from the other side had stolen his entire cache, even his tent. He had spent his last cent in the world, and now he had lost everything. Addison's mother, to whom he recounted these stories, did not like them and said so. After that his letters told no more of tragedy along the trail. (He also made other editorial decisions, such as refraining from mentioning the existence of Rena Fargo. Mama Mizner never knew her twenty-one-year-old favorite had been accompanied throughout the trip by a nightclub singer.)

The trip from Dyea to Dawson covers roughly six hundred miles. It took Addison over six months to get there. He lost thirty pounds and nearly died in the process. Yet the hunt for gold had not even begun.

CHAPTER 7

"THIS IS A COUNTRY FOR THE YOUNG, STRONG AND STUPID."

Dawson City was a typical gold rush town. With the news of the strike, its few shacks and stores had been transformed overnight into a community of twenty thousand frenzied prospectors. When Addison arrived in June 1898, rows of dirty tents were springing up everywhere, along with "hotels," saloons, and gambling halls and the usual bottom-feeding personnel to go with them. "In a month," Addison wrote, "the place had changed from a struggling little village into a metropolis." In fact, one of his first urban planning jobs was to help stake out roads for the booming city.

By the time Addison and Louis Jonke arrived, Edgar and William were already on the trail of a claim. Edgar had left his brother a letter about his cabin's whereabouts and enclosed a "poke," a moose-hide sack filled with gold dust. Addison described it as a "little wad of yellow gravel."[1] Edgar's letter explained that the poke held thirty ounces of gold dust at thirteen dollars an ounce—three hundred and ninety dollars. Addison paid for his first meal that night—corned beef hash, bacon and potatoes, a cup of coffee, yeast bread, and a small wedge of soggy pie—with two and a half ounces of that yellow gravel. Dawson City was not going to be cheap.

Nor was Dawson City going to be a resort. As in any frontier town, gunfights, thievery, and drunkenness were endemic. Long wild nights in saloons with imported entertainers like Rena Fargo whiled away the weeks as the men waited to find a strike or for reasonable weather to make the journey to a claim. Addison could deal with the rough characters in town. But as a passionate animal lover, he found almost unendurable the dogfights that took place in the streets. "They always fight in packs," Addison said. "The 'inside' [i.e., local] dog [malamute and husky] fights like the wolf, standing at a distance, closing for engagement, snapping like a bear trap, with a snap of the teeth that would make yours ache to hear; and then retiring for a new rush. The 'outside' dog fights in the same old way so you can imagine what the streets of Dawson are like." Jack London, who visited Dawson for a month in May 1898 (he left just as the Mizners arrived), immortalized some of these dogs in his two masterpieces, *The Call of the Wild* and *White Fang*, describing how miners turned the dogs' aggression into profit, brutalizing the creatures into fighting to the death on a bet.[2] When the Dawson authorities finally ordered the dogs off the streets, the change was so great that Addison compared it to going behind the scenes in an orchestra: "How different everything looks." Addison owned some sled dogs himself for a while. He wickedly named them after the menu that he most craved—Scrambled Eggs, Oysters, Salad, Mushroom, and Cake. As he summoned his dogs, the tantalizing litany of those delicious dishes rang through the streets of Dawson, reaching the ears of the hungry prospectors. "It made the fellows you passed furious to hear one call them by name and incidentally, led to several battles."

Addison soon learned the cutthroat culture of gold mining. First, you had to obtain a miner's license, which was valid for one year. Then, if you were lucky, you found a creek bed that held gold dust, staked a claim to that area, and mined it as fast as you could until you had dredged it dry. Inexperienced gold hunters soon found that most of those opportunities had long been closed off by faster-moving prospectors. The alternative was to stay close to the commissioner's office in Dawson, where every new strike had to be registered. As soon as a man came in and named a claim, all the eavesdroppers, already equipped with packs, food, a hatchet, and a pencil, rushed as fast as they could to reach the location and share in the discovery. Needless to say, it often became a violent business.

For the first few weeks in Dawson, Addison decided to forgo the idea of finding gold and took a job in the food store of the Alaska Commercial Company (which Edgar ran), doling out provisions. The supplies were shipped in by steamer, and whenever the boats came into town, there was a near-riot at the docks. As well as food, the steamers brought mail, newspapers, and "cargo after cargo of ladies, naughty, naughty ladies," as Addison put it, adding, "and if the good Lord will only explain to me how with their faces they ever went wrong, I think I would have many interesting stories to tell." When the steamers departed, emotions ran equally high. People went to watch, to weep, to wave at those departing for the "outside." Miners talked about "outside" and "inside" as though Alaska were a jail, but Addison was feeling no pangs of homesickness as the steamers sailed away. He was determined to make a success of the adventure.

A lucky break soon came his way. His work at the Alaska Commercial Company not only provided him with a small income but also brought him in contact with some of the miners. One day a friend gave him a tip about a discovery in Dominion Creek. Addison, knowing the drill, crept out of Dawson at five A.M. to find the place. It was forty-five miles to the edge of the creek, and when he got there, he discovered that thirty-six men had already staked downstream from what was called Upper Discovery, and twelve had staked upstream from Lower. "This left me only 202 feet, which I staked as 'Thirteen above Lower.' " Exhausted after his long hike, Addison fell asleep. In half an hour, almost frozen, with ice forming all around him. He lit a small fire and kept himself awake until sunrise, then managed to crawl back to Dawson to register his claim on June 15, 1898.

Now a bona fide stakeholder (he generously shared the claim with Edgar, his employer at the Alaska Commercial Company), Addison resigned from the company and started to prepare himself for the long task ahead—mining the gold from his claim. It was still June; he would have to wait several months for the water to freeze. Digging in ice, while unavoidable, doubled the miners' difficulty, since it took both time and physical strength to thaw out a hole, run a bucket down the hole, and then hoist it up again. The work could not be done by one man, so Addison's first challenge was to find a partner or partners to join him.

His brothers were not available. William had become increasingly disenchanted with the whole idea of gold. He was "dead sick" of the country, he told Addison. When Addison first saw him in Dawson after they had separated on the trail from Dyea, he hardly recognized his older brother. "William is so thin that I passed him in the street not knowing him at all after his shave." William decided to leave as soon as he could. He managed to get an assignment taking a sum of money out of Dawson for a client and on June 23 took the steamboat for home. His parting words to Addison said it all: "This is a country for the young, strong and stupid."

Edgar had fared better. As boss of the Alaska Commercial Company, he had gained a reputation for being extremely tough and authoritarian, so much so that he was nicknamed "The Pope of Alaska."[3] Wilson reported that his brother was hated from one end of the Yukon to the other, a distance of twelve hundred miles. Like Wilson, Edgar also had considerable success with the ladies in Dawson, although his most significant romance, one Grace Drummond, dumped him after a miner known as the Lucky Swede promised to pay $15,000 into her bank account if she would marry him. (He did, and she did. He later built her a huge castle in San Francisco.)[4]

Edgar then made a serious error of judgment that damaged his career in Dawson. For some unexplained reason, he refused to provide an Austrian prospector, Antoine Stander, with food and supplies in exchange for a percentage of a claim. The claim turned out to be worth millions of dollars.[5] It was also said that Edgar lost his job at the Alaska Commercial Company after losing $20,000 at the roulette wheel.[6] Edgar was disappointed by his experiences and left with William at the end of June, although he made plans to return.

If Addison felt sorry to see his brothers go "outside," he put a brave face on it to his mother, saying, "With Edgar and William both going out, it leaves me with one of the finest outfits of furs, books and medicines in the country." (Addison had already requested that his mother send him books—Shakespeare, Dickens, Thackeray.) "I also have a paid-for ticket entitling me to nursing, board, lodging and washing if I am ever ill at the Catholic Hospital. So you should not worry about me in the slightest for I am as happy as a clam at high tide."

Wilson, however, remained. But Mama's Angel Birdie, like William, had come to the conclusion that it made no sense to risk life and limb scrambling down a gorge and digging through ice in hope of finding gold dust. He thought it a much brighter idea to take the gold dust off the miners after they had brought it back to Dawson City. And what better way to do so than by running a gambling joint, with liquor and women on the side? As Wilson put it, "Flesh beats scenery."[7] He set himself up in the Dominion Hotel and was soon a well-known figure in Dawson's rugged night world. Rena, who had stuck by him throughout the terrible journey from Dyea, was dismissed and replaced by Nellie Pickering, part of a song-and-dance trio called the Petite Sisters Pickering. "Nellie the Pig," as she was unkindly but affectionately known, "was kindness itself, when she wasn't drunk, and I saw a good deal of her," Addison said circumspectly.[8] Wilson, who had a torrid romance with Nellie, was crushed when she went after "Swiftwater Bill" Gates, another gambling house proprietor, who first married Nellie and then married the two other Pickering sisters, one after the other.

Wilson Mizner got quite a name for himself. His youth, flamboyance, and talent as an entertainer made him the bad boy of the town. A young farmhand called Jack Kearns, newly arrived in Dawson, never forgot the first time he saw Wilson, "a husky young man with a large, leonine head. He was standing at a bar with two other scantily-clad women. They laughed and chatted and, after some urging, the young man picked up a banjo and began to play and sing."[9] Kearns was dazzled by Wilson, who called him "the Kid" and lent him money. He also taught him to become a weigher, one of the most important jobs in Dawson. A weigher was responsible for weighing out the pokes of gold dust brought in by the miners and writing down the number of ounces read out on the scale. It was a vital record. Not only was it proof of a miner's take, but it was also the currency in Dawson; customers paid in ounces, not in cash.

Wilson had other motives besides kindness in providing his protégé with an occupation. He told Kearns to put syrup into his hair every day before he went to work. "Then, when you weigh the dust, get as much of it on your hands as possible, and right quick run your fingers through your hair. Kid, every night you'll be able to wash gold out of that mop of hair like it was dandruff."[10] He did.

When Addison found out about his brother's scam (and this was not the only one), the discovery shocked him so deeply that he poured out his anxiety to the only one of his brothers who might genuinely care as much as he did. Clergyman Henry was appalled at Addison's story. "Though not entirely unprepared yet I cannot describe to you the effect the news your letter brought had upon me," he wrote back. "Mama knows that Wilson has been in the habit of associating with disreputable women but that he could be in the slightest degree dishonest or sink to his present level I do not think she could be made to believe." Addison had wondered whether he should tell his mother what was going on. Henry said no. "We may as well spare her this as long as possible." Henry's advice was to keep the lines of communication open with Wilson. "Through the force of circumstance and not a little thro' our fault he did not have quite the same bringing up as we did—and he was our fallen favorite son. We must stick to him as long as we can."[11] Addison followed Henry's guidance. Hoping to take Wilson away from the scenes of his debauchery, Addison begged his young brother to come to the creek with him that winter. Wilson reluctantly agreed.

In August Addison's life in Dawson took a more interesting turn: he began to work as an architect. "At present I have two buildings under way. . . . The office building is the first building ever built in this country that had a plan drawn for it. The first floor is of logs, the second two of rustic and I think will make a rather pretty building. My drafting table is on a counter in the ladies department which is upstairs and at present they are very busy unpacking and tagging woman's stuff. You would simply scream to see the things that are scattered about here." The image of Addison working on his drawings, surrounded by piles of ladies' underwear, is marvelously appropriate to the bizarre world in which he had found himself.

While brushing up his architectural skills (there is no record of his plans being built), he was distracted by the arrival of two grandes dames from New York, Mrs. Van Buren and Mrs. Hitchcock, who brought with them pigeons, dogs, phonographs, and, according to Addison, a bowling alley. Not surprisingly, Addison got along very well with this "queer couple," as he called them. "They have a tent 70 by 45. It looks like a circus tent. The 'girls' (50 and 40) are great fun. This morning I went over in a canoe. . . . This evening Mrs. H. gives a large dinner to all the officials, to which I am going. I took them to the opening of a dance hall the other night. The performance was something terrible." (Mama Mizner, ever watchful for useful social connections, was gratified to discover that Mrs. Hitchcock was a cousin of Rhode Island Governor Elisha Dyer and widow of one of America's naval heroes, Captain Roswell D. Hitchcock, while Edith Van Buren was a great-grandniece of President Martin Van Buren.)

By September the level of the river was falling daily, and soon the boats would not be able to go all the way through. Addison sensed change in the air. "Until yesterday, men stood on the streets in their shirt-sleeves, but last night a thin filmy scum of ice formed on the pools and warned us that the great crouching tigress of the North was crouching nearer, preparing for her final spring." Visitors to Dawson were making hasty plans to get on board the last steamers for the outside before it was too late. Edgar, who had briefly reappeared with a Christmas box for Addison from their mother, left again on September 5. Friends from New York and San Francisco left too. Mrs. Hitchcock and Mrs. Van Buren managed to get on a late steamer. "They are nice people," was Addison's conclusion, "but the biggest pair of cranks and erratics that ever existed."

For those waiting to get to the frozen river, the time seemed finally to have come. Now it was only the stalwarts, the determined ones, the tough ones who stayed inside, prepared to take on the arctic winter in order to satisfy their thirst for gold. In the end it was Addison, the unlikeliest brother, the artist, architect, aesthete, wit, and party boy of San Francisco, who stayed with these men. While William, Edgar, and Wilson, the brothers who had initiated the project, lost their nerve, Addison stood fast and faced the lonely task ahead, sticking to the Mizners' original dream of making their family rich. Moments like these form a man's character. Addison had failed most of his schoolwork, but when it came to resolve, he proved at this juncture that alone of all the Mizners, he could pass the test.

On September 22, after the arduous forty-five-mile hike through the waterlogged canyons and steep inclines along the banks of the Klondike, Addison along with the three men he had hired arrived at 13 Above Lower, Dominion Creek, and set up their camp for the winter. Addison's companions were of Swedish descent. Their first task was to build a cabin. It was about fourteen feet square and about six feet high at the eaves. They installed two large logs through the center as support for a very slightly sloping roof, which was covered with moss and eight or ten inches of dirt. Prefabricated windows were set into the sides of the cabin. Since Addison and the Swedes were all six feet tall or more and weighed over two hundred pounds, the cabin was certainly not too roomy.

The men's size and strength were critical for the mining work they had to do. First, they had to dig a hole down to bedrock (about six feet deep). Only the last bottom four or five feet contained the gold. Then twice a day they built a big fire (cutting enough wood was a permanent problem) on which they piled large rocks. When the rocks were hot, the men flung them down the hole, where they steamed and sputtered for an hour or so. When they were cool, twelve or eighteen inches had been thawed out and a bucket could be sunk, dragged along the loosened gravel, and hoisted up. Then the men combed through the gravel for gold.

Addison almost immediately struck it lucky. A week after they started to mine, he was able to write triumphantly to his mother, "When I hoisted the last bucket this morning you could see the gold shining in the sun. Panning it out we got $2 to the pan, which shows that we are on the 'pay.' A pan equals about a shovelful."

For most of October the pattern was the same. Dig, make the fire, put down the bucket, and hoist. Addison was the strongest of the "hoisters," and while he averaged 175 hoists a day, he would sometimes go over 200. The weather grew colder and harsher, and blankets of snow fell. Other miners would stop by. Addison or his companions would make trips to Dawson for supplies, the forty-five-mile journey becoming more and more difficult to negotiate in the ice and snow. Trails were covered, bridges collapsed. By November, although the men were still finding small pans of gold, even Addison's indomitable spirit began to sink. The monotony of the physical labor involved in shaking out the elusive yellow gravel from the frozen river muck was increasingly depressing. The idea of gold mining might be glamorous, but its reality was mind-numbing boredom and fatigue. Addison disliked his huge cabin mates, yet when they went to Dawson for supplies, he found himself lonely without them. His exhaustion at the end of the day made him unable even to read. As he thought of his upcoming twenty-sixth birthday and Christmas so far from home, he became melancholy.

On a December trip to Dawson, he found Wilson and managed to persuade him to come back with him to Dominion Creek. There he was put to work cutting wood for the fires. Addison hoped that his younger brother might work with him there until the spring, but as usual with Wilson, it was wishful thinking. Wilson explained that he had to return to Dawson on Christmas Eve in order to appear in a minstrel show. Addison was left to celebrate a freezing Christmas Day without him. The Yukon poet Robert Service had been there:

On a Christmas day, we were mushing our way over the Dawson trail,
Talk of your cold! Through the parka's fold it stabbed like a driven
nail.

But Addison refused to give in to despair. He and the Swedes decided to put on a good show for Christmas Day, and they invited miners from the nearby claims to their cabin for an all-day party. Addison concocted a creative menu from his meager pantry: "Caviar and anchovies (frozen in a can); frozen oysters; Bouillon (out of capsules); asparagus (straight from the can); grilled sardines; roast of moose, plum pudding (made by Addison); cheese, coffee (from home)." Since turkey was only $2.50 a pound, there was turkey too. The Swedes had a stash of liquor that was passed around. Various people dropped in throughout the day, and twenty more arrived after dinner. "The moon was round and genial," Addison wrote to his mother, "seeming to almost smile out its merry Christmas."

This heroic effort at celebration took its toll: on New Year's Eve, Addison's mood was more wistful. "Poor old '98 is almost gone," he wrote his mother. "What a lot have I learned in its 12 months—What fun I have had and how often I have thought of you and wished to be with you can never be reckoned. . . . Everyone is asleep so I won't dare shriek Happy New Year, so when the watch just hits the minute I will write it here. Happy New Year. Happy New Year. Happy New Year. Happy New Year. '99."

Even to his mother he could not entirely conceal his desolation. Between the lines is the reality of Addison alone, cold, tired, longing for fresh food and drink and a hot shower, huddled up in his furs in the smelly cabin with the snoring Swedes, and writing almost to himself during the long dark night of the arctic winter.

Perhaps the worst moment of all came in early January, when he overheard the Swedes plotting to kill him. A few days later Addison confronted them and told them he had sent a letter to Dawson describing his murder, and that they would never get away with it. He added with typical bravado that they didn't have enough guts to kill him anyway. He was right. They continued to work the claim to the end, sullen and silent, but one can only imagine the atmosphere for poor Addison after that.

Life in Dawson wasn't much more cheerful. While Addison was on a brief visit there in February, one of Wilson's close friends shot his girl-friend and then shot himself. It was the first murder-suicide ever in Dawson. Addison went to the crime scene and was overwhelmed by what he saw. "A cheerless dreary little room with walls of the cheapest and smallest figured paper, with a haggard, worn-out woman of the dance hall cooling her life blood in little pools on the floor. . . . The candle on the washstand kindly cast a shadow on the upper part of the body, blotting out the ghastly wounds on the head—that head that was resting for the first time in many a year . . . with its eyes staring in a terrible gaze [on] her murderer, who in turn gazed back with the awful realization of his deed written on his face." Addison later wrote a sad little story based on this tragedy, which had clearly shocked his sensitive soul to its core. Wilson's response is not recorded.

Gradually the weather grew warmer, the ice thawed, and the holes began to fill with water. Addison and his crew kept on digging as long as they could, making a dam to prevent the water from flooding their holes. Finally, the clean-up began. Before the mining inspector from the Canadian government would give them permission to leave, they had to close their mine shaft and dam. But eager as Addison was to move out, obstacles still remained, including damaging floods that destroyed their efforts to clear up the dam.

Another more serious problem arose over complaints from the Canadian government that Addison had mined over and beyond the boundaries of his stake, and thus the extra gold belonged to the government. It turned out later that the Swedes had lied to the mining commissioner about the boundaries in exchange for a cut of the take. (Many Canadian officials in the Yukon territory were corrupt, but few were ever indicted.) One of the most draconian restrictions placed on the mining community was that if you were in debt, you were not allowed to leave the country. Men were literally hauled off steamers because they had left behind outstanding bills. The idea of an enforced stay depressed Addison enormously. "It's my sincere prayer that I will be able to pay off all I owe and make enough this next winter to get out of this infernal 'Hell Hole.' "

Long disillusioned by the treacherous Swedes, Addison had cunningly hidden some of the gold he had hoisted from the creek. With it he was able to pay off his personal debts and the legal bills arising from the claim boundaries issue, and when everything was sorted out, he had a profit of over $34,000 (of which 10 percent was paid to the government of Canada as a royalty). In June 1899, almost to the day his one-year miner's license expired, Addison left Dominion Creek for good.

Greatly relieved to be back in Dawson, which had become a far more sophisticated town during the long months he had been away, Addison's spirits soon revived. While waiting for passage on a steamer, he took a small cabin with a friend and immediately threw himself into decorating it: "I lined the walls with a plaid gingham and used a brighter red and white plaid for curtains. A narrow shelf runs all around the cabin dividing the gingham for the rough roof with its heavy log rafters. It makes a very clean and not unattractive cage."

But even though he had settled his bills, he still could not leave. One of his Swedish "partners" brought a case against him claiming that he deserved a half share of Addison's take because he had worked so hard. Addison was forced to wait for the hearing. The result was in his favor. He left with his profit intact, and finally, on July 24, just over a year after first arriving in Dawson, Addison boarded the steamer *Hanna*, which would take him down the Yukon toward St. Michael's and a boat home. His last letter to his mother from the Yukon sounded the jubilant call: "Mudder, dear Mudder, I'm coming home to you now."

CHAPTER 8

"WHY NOT FRESCO SOMEBODY'S WALL?"

Addison had written regularly to his mother during his year in the Yukon, often once a week, in spite of the extremely hostile conditions. While his literary skills were not those of Jack London or Rex Beach, both of whom made careers out of their Klondike experiences, Addison's letters retain an immediacy, a strong sense of his surroundings, and a shrewd sense of human nature that reveal as much about the man as they do about the rugged world he describes. (He was a very sympathetic observer. Once, watching people on the wharf at Dawson making their sad good-byes to the passengers on a departing steamer, he noticed two drunken women in black satin and lace hats, "turning away to 'have another,' with a glisten in the eyes.")

What one senses most clearly from the hundred or so letters that survive is his basic sweetness and good nature. When his brothers abandoned him to soldier on alone; when the Swedes tried to kill him; even when he was sick and depressed and thought he would never be able to get out, he never wrote a bitter or angry word. Admittedly, these letters were to his mother and therefore were edited; but while some sons might have been willing to expose vulnerability at times of stress, Addison never lost his sense of humor or his sturdy equanimity. The only glimpse of his dark side appears in this brief paragraph in his memoir. "The greatest gift God has given me is to forget the horrible things, remembering only the funny ones," he wrote, fleetingly letting down his guard. "I have just made the mistake of looking over my old letters to Mama Mizner—and a shadow is across my vision—let me shove the letters aside, and wander on from memory."

While Addison determinedly offered a romantic and whitewashed version of his experiences to his mother back home, she had another agenda. In a torrent of letters written to her beloved boy in Alaska during his one-year absence, she made crystal clear her hopes and fears about her sons. Shortly after he departed for Dawson City in the summer of 1898, she wrote, "I am so anxious and have such a *heartache* over this exodus of my children. You will all do well, I know, and if you pledge yourself not to drink anything or go into, or gamble, in a public gambling place there is no doubt of your success. As for the rest, 'noblesse oblige,' have a goal, my son, and work up to it and cultivate as much as possible the refinements of life. . . . Avoid even the appearance of evil and help Wilson to do what is right always. . . . I hope I shall live to see my sons noble, true and successful men. Your picture of a sweet little home of our own is very alluring and I pray the dream may be fulfilled."

Ella Watson Mizner's burning ambitions for her sons were both high-minded and practical. Money was a constant theme in the letters. She was still spending most of her time at Stag's Leap, where the situation had not improved. She could not afford to move out, let alone help pay for her sons' mining gear in Dawson, on which they had counted. Ever on the prowl for ways to promote her sons' financial interests, she heard that one of Edgar's friends was earning up to $35,000 a year as an agent for the Rothschilds and was staking out railroad interests. She urged Edgar to follow up. *Let nothing escape,"* she implored. "Do whatever you can find to do *honest* good work so that your mother may never blush for you."

One solution to the family's money problems, of course, would be for one or more of her sons to make a good marriage. Mama Mizner no doubt regarded with some frustration the unbecoming prospect of five unmarried sons. Lansing, still single at forty-one, had become his mother's companion and escort to parties at home—a bad sign. Edgar and William were well over the age of consent, but although popular in town, they had shown equally few signs of matrimonial intent. Mama Mizner had begun pinning her hopes on Addison, whose rich San Francisco friends provided a deep pool of potential brides. In particular, the young Miss Gwin had shown an interest in Addison, and Mama Mizner did not let him forget it. "Mary Belle Gwin with her mother is traveling in the East (they expect to go to all the fashionable watering places)," she wrote pointedly to her son. "She is having a fine time and I suppose is expected to make a brilliant match." (She did. Mary Belle married Kenneth Kingsbury, president of the Standard Oil Company of California.)

Mama Mizner also encouraged her son to continue painting and doing miniatures of people—maybe, she suggested somewhat fancifully, he should "fresco somebody's wall." Addison sent her a poke with some of the first gold dust he earned in Dawson, which she said she put away, "keeping it for you when you become rich. I have visions already of a dear little house somewhere with you, my beloved son." She then added, "I believe you have strength to resist temptation which is most necessary of all in that miserable place Dawson City."

In urging self-denial on Addison, she was clearly dwelling with far more concern on her other precious son. She frequently told Addison that Wilson had not written her one word since arriving in Alaska, which only increased her anxiety. "Do not quarrel with [Wilson]," she begged Addison. " 'United we stand, divided we fall,' should be our motto as well as our country's. Try to have a good influence over him. Have patience with him and remember he has been without a home for five years, practically for nearly eight years. Persuade him to read good literature, associate only with his equals. You know, my darling son, how my heart is in this. I know there is much good in Wilson if we only knew how to reach his heart, to cultivate his love."

Wilson, with all his dissolute ways, was not yet twenty-three years old. But by the middle of 1899, Addison's patience with him was almost exhausted, and he finally exposed his feelings to his mother. "The truth is," he told her, dropping any pretenses, "his friends are not mine, and all I know is that he has acted very foolishly in here, under the delusion that he was clever." The despairing note in Addison's letter reflects not only impatience with his younger brother but a profound concern. This duality of feeling, both love and frustration, had been Addison's cross from the beginning. While the other brothers turned their backs on Wilson's misdemeanors, Addison was never able to escape the conflicting emotions aroused by Mama's Angel Birdie. Brought up together, Addison had monitored with a mixture of admiration and anxiety his brother's defiant and lonely journey toward independence. With his mother's emotional pleas for understanding ever in his ears, he could not abandon his feeling of responsibility toward the prodigal.

Later that summer Wilson, disenchanted with the new rules and regulations that were making Dawson much too respectable for his taste, moved north to Nome, on the Bering Strait. Even though Addison had completed his business at Dawson and was eager to take the steamer home, he responded to his mother's instructions and took a detour to Nome to check on his brother. Nome was the kind of rough-edged starter mining town that Dawson once had been. A new strike had been reported in the area, and the usual eager fortune-seekers and attendant riffraff were flocking to this, the latest El Dorado. Lanier McKee, who wrote about Nome in 1900, said, "I heard old-timers who had visited all the principal mining camps in recent years remark that this Nome was the 'toughest proposition they had ever encountered.' "[1] In other words, a perfect place for Wilson.

By all accounts, Mama's Angel Birdie did his best work there: he built a gambling casino called the McQuestion, managed boxers, and dealt faro. "He was considered a boulevardier, sending for suits and linens," wrote Richard O'Connor in *High Jinks on the Klondike*. "Once he lured a jazz band—on credit—to welcome ashore an especially dazzling group of actresses and dancing girls."[2] O'Connor reported that one of the actresses claimed that Wilson had married her, but the young libertine denied it.

Wilson stayed in Nome for two years, then returned briefly to the States and in May 1902 sailed again for Nome on the *Portland*. Shortly after its departure, the steamer became stuck in an ice floe and began drifting northward. For two months it was out of communication, and all the passengers were assumed dead. Mama Mizner was in deep mourning. But to everybody's relief, the ship arrived safely in Nome on July 2. Wilson, for a change, emerged as the shipboard hero: he had kept up the passengers' spirits with a constant stream of theatrical shows and entertainments.

Addison stayed in Nome only a few days, long enough to see that Wilson needed no help from him. Upon returning to San Francisco in September, he arrived at the same time as a large number of troops from the Philippines, who were being welcomed home after the successful conclusion of the Spanish-American War. The soldiers' greeting at the Golden Gate included a flotilla of ships and a wild explosion of cannons and whistles. "At first, I thought it must be for me," Addison quipped. He had heard only vaguely about the war through newspapers and his mother's letters. Alone of the Mizner brothers, Henry had tried to join up, but his papers did not come through in time.

Addison's homecoming was hardly that of a triumphant warrior. Although he was financially better off than when he had left, thanks to his gold profits, he still had no career prospects. During his year in Alaska, he had thought about the problem, casting about for ideas. His family praised the letters he had written home (his mother had disseminated them to all), so he was once more thinking of becoming a writer. He sketched out some stories based on his experiences in the Klondike. One of these was a fairly proficient Jack London–type tale of a miner named Linn and his yellow malamute dog, which Addison named Scrambled Eggs after one of his own sled dogs in Dawson.[3] He confided to Henry that he would rather be able to write well "than anything else going." Addison then suggested to his mother that she ask Lansing if he could wangle him a writing job at the *San Francisco Examiner*. He also floated other ideas. "If you have any way of finding out," he asked her, "look into the qualifications of a consul or the possibility of getting an attache's position in any country in Europe."

A writer? A diplomat? As jobs failed to come his way, architecture slipped back into his life. During the summer, Addison had learned from his mother that his friend Andrew Martin was very sick. "What does Min mean when she says that Andy will not live through the year?" he asked in agitation. "What is the matter with him? If there is anything you can do for him please do it for he has been mighty nice to me." Andrew had become ill with pneumonia while traveling in the East with his mother, and after a hasty return to California, he had moved from San Francisco on doctor's orders to the warmer, dryer climate of Santa Barbara. Andrew told Addison merely that he had a spot on his lung—and that he had more important news: he had become engaged to Genevieve Goad (the "California Venus" and sister of Addison's onetime love Aileen), and he wanted Addison to be his best man.

So shortly after his return in September, Addison ordered some fine new clothes, which, thanks to his "yellow gravel," he could now pay for (to the surprise of his tailor), and with a new dachshund named Amsel in tow, he took the train to Andrew's house in Montecito, just north of Santa Barbara. Andrew seemed in better health than expected, but Addison sensed that his friend would never be entirely well again.

On September 16, 1899, Andrew Martin married Genevieve Goad at the Goads' family house at the corner of Gough and Washington Streets in San Francisco. It was the marriage of two very great fortunes, but because of Andrew's health, the event was only a small family affair. After the wedding, Addison stayed on with his friend in Montecito to help design the house Andy had bought in Palm Springs, where his doctor had recommended the couple live. Addison may have been uncertain about his career, but Andrew Martin had no hesitation in giving him the commission.

In early October, Addison moved to Palm Springs to work on the house. At this time Palm Springs was considered a remote, arid outpost with little to recommend it. Addison saw it very differently: "Palm Springs is an oasis in the desert with a hot mineral spring discharging several thousand gallons per hour. The spring itself is surrounded by mammoth palms. Then 3 or 4 blocks in every direction are covered with a huge grove of cottonwoods, peppers, oranges, figs, and palms. Oleanders grow into huge trees, and water is all that is needed to turn this into the rankest greenhouse. . . . The desert is skirted with pyramid-like mountains that rise straight from the plain without a tree or foothill, rugged and rocky. The village consists of as near as I can find out, of 14 people, when fully populated."

Addison worked not only on the exterior of the Martin house but also on the interior. He was proud of the results, which showed some evolution from the red-and-white-gingham cabin in Dawson. Genevieve's room was decorated with cream enamel woodwork and big panels of green hydrangea–covered cretonne. Between the panels stood French gilt candlesticks. The bed was a brass four-poster, with a deep valance of white organdy around the top, matching the curtains. The tester was swagged in green lawn, with cerise bows and green taffeta ribbons. He covered the dining-room walls in blue burlap decorated with a big stencil of green and purple grapes. A corniced redwood shelf held pretty china, and the doors, mantel, and ceiling were made of redwood. He hung blue and white crepe from the windows. "I thought all the while," he wrote his mother, "how nice it would be if it were only in San Francisco and for you and me." Andrew also asked Addison to design two other houses on the compound, one for guests and the other for staff. These commissions catapulted Addison into the local headlines, with announcements that "Addison C. Mizner, the well-known Montecito architect," was working on the Martins' lodge. He had become, at last, an architect.

The assignments kept Addison in Palm Springs for the rest of October and into early November, living quietly with the Martins in this isolated "Colorado desert station," as the *San Francisco Examiner* described it. In the second week of November, after a sunny picnic turned rainy, Andrew caught a cold. Three days later the twenty-three-year-old bridegroom was dead. There was a big funeral in San Francisco.

This tragedy for the Martin family was also a severe blow for Addison. Once again, just when an architectural career was within his grasp, disaster struck. To add to his woes, money that he was expecting from Dawson did not show up. With his twenty-seventh birthday and the beginning of a new century looming, Addison felt little cheer.

At times like these, his reaction was usually to turn to the next opportunity that came his way, however unlikely it was to lead to a career. After the Guatemalan architectural commission had fallen through, he left for Alaska on a harebrained scheme of finding gold. Now, after Andrew Martin's death, he found an equally unlikely opportunity abroad. He met a doctor from Honolulu who wanted him to help build a huge hotel there, as well as a private house for himself. This stranger promised Addison a great architectural future in Hawaii. Addison believed him, once more grasping at a new opportunity with unthinking enthusiasm. The offer was surely dubious, but the alternative—once more scrounging for jobs in San Francisco—did not appeal. Moreover, after a year in the frozen North, the idea of Hawaii must have seemed very seductive.

After he arrived in Honolulu, Addison realized he had been taken for one of the suckers with whom Wilson so liked to keep company. The "doctor" promptly disappeared; there was to be no hotel and no money. But Addison was not about to go home to Mama Mizner with another sorry tale of failure. He decided to stay and, Californian to his boots, look for some post-Klondike lucky strike.

Addison's parents had known the Hawaiian queen Liliuokalani and had attended the first anniversary of her accession in 1892. But a year later, she was deposed, so when Addison arrived in early 1900, that connection would get him nowhere. But when he went to visit the royal palace, he noticed that the queen's pictures (some by important artists) were still hanging in place but were sadly neglected, with canvases flapping and surfaces torn or moldy. An old gentleman with a long white beard passed by, and Addison asked him who was responsible for the collection. The gentleman answered, "I don't know, unless I am. I'm President Dole." The upshot of this exchange was that Addison was put in charge of restoring the paintings. He would get no fee, but he would get free supplies from the local art store.

Addison had no training as an art restorer, but fearless in the face of a new challenge, he went to work with characteristic energy and enthusiasm. He had spent time with artists and done some painting himself, and for the next year he worked on the royal collection, learning as he went. Having rescued more royal pictures from attics, basements, and even lumber piles, he carefully soaked, patched, and varnished at least seventeen of them until they were almost back to their original condition. (He kept photographs of them, and their impressive appearance confirms his skill in restoration.) He then paid a call on the ex-queen who, although hostile to Americans for having conspired in her removal, fell for Addison's charm and was pleased that he had preserved her family treasures. She had left behind in the palace a box of medals and decorations, and he smuggled them out for her by concealing them in his clothes. She was so grateful that she awarded him the star of Kalakau.

But Hawaiian medals did not pay the bills, and Addison was desperate for work. Still clinging to his hope of becoming a writer, he sent in a story to the *San Francisco Call,* which rejected it. ("I would say that I hardly think the story you suggested is worth anything near the amount you asked for it.")[4] Falling back on the artistic talent that he had nurtured in the Yukon, he eked out a living carving ivory miniatures of prominent people on the island. This not only kept him in food and lodging but also exposed him to the upper echelons of Hawaiian social life, where, with his quick wit and entertaining ways, he quickly made a name for himself. Hawaii was a popular vacation spot for rich Americans, especially from the West Coast. Many of them knew or had letters of introduction to Addison, who would take them around the island and generally amuse them. He soon became known as the Ward McAllister (New York's preeminent social arbiter) of Honolulu.

One of these visitors from the United States was Ethel Watts Mumford, a twenty-six-year-old divorcee who, with her young son, had come to Hawaii to find inspiration as a writer. (She later became a successful playwright and novelist.) She took a house on the beach at Waikiki, and soon her place was a center for the liveliest people on the island. Addison was very taken by Ethel, whose sparkling personality and sense of humor reflected his own, and they spent a lot of time bandying jokes and epigrams together. Out of these exchanges came the idea for *Cynic's Calendar,* a compendium of sayings and proverbs updated for the new century, which the two creators thought would make good Christmas presents. Oliver Herford, a well-known illustrator and writer, who had produced similar small books of light verse and aphorisms, was brought in as coauthor to give the project weight.

The result, with illustrations by Addison and Herford, was prettily produced by the San Francisco publisher Paul Elder and became an immediate success. Each month had a quotation such as "March: Too good to be new" and a list of Prognostications such as "Jan. 25—Lucky. Jan. 26—Lucky till 7 pm. Jan. 27—Avoid pawnbrokers. Jan. 29—Avoid dentist" and so on. At the beginning of each entry a paragraph laboriously parodied astrological readings ("Towards the middle of this month the nebula of the Pledgides partially disappears and the Bowl Star is visible to a strong glass").

The royalties from this little calendar, which was reproduced with different coauthors and titles each year for eight years, provided Addison with pocket money, but not enough to live on. In 1902 an investment he had made in San Francisco was supposed to mature, but until then he still had to find a way to keep going. For a while he made charcoal copies of photographs of Hawaiian scenes and sold them in tinted frames to tourists. A little ashamed of these tacky efforts, he did not put his name to them. His partner in this venture was a photographer named Melville Vanaman, who, like Addison, was hustling his way through the South Seas. When the charcoal ran out, strong and burly Addison got the job of transporting Vanaman's new invention around—a huge camera that could take pictures six feet long. The Inter-Island Steamship Company hired them to take photographs of the islands, but when the company's chief executives heard that Addison had called them the "Inter-Island Pukers" (Addison suffered badly from seasickness), he lost the job.

Addison decided to move on. By this time, his investment was ready to deliver dividends, so he wired the bank in San Francisco to send his money to Samoa. Then he said good-bye to his friends in Hawaii and, foolishly confident, made his way by trading steamer to Apia. But Addison's investment turned out to be but a dream; there were no dividends. Once more Addison had to use his opportunist skills to stay alive. This time he stumbled upon a "second-rate" Englishman calling himself Professor Collins, who was making a living by coloring lantern slides. Addison could do the work ten times faster, so the two went into business. It worked so well that they decided to expand their market and took a steamer to Melbourne, Australia.

In Melbourne the two quarreled and broke up. Addison, once more on his uppers, began to hang out at a local saloon that was frequented by boxers. His size and weight made him a likely candidate for the ring, and when one of the boxers reneged on a fight, his frantic manager talked Addison into taking on "the Pride of Australia." As usual, Addison's qualifications were not exactly reassuring, but he had known Wilson's boxing friends and seen a few fights in Benicia and San Francisco. So, calling himself "Whirlwind Watson from Frisco" (after his grandfather), Addison managed to earn $150 by beating "the Pride" in twenty rounds. Eager for a return bout, the manager again appealed to Addison, who negotiated a better financial deal the second time but made the serious tactical mistake of completely knocking out the Australian champion. Fleeing the angry crowd, Addison made his way to the docks and managed to scramble on board a steamer just as it was pulling away from the pier. The ship's destination was Shanghai.

Broke in Shanghai, he picked up yet another suspicious character. This one assured him he could make money by attending an auction of unclaimed steamship storage. The auction was "blind" (i.e., the buyer did not know what he or she was getting), so naturally the risk appealed to Addison, and he enthusiastically bid on a very large and heavy box, which he got for under five dollars. In it were a dozen sets of coffin handles, six to a set. Undaunted, Addison, who had picked up a smattering of Chinese from his old cook, Ying, set out to sell his seventy-two coffin handles—as door handles, towel racks, whatever he could think of—and managed to make a small profit. Pleased with his success, he boarded a steamer, this time making sure of its destination: San Francisco.

He arrived home in the summer of 1902. He had been in the Pacific for a wild two years that once again were hopeless in terms of career prospects. He was nearly thirty years old and had hardly made a dent as an architect, let alone in any other pursuit except selling coffin handles. He had, however, honed a vital skill: the ability to enter into and complete seemingly impossible assignments. His opportunism, combined with his natural confidence and optimism, had worked to his advantage as he knocked around the South Seas. Although he came home empty-handed, he had seen and absorbed aspects of other cultures that would become very useful when he finally did find his calling.

Back in San Francisco, he picked up some drafting jobs and reconnected with friends. He also began a romantic dalliance—something he had avoided since the Ella Hobart affair. The new focus of his attention was Bertha Dolbeer, a local girl whose millionaire father, a lumber baron, had just died, leaving her his fortune. Newspapers said she was worth $5 million. (Mama Mizner must have been crossing her fingers.) Addison had known and occasionally corresponded with Bertha since he was eighteen years old, but now he saw her through different eyes (was it partly the money?) and courted her assiduously throughout 1903. But he had about as much success as he had achieved with Aileen and Ella. Addison was fair-haired and blue-eyed, stood six feet three inches tall, and weighed 270 pounds[5]—proportions more appealing to those with a taste for bear-hugs than for sinewy Latin embraces. Bertha saw him regularly, and like most of his friends, she found his company amusing, but she showed no signs of reciprocating his passion, saying kindly but unromantically that he was "the funniest man in town."

In the winter of 1903, Bertha took a vacation at the Hotel del Monte in Monterey, a fashionable summer resort. Addison decided to follow her. He set off with his close friend John Rush Baird (known as Jack) in an automobile, still a very newfangled machine. The vehicle went well enough on flat roads, but it could not make the hills toward Monterey and had to be towed into town by a team of horses. Addison spent two days in distant pursuit of Bertha, but to his chagrin on the third day a rival arrived in town who was clearly more successful with the young heiress. Jack advised Addison to make her jealous by leaving her and driving on to Santa Barbara where some other attractive females were staying. "No one had ever made the trip from San Francisco to Santa Barbara in an automobile and it would be wonderful to be the first," Addison said, delighted by his friend's proposal. They arrived in Santa

Barbara with much fanfare after a ten-day drive over the San Luis Obispo Pass, and stayed for several nights in a stylish suite of rooms at the Hotel Potter.

By this time Addison was reliable fodder for the gossip columns. One Sunday in February, Jack wagered a new suit of clothes that Addison would not go fully clothed down the slide into the swimming pool of Santa Barbara's Delmar Plaza Hotel. Addison immediately flung himself down the slide into the pool. The newspapers had a field day with the story, with the *San Francisco Examiner* calling him "three hundred pounds of the most exclusive society in San Francisco." The reporter went on, "Had the remains of the Russian fleet been stationed in the plunge, the vessels would have sunk, so stunning was the impact of the San Franciscan. For a moment two shining shoes beneath which peeped out two black ankles ornamented with little sprays of pink roses kicked above the water." Addison emerged and, dripping, walked with dignity through the lobby of the hotel to wild applause. "I think I win" was his placid and only remark.

The next day, on reading this story, he was less placid, taking issue with the newspaper's report of (a) his weight, which he claimed was thirty pounds in excess of the truth, and (b) his stockings, which, he declared, *never* matched.

Bertha was not impressed and told Addison that she would never marry anyone who had no purpose in life. He could not argue with her. As he said himself, "You couldn't ask a girl to knock about the world on an off chance of painting lantern slides or selling nickel-plated casket fittings." He concocted a new plan to make his fortune: he would become a coffee importer. American coffee was generally undrinkable, and the best coffee came from his old stamping ground, Guatemala. After co-opting some of his rich friends as investors, he told Bertha his idea and asked her: if he made $3,000 and owned part of the business, would she consider him as a suitor? She left the door open. Then in April 1904 Bertha, accompanied by her close friend Etta Warren, left San Francisco for an extended trip to Europe. Addison went to Benicia to see her off, and they parted on friendly terms. Shortly after, Addison, with Jack Baird and two other friends, left for Guatemala. They planned to be away for six months.

While coffee was the main item on Addison's agenda, he followed another impulse that turned out to have a decisive impact on his future. Because of political restrictions imposed upon the Roman Catholic Church in Guatemala, he discovered, many of the country's great churches had been reduced to poverty, and their vast treasures of gold, silver, and furnishings were badly neglected. In addition to the political problems facing these religious institutions, the marvelous Spanish colonial palaces and churches in Antigua, the beautiful Baroque city that had once been the capital of Guatemala, were mostly deserted owing to a violent earthquake in 1773 that had caused its inhabitants to abandon the city. After several attempts at repatriation and rebuilding, Antigua, once the country's intellectual and social capital, remained a ghost of a city, its religious monuments closed, its priests bankrupt. On visiting this still-beautiful ruin, which Aldous Huxley in the 1930s called "one of the most romantic cities in the world," Addison realized that in its tragedy lay his opportunity, and he immediately started negotiating with the priests to buy their treasures. He assured his friends that this was perfectly aboveboard, since the parishes were close to starvation and desperately needed cash.

In the manner of Gilded Age millionaires like Henry Clay Frick and Cornelius Vanderbilt, who extracted complete rooms from English and French stately homes and brought them back to their American palaces, Addison decided to purchase an old monastery near Antigua—the whole building. "The reason I wanted it was that eight of the side chapels of the church were intact and in each stood, thirty feet high, carved wood altars with heavy gilding." Addison's decision to make such a large investment indicates his strong belief in the value of these artifacts. He was opportunistic, yes, but on this occasion also very shrewd. These treasures, so much easier to acquire than gold dust from the bottom of the Yukon River, would be the foundation of his future career.

This return visit to Guatemala was hugely stimulating for Addison. He made a scrapbook of the trip, in which he placed photographs of every aspect of the landscape—gardens, fountains, Baroque ruins, donkey carts, cathedrals, thatched roofs, local boys smiling at the camera, religious processions. He also made a wonderfully sensitive series of pen-and-ink sketches of the glorious architectural features of Antigua. Looking through these old album pages, one senses not only his love and respect for Guatemala's art and culture, but also that his most important talent was finally beginning to take hold. Whether he admitted it or not, his romance with architecture would not die.

In early July 1904, in the midst of his negotiations over the Guatemalan treasures, he received a telegram from Jack telling him that Bertha Dolbeer had died. After her return from Europe, she had fallen from a high window in the Waldorf-Astoria in New York and was instantly killed. After receiving the telegram, Addison continued to receive letters from her, as though from a ghost, telling him of her European trip and how she looked forward to seeing him in New York. The shock caused him to speed up plans to go home, and after completing his coffee contracts and arranging for shipment of all the religious artifacts he had acquired, he sailed directly for New York.

Bertha had left all her fortune (something in the realm of $2 million) to her friend Etta Warren. Bertha's aunt, Mrs. J. L. Moody, contested this disposal of the Dolbeer millions, declaring that her niece was not of sound mind at the time she made the will and that her death was a suicide. At a hearing in New York, evidence was presented that the deceased had suffered from "melancholia" after the death of her father. Warren admitted that her friend had often said she wished she could join him. She also said that Bertha had been treated in Paris for neurasthenia.[6] The trial then moved to San Francisco, where, in a dramatic move, Addison was summoned from New York by Warren's lawyers, who put him up in a small room at the St. Francis Hotel.

His appearance at the trial was an unwelcome surprise to the Moody lawyers. Addison established that he had enjoyed a close relationship with Bertha, then told the court that he had had a conversation with her over tea one afternoon in April, just before she sailed for Europe. In that conversation, he testified, she discussed her will: she told Addison that she had left everything to Etta Warren, who was "mother, brother, sister and father" to her. Addison also testified that Bertha was entirely sane throughout his friendship with her, a view that was corroborated by other witnesses. (Many friends who had seen her in Europe also disputed the suicide. On the day of her fall, July 9, she had visited her bank and drawn out $800. The cashier testified to her unremarkable behavior on that occasion.)[7] Although the cause of death remained unresolved, Etta Warren won the case.

Addison's appearance at the trial confirmed the news, presumably known to friends and family, that the surprise witness was now a permanent resident of New York City. The San Francisco newspapers made headlines out of their former social favorite's temporary return to his hometown, while "industriously prosecuting his clever work in a studio in New York."

Was this a sudden decision on Addison's part? After his Guatemalan trip, he had certainly planned to meet Bertha in New York. But to stay permanently? He must have made the decision while he was still in Guatemala, for while he was there, he arranged to have his effects sent on from San Francisco to New York. Probably the decision was easier to make while he was a very long way from home—and out of range of the siren call of his mother.

For much of his early life, Addison had not taken architecture seriously as a profession. Whenever possible, he had looked for alternative occupations—for good reason. He saw at first hand how Willis Polk, so richly talented, had struggled to achieve success as an architect. His own lack of experience and qualifications continued to be a serious hurdle. Whenever he had managed to obtain a commission, he had had to abandon the project because of bad luck or bad timing. The omens were not encouraging.

Yet the evidence of his extensive scrapbook and of his acquisition of religious antiquities in Guatemala testifies that he was at last seriously focusing on architecture and design, and notwithstanding the cultural merits of San Francisco, New York offered far more opportunities in this field of endeavor. Whatever his other ambitions, the trip to Guatemala in the summer of 1904 hardened his resolve. When he returned, it was to say good-bye to his life in San Francisco, and by October, two months before his thirty-second birthday, he had taken another plunge into the unknown and was living full time in New York.

PART TWO
NEW YORK
MANSIONS AND MONKEYS

BEACH HOUSE DESIGN (WATERCOLOR AND PENCIL) FOR
ALVA BELMONT, GREAT NECK, NEW YORK.

(Courtesy of the Kim Mizner Hollins family)

CHAPTER 9

"THINGS ARE VERY COMFORTABLE HERE AND THE SERVICE IS EXCELLENT."

Addison did not know many people when he first arrived in New York in the fall of 1904, but it did not matter. His old friend, Mrs. Hermann Oelrichs, the former Tessie Fair of San Francisco, was able to hand him his "naturalization papers," in Proust's expression, gaining him immediate entrance into New York society—and, if he played his cards right, a career as an architect.

Tessie Oelrichs had become a figure to be reckoned with, both literally and metaphorically. When she first arrived in New York in the 1890s as the very young bride of Hermann Oelrichs, she had been dubbed the "Bonanza Heiress" and was regarded with some suspicion. That she possessed "Western magnificence," as the press put it, while sounding Henry Jamesian, was not necessarily a compliment. But she soon won over the social set, thanks to her enormous New York apartment, her lively personality, and her Comstock mining fortune, supplemented by that of her husband, who had ceded to her the authority to spend as much of it as she needed to achieve her ambition of throwing better parties than anyone else.

She accomplished her goal with the help of Rosecliff, the house she built in 1898 in Newport, where all her friends were building second homes. Building a house was a sure way to elevate one's standing in New York, and Tessie Oelrichs knew that as well as anyone. Originally she had loyally assigned the work to her hometown architect A. Page Brown. He drew a plan for a handsome house that, like much of his work, reflected his regional bias: a mission-style structure with tile roof, balconies, and arches. But then Tessie met with the very famous Stanford White, who persuaded her to change her mind and her architect. In 1901 McKim, Mead & White gave her the mansion for the precise purpose to which she was fastened.

White replaced Brown's Spanish mission style with that of the Grand Trianon at Versailles. The exterior was of white tile in contrasting glazes, such as White had used for his architectural masterpiece, Madison Square Garden. The ballroom was the largest in Newport, with a heart-shaped staircase for Tessie's dramatic entrances and a triumphal arch through which guests processed, like gaudy prisoners, to offer tribute to their doughty conqueror. Thanks to White's presiding genius, the house was lighthearted in spirit, in spite of its grandeur, with pleasing proportions and a sense of ease; the French influence was subtly incorporated into his idiosyncratic design.

As Rosecliff's chatelaine, Mrs. Oelrichs was frequently mentioned in the gossip columns, and the uniforms of her chauffeurs were exhaustively discussed in the pages of *Vogue*. But true to the old saw, Tessie's money did not buy her happiness. Hermann Oelrichs preferred to spend his time away from his wife, often back in San Francisco, where he had met and married her. Even before his death by a heart attack at sea in 1906, Tessie was often left to go about her social engagements in New York without a chivalrous arm to guide her out of her carriage or in to dinner. Not that this would stop her, of course. But Addison's sudden appearance in New York was nothing less than providential.

His social entree assured, Addison's first problem was sartorial. Having arrived in New York directly from Guatemala, the clothes he had with him were (a) unsuitable for a New York winter, and (b) ruined by a hurricane that had practically sunk the steamer that brought him back to the United States. Since he had spent most of his life in California, he did not even own an overcoat. (The Alaska furs were long gone.) Once these delicate matters were sorted out by a tailor who could deal with his huge person, he was ready to greet New York.

In November 1904 Tessie Oelrichs eagerly awaited him in her box at the horse show at New York's most glamorous venue, Stanford White's Madison Square Garden.* There Addison was introduced to a string of

---

*Sadly, Addison arrived in New York too late for the Bal Blanc, Tessie's most famous party at Rosecliff, in August 1904, when everyone and everything was white.

socially prominent people whose names "were headliners in every social column in America. . . . I had hit the social top and I was in the 'seventh heaven' of astonishment and delight." Almost instantaneously, however, Addison's celestial elevation at Madison Square Garden was darkened by a shadow—a large and noisy one. It couldn't be—but it was—Mama's Angel Birdie (or Mama's Jail Birdie, as some saw fit to call him).

Wilson Mizner had last been seen in Nome, Alaska, running his own private red-light district. Was he really now in New York? Addison could hardly believe his eyes when he spotted the tall, gaunt figure in the crowd at the horse show, dressed to the nines with a gardenia in his but-tonhole and a silk hat. It had been six years since he had seen his brother. Addison left the box, and the brothers greeted each other warmly. Addison promised to meet him later and hastily returned to his new friends. "Who was that?" they asked. Addison tried to deflect their interest, but Wilson was looking his elegant best, and the grand ladies were curious to know more. Addison was directed to bring him to the box. The brothers later gave different versions of what happened. Addison said he found Wilson in a bar and Wilson told him he was a fool to be appearing at Madison Square Garden with two "old madams." Wilson's version was that he met the "old madams" and calmly informed them that he was living in a cathouse at Broadway and Forty-second Street where "I just sit there all day reading my beloved books and smoking opium."

Both versions expose the same troubling issue: Wilson was back in Addison's life.

The following night Addison was invited to join a box at the theater as the guest of Myra Yerkes, the wife of Charles T. Yerkes, whose millions had been made in the transportation industry. Addison quickly took the measure of Myra Yerkes. She was swathed in an enormous velvet cloak, trimmed with yards of silver tip fur. Upon her big black lace hat, an enormous emerald held in place a long white ostrich plume. When she took the cloak off, she revealed two strings of enormous pearls (Addison called them "moth balls") and an emerald pendant "big enough for a crème de menthe for a cow." Addison also noticed that Mrs. Yerkes was drunk. In the second act of the play, she shouted at the actors so loudly that the management came to the box to quiet her, after which she fell asleep.

Undeterred, Addison accompanied his revived hostess back to her mansion at 864 Fifth Avenue for a party after the theater. He was unprepared for what he found. "The view was astonishing. A huge court rose two stories, with huge red marble columns supporting a glass dome. Directly opposite was a cascade of water, dropping down one story from a beautiful garden of orange trees and palms that seemed infinite as it reflected its white marble peristyles in huge mirrors." But while the architecture was staggering, it was the art that most impressed Addison. "At the back of the house supporting the hanging gardens there were two picture galleries, each one a hundred and twenty-five feet long and thirty feet wide, hung solid with Rembrandts, Franz Hals, Van Dycks, and many other old masters, along with Italian primitives and early Spanish pictures. It was the first private gallery I had ever seen that wasn't two-thirds Barbizon horrors."

It turned out that Myra Yerkes, like Tessie Oelrichs, had a wayward husband. Charles Yerkes at this time had more than a passing interest in a young actress called Emma Grigsby, so Addison was immediately pressed into service as Myra's escort. Every night he attended her at social functions. Every day she talked to him on the phone. Even for Addison, the attention was a little overwhelming. About five weeks after they met, while Wilson was visiting Addison, she telephoned about a dinner party. Addison made the excuse that he must dine with his little brother. Myra insisted that Addison bring this little brother with him. Addison, not surprisingly, was somewhat apprehensive, but Myra Yerkes found Wilson even more entertaining than Addison—and considerably thinner. The two became inseparable, and Addison was unceremoniously dumped.

He didn't mind. Despite her mansion and her artworks, Myra Yerkes was not his favorite companion. She was neither amusing nor intelligent, and she tended to make scenes in public (often because of too much "dipping the beak," as Addison described it). He preferred the redoubtable Mrs. Stuyvesant Fish. Many people were intimidated by Mrs. Stuyvesant Fish, but Addison was rarely intimated by anybody, certainly not older women, with whom he had always felt at ease. (In his teenage diary, he relates many occasions where he spent time with women his mother's age and enjoyed their company.) The feeling was mutual. New York society ladies found Addison definitely refreshing. He was, after all, a Californian, part of that "tough lot," as the New York newspapers had described Tessie Oelrichs's early suitors—somehow reeking of gold dust and barroom brawls and a machismo that refined easterners could not match. Thanks to his mother's tutelage, he was a good dancer. Large and raffish, he also brought to the party a raconteur's talent. His humor could be bawdy, although not much remains in print to prove the point. (As in many cases where verbal wit is at issue, reported examples rarely convince. When Addison published his memoir, friends regretted that so much of his lively conversational style failed to communicate on the page.) Mrs. Fish in particular liked his forthright manner. They were equally outspoken, and Addison grew to "love her terse humor and her direct way of putting things." He called her "Miss Mamie," and they became firm friends. With Mrs. Oelrichs and Mrs. Stuyvesant Fish as his patrons, Addison's path through New York was soon awash in champagne and ostrich feathers.

His first New York apartment was in the Livingstone House, at 30 West Twenty-fourth Street. He lived there with an adoring housekeeper whom he always referred to in his memoir as "Miss A. Louise Darry." An apartment with staff? It seems rather an expensive way of life for a man who had recently arrived in the city without work, even if he was moving in extremely grand circles. How did he pay the rent and household expenses? For a change, it appears that Addison had money in the bank. Although he had no job, he owned a large number of very beautiful objects—the treasures he had brought back from Guatemala—with which he filled his apartment: rich velvet and damask vestments, ornate carved church paneling, reliquaries, gilded candlesticks, and other rare ornaments, all of which created a powerful effect on visitors. When they showed particular interest in an object, he was pleased to inform them that it could be purchased. For instance, he sold fifteen yards of red damask for two dollars a yard; two thousand yards of yellow for two dollars and a half; and a quantity of priests' robes and oddments at unnamed but no doubt handsome prices. Like a design showroom, his apartment was for sale, and very soon he was making good money on the rare items he had rescued from the poor priests in Antigua. In addition to these profitable ventures, his Klondike take was steadily increasing in value. Enjoying one of the upswings of his roller-coaster financial fortunes, Addison could for the time being afford to take advantage of what the city had to offer.

The early 1900s were good years to be in New York. Frank Crownin-shield, social observer and editor of the first *Vanity Fair,* called the years 1901 to 1914 the bonanza period in New York's social progress, "ushered in by the sale of the Carnegie Steel Company to Mr. J. P. Morgan and his associates for approximately half a billion dollars (a tenth of the national wealth). Others followed. It was estimated, during that period, that more than a thousand men in America amassed a million dollars between the years 1898 and 1907, and that three hundred of those captains of industry had gravitated to New York."[1]

One consequence of this bonanza was an unprecedented explosion of real estate development and its salutary effect on the architectural profession.[2] But although several "high buildings" (the original name given to the new office blocks sixteen or more stories high) were beginning to change the face of downtown, the residential areas of the eastern metropolis remained firmly traditional. The wealthy inhabitants of early-twentieth-century New York wanted French chateaux, English stately homes, and Italian palazzos—the nostalgic European ideal upon which American taste had so long relied.

The architects to whose work Addison was exposed as he strolled the New York avenues offered similar forms of historicism: Horace Trum-bauer, Whitney Warren, John Russell Pope and Carrère & Hastings were all hired to create a range of Victorian or neoclassical mansions for their clients. Richard Morris Hunt, perhaps the favorite architect of the so-called Gilded Age, built gratifyingly extravagant mansions for the Vanderbilts and the Astors in an eclectic range of European styles. Many of the architects mining this rich lode during the first fifteen years of the twentieth century, like the landscape designers working alongside them, were as well born as their clients. Ogden Codman, for instance, came from the best of Boston families. Wedded to the eighteenth century, Codman designed houses that were sometimes called Colonial Revival. They were beautiful, elegant, symmetrical, and built largely for his friends. (Codman also wrote a book with another socially prominent colleague, Edith Wharton, called *The Decoration of Houses,* which proposed that American interiors should be released from Victorian excess and made simpler and more practical.)

Stanford White was the prototypical exponent of the delicate marriage between society and architecture. In 1905, when Addison was starting to make his connections in New York, White, scion of a respectable literary New York family, was nearly ubiquitous. The list of his commercial buildings in New York alone is quite dazzling: the Metropolitan Club, the Century Club, the University Club, the Lambs' Club, the Tiffany Building, the Washington Square Arch, the Bowery Savings Bank, Sherry's restaurant, and the Herald Building were just some of them, and the noncommercial buildings include the charming Madison Avenue Presbyterian Church and the great Spanish Renaissance palace (now long gone) Madison Square Garden.

The list of private residences he built is equally impressive. As well as Tessie Oelrichs's Rosecliff in Newport, he designed, for instance, Southside in Newport for the Robert Goelets, Harbor Hill in Roslyn for the Clarence Mackays, the Orchard in Southampton for the Jimmy Breeses, and many townhouses, one of the most famous being Mrs. Fish's "Palace of the Doges" at 25 East Seventy-eighth Street. Dependent on social connections for his commissions, he became intimate with his clients, who entertained him in the great mansions he had created for them. Thus patron and artist generated a symbiosis of art and money, not unlike that which had inspired the great European cultural flowerings of the past.

While his wife remained in their country house—Box Hill, in St. James, Long Island—"Stanny" supported artists and playwrights, assiduously attended plays and musicals, and amused himself and his bachelor friends with riotous parties of a somewhat scandalous nature in the bordellolike studios he owned around the city, or in his sumptuous suite of rooms in the tower of Madison Square Garden. A familiar sight with his six-foot-three-inch frame, upbrushed red hair, and electric personality, Stanford White epitomized the raw energy and talent that fueled the cultural life of New York in the early 1900s.

It was inevitable that Stanford White and Addison Mizner should meet. According to Addison, he was introduced to White by Tessie Oelrichs, although it could just as easily have been Mrs. Fish or one of the other members of their social circle. Some of Addison's old friends were now socially well connected too. For instance, Richard Harding Davis had by this time become hugely successful as a foreign correspondent and writer of best-selling adventure stories and was a well-known figure at New York's intellectual and artistic gatherings. Davis knew Stanford

White well, spending weekends in his house on Long Island and traveling with him in Europe.[3] Davis was also a partner in White's late-night sex parties. A letter from White to his friend, discussing the cost of a "shindy" in 1895, proposes that "I will take Miss Clews into my party. We can divvy on the other three girls."[4]

Another friend from Addison's past, Helen Benedict, had moved to New York and now belonged to the architectural fraternity by marriage. Her husband was Thomas Hastings, who, with his partner, John M. Carrère, had apprenticed at McKim, Mead & White and then formed their own firm. The two men were now making their own bid for fame, building the New York Public Library, which was completed in 1911. Helen Benedict had also known Stanford White before her marriage, buying from him a tapestry for $125 in 1899.[5]

Stanford White was fifty-two when Addison met him, nineteen years older than the import from California. They must have made a striking pair, both well over six feet tall, verbal, charismatic, and full of energy. "I got to know Mr. White well," Addison recalled, "and as I was not pushing for jobs, he used to like to sit and talk architecture to someone who knew so little about it. I worshipped, for he was my god." "Pushing for jobs" would have done Addison no good, for at this point White was in no position to help anybody. Thanks to his reckless private life and inefficiency in business management, he owed hundreds of thousands of dollars to landlords, restaurants, wine merchants, building suppliers, draftsmen and designers. As a last resort, to raise money to pay some of his bills, he assembled all his best furniture, tapestries, paintings and objets d'art in order to sell them. On February 13, 1905, around the time Addison met him, fire broke out in the warehouse where White had stored all his treasures. The blaze destroyed almost every valuable possession he owned. With his insurance mostly lapsed, the loss was estimated at something on the order of $300,000, a devastating blow to the architect. In desperation, to help protect the firm from liability to his creditors, he offered to separate himself from the partnership and to take a monthly salary instead.[6]

How much Addison knew of White's humiliation is not clear. He certainly did not see much of White at this time, since in March 1905 Addison went to Europe with Tessie Oelrichs, and from June to August White himself was abroad. Addison says that White found a few jobs for him during this period, but they were inconsequential ("I only got bungalows and warehouses to build at first," Addison conceded later), and Addison's name does not appear at all in Stanford White's extant correspondence. But, Addison deeply admired White (his "god") and studied almost every commission completed by the famous architect's firm, pasting pictures of them in a scrapbook. Devoted to United States architecture, the book's first twenty pages are filled exclusively with the work of McKim, Mead & White. Alongside photographs of the Columbia University Library, Rosecliff, the Union Club, the Brooklyn Museum, and others, Addison added his own pencil drawings of their design details and indicated distances between columns, projections, and the like. He drew a quarter section of White's Madison Square Garden dining room, noting "garlands of oak or laurel, embossed ribbons, stems gilt, fruit old red-pink, leaves chocolate." He also sketched the Italian mantel that White installed in the Lambs' Club. These studies were the work of a diligent student, and those who later criticized Addison for his lack of professional training needed only to look at these pages for proof of his self-taught draftsmanship and technical skills.

Perhaps Addison's most useful lessons were derived from his direct experience of several of White's best houses. As a guest at Rosecliff, Tessie Oelrichs's house in Newport, for instance, Addison could examine at his leisure how White had designed the H-shaped floor plan to embrace the ocean view, how he had used two glazes in the exterior tile, how the cloud-and-blue-sky ceiling lightened the effect of the forty-by-eighty-foot ballroom, and how the oak paneling in the library had been pickled to make it lighter. Was there not a nod of recognition when Addison saw the religious decorations (such as chasubles) so similar to his own Guatemalan decorative objects, that White had hung beside the tapestries on the walls of the first-floor gallery?

Newport in fact was a walking tour of Stanford White's architectural career. Addison could stroll down Bellevue Avenue and look at the Isaac Bell house, a very early shingle-style work by White's firm, or Southside, the summer residence of Robert Goelet, or E. D. Morgan's Beacon Rock. Or he could visit Kingscote and admire White's gloriously proportioned and textured dining room, with its Tiffany glass, cork ceilings, and cherrywood floors. These houses, and those in New York, such as Mrs. Fish's luxurious palace, allowed Addison to conduct hands-on research into the secrets of the masters.

In February 1905 Tessie Oelrichs invited Addison to meet her in Paris and join her on a drive through Italy. Having never been to Italy, Addison was thrilled. Carrying a letter of introduction to the pope from Countess Leary in New York, who had papal connections, he and Tessie managed to obtain an audience with the pontiff, "a fine looking old man with sad eyes," he said. Addison and Tessie then went on to Venice and then back to Paris, where Addison met his old friend Frank Goad, brother of the three famous Goad sisters. ("Ella, Aileen and Genevieve were beautiful, but his parents had gone into the red with Frank," Addison said with typical bluntness, adding that Frank was the most delightful traveling companion one could have.) Leaving Tessie in Paris, the two Californians continued together to Spain, a country Addison loved, "even when I was at Salamanca and supposed to be studying hard," and Morocco.

This and subsequent trips, which he made each year, were critical to Addison's architectural growth. He collected postcards and photographs of the places he saw—castles, palaces, churches, fountains, furniture, sculpture, moldings, and the like—and glued them in scrapbooks on his return home. In later volumes, he would add tearsheets from magazines to supplement what became his own private architectural reference library. At his death, he had twenty-seven scrapbooks in all, with titles such as *Moorish and Near East*; *Byzantine-Romanesque*; *Ceilings, Murals, Paneling, Doors*; *Cloisters*; *Aztec-Primitive*; *English Gothic*; and so on— the visual autobiography of an architect.

The pencil annotations that he made on many of the pictures, describing his aesthetic and emotional responses to these riches, shine a useful light on his mind at this stage in his architectural education. Commenting on the interior of San Miniato in Florence, for instance, he wrote, "Wonderful both in color and design. Notice that the capitals do not fit the columns, probably spoils of different pagan temples." On a picture of the doors of the Baptistry in Florence: "Michelangelo truly said that they should have been the doors of paradise." About Genoa: "I think Genoa is the most lovely from the outside. The palaces much more livable and refined." Of the Medici Chapel in Florence: "The most marvelous effect in color imaginable. Every stone known with mother of pearl and colored corals." The chapel's interior, with the Michelangelo statues, pleased him less: "This looks better in a photograph than in reality. Black marble etc. but the plain spaces are dirty white plaster."[7]

Mama Mizner at thirty.
(COURTESY OF THE KIM MIZNER HOLLINS
FAMILY AND THE OAKLAND MUSEUM OF
CALIFORNIA)

Addison, aged three.
(COURTESY OF THE KIM MIZNER
HOLLINS FAMILY)

The Mizner family in their Benicia garden. BACK ROW: Edgar.
THIRD ROW, LEFT TO RIGHT: Ella Watson Mizner, Lansing Jr., and William.
SECOND ROW, LEFT TO RIGHT: Lansing Mizner, Wilson, Minnie, and Henry.
FRONT ROW: Addison. (COURTESY OF THE HISTORICAL SOCIETY OF PALM BEACH COUNTY)

The Mizner estate in Benicia, illustrated in Thompson and West's atlas of Solano County, 1878. (COURTESY OF THE CAMEL BARN MUSEUM, BENICIA, CALIFORNIA)

The Mizner estate in later, less prosperous years. (COURTESY OF THE CAMEL BARN MUSEUM, BENICIA, CALIFORNIA)

Addison Mizner, aged about fifteen. (COURTESY OF THE KIM MIZNER HOLLINS FAMILY AND THE OAKLAND MUSEUM OF CALIFORNIA)

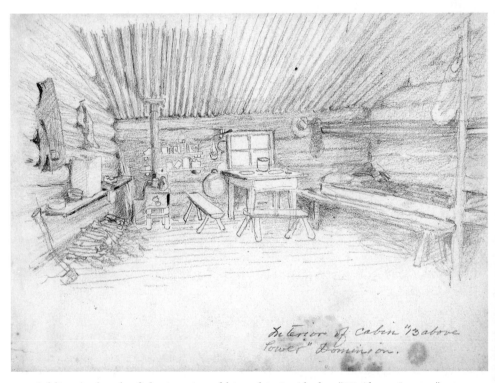

Addison's sketch of the interior of his cabin in Alaska, "13 Above Lower." Dominion Creek, 1899. (COURTESY OF THE KIM MIZNER HOLLINS FAMILY)

ASIDE DAM'S NOT BY A DAMSIDE

Looking up Dominion Creek, Alaska, June, 1899—Addison (seated, right),
with colleagues and dogs. (COURTESY OF THE KIM MIZNER HOLLINS FAMILY AND THE OAKLAND
MUSEUM OF CALIFORNIA)

Klondike
bound,
prepared for
the cold.
FROM LEFT TO
RIGHT, Addison,
William,
Wilson. (COURTESY
OF THE KIM MIZNER
HOLLINS FAMILY)

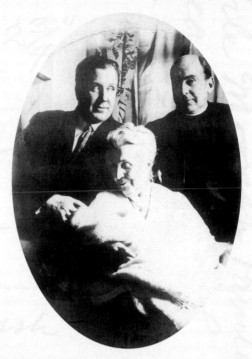

Mama Mizner with her sons Addison (left) and Henry, and her grandchild, Henry's daughter, Alice. (COURTESY OF THE KIM MIZNER HOLLINS FAMILY)

Addison the art restorer, working on Napoleon III at the Iolani Palace, Honolulu, 1900. (COURTESY OF THE KIM MIZNER HOLLINS FAMILY)

Minnie with her husband, Horace Chase, and their two children, Ysabel and Horace Jr. (COURTESY OF THE KIM MIZNER HOLLINS FAMILY)

Wilson with Anita Loos in Palm Beach. (COURTESY OF THE KIM MIZNER HOLLINS FAMILY)

RIGHT: Addison during his palmy, portly days in Palm Beach, circa 1922. (COURTESY OF THE KIM MIZNER HOLLINS FAMILY)
BELOW: At sea. Addison with Alex Waugh on a shopping spree to Europe. (COURTESY OF THE KIM MIZNER HOLLINS FAMILY)

Wilson (left), Addison, and Marie Dressler—one of the few photographs
of the two brothers together. (COURTESY OF THE HISTORICAL SOCIETY OF PALM BEACH COUNTY)

Addison at the Del Monte race meet in California. The newspaper caption that ran with this photo reads, "Mr. Mizner is a brother of Wilson Mizner, the wit." Wilson sent the clipping to his brother with the comment, "This should put you in your place." (COURTESY OF THE KIM MIZNER HOLLINS FAMILY)

Addison at a ball in Palm Beach with Louise Munn and William Rhinelander Stewart Jr. (COURTESY OF THE KIM MIZNER HOLLINS FAMILY)

Friends in Palm Beach.
From left: Addison, Mrs.
David R. Calhoun, Joan
Singer, Paris Singer.
(COURTESY OF THE HISTORICAL
SOCIETY OF PALM BEACH COUNTY)

Mama Mizner toward
the end of her life with
one of Addison's furry
friends in Port
Washington. (COURTESY OF
THE KIM MIZNER HOLLINS FAMILY)

ABOVE: Paris Singer. (COURTESY OF THE HISTORICAL SOCIETY OF PALM BEACH COUNTY) RIGHT: Addison with one of his pet kinkajous. (COURTESY OF THE KIM MIZNER HOLLINS FAMILY)

ABOVE: Very early Mizner: Addison's design for Ralph Thomas's tennis house, Sands Point, New York, 1911. (COURTESY OF PLAIN TALK) OPPOSITE: Addison in his prime. (COURTESY OF THE HISTORICAL SOCIETY OF PALM BEACH COUNTY)

Addison's watercolor rendering of a French chateau proposed for Alva
Belmont in 1912. She rejected it. (COURTESY OF THE KIM MIZNER HOLLINS FAMILY)

One of Alva Belmont's consolation prizes to Addison—the commission for a beach house in Newport, R.I., the side elevation shown here in a watercolor sketch. (COURTESY OF THE KIM MIZNER HOLLINS FAMILY)

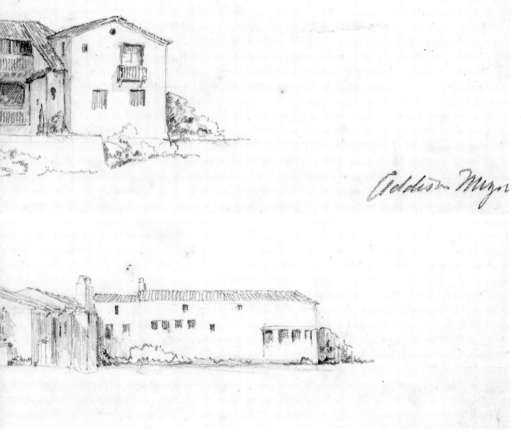

Addison's signed drawings of the front and rear facades of Casa Serena, John R. Bradley's house in Colorado Springs. (COURTESY OF THE KIM MIZNER HOLLINS FAMILY)

Project of Touchstone
Convalescent Soldiers' Club

THIS Clubhouse shown above is the Central Building of a Group of Cottages being Built at Palm Beach, Florida, Which Constitute The Touchstone War Service. The Clubhouse as well as the Cottages Have Been Designed By *Addison Mizner*, Who Is the Architect of The Association. :-: :-: :-:

For Further Information Address The Editor of The Touchstone.

ABOVE: *The Touchstone*'s announcement of the Convalescent Soldier's Club (the Everglades Club's first incarnation), with Addison's original pen-and-colorwash sketch. (COURTESY OF THE KIM MIZNER HOLLINS FAMILY) OPPOSITE: Addison's Palm Beach debut: The Everglades Club, circa 1919.

The living room of La Ronda, Percival E. Foerderer's mansion in Bryn Mawr, Pennsylvania. This is one of Addison's last and most spectacular houses. (COURTESY OF THE KIM MIZNER HOLLINS FAMILY)

The height of the season at the Everglades Club. (COURTESY OF THE HISTORICAL
SOCIETY OF PALM BEACH COUNTY)

Guests admire the elegant canal and gardens of El Mirasol, circa 1929.
(COURTESY OF THE HISTORICAL SOCIETY OF PALM BEACH COUNTY)

One of the charming allees of Via Mizner. (COURTESY OF THE KIM MIZNER HOLLINS FAMILY)

The stair tower of George S. Rasmussen's Casa Nana—stairs Addison was wrongly accused of having "forgotten." (COURTESY OF THE KIM MIZNER HOLLINS FAMILY)

A catalog for Mizner's handmade pottery. (COURTESY OF THE KIM MIZNER HOLLINS FAMILY)

RIGHT: One of Addison's pots displayed on a tiled stairwell in Via Mizner. (COURTESY OF THE KIM MIZNER HOLLINS FAMILY) OPPOSITE: The courtyard opposite Villa Mizner was a splendid place to promote Addison's wares. (COURTESY OF THE KIM MIZNER HOLLINS FAMILY)

LEFT: Addison's drawing of a Gothic window for the Foerderer living room. BELOW: Sketches of various architectural details (some copied from churches in Burgos and Barcelona) for the patio addition of Playa Riente Addison made for the Dillmans. (BOTH: COURTESY OF THE KIM MIZNER HOLLINS FAMILY)

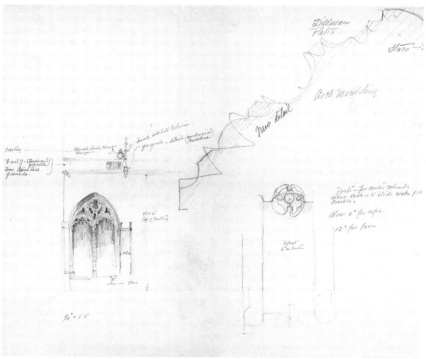

OPPOSITE: The cloister of the Ritz-Carlton/Cloister Inn, Boca Raton, showing the columns installed upside down. (COURTESY OF THE KIM MIZNER HOLLINS FAMILY)

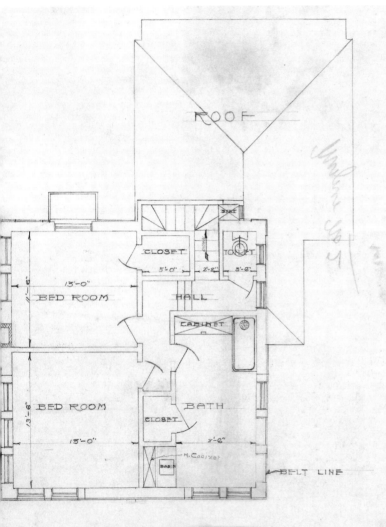

ROOF

CLOSET
5'-0"

TOILET
2'-2"   5'-6"

13'-0"
6"
BED ROOM
HALL

CABINET

BED ROOM
13'-6"
BATH

CLOSET
13'-0"
2'-6"

M.Cabinet
BASIN

BELT LINE

THIRD FLOOR PLAN
SCALE - ¼" - 1'-0"

MIZNER #

Floor plan for one of the small houses Addison designed to be built in
Boca Raton. (Courtesy of the Kim Mizner Hollins family)

ABOVE: Addison's drawing of his great living room in the Villa Mizner, scene of so many musicales and entertainments. BELOW: Coffered pecky cypress ceiling, tiled floor, carved stone fireplace, Spanish portraits and furniture: Mizner's signature decoration for the living room of William Gray Warden's Palm Beach house, 1922. (BOTH: COURTESY OF THE KIM MIZNER HOLLINS FAMILY)

ABOVE: Addison's saucy design for his personal book plate. (COURTESY OF THE KIM MIZNER HOLLINS FAMILY AND THE SOCIETY OF THE FOUR ARTS, PALM BEACH, FLORIDA)

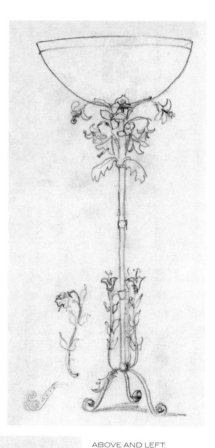

ABOVE AND LEFT: Sketches found in Addison's scrapbooks of furniture and decorative details, typical of his focus when traveling abroad. (COURTESY OF THE KIM MIZNER HOLLINS FAMILY)

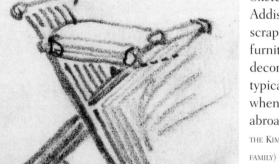

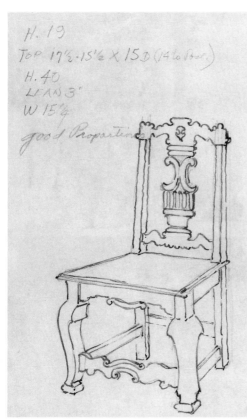

H. 19
Top 17½-15½ X 15 D (14 [illegible])
H. 40
L. AN 3"
W 15¾
good Proportions

LEFT AND BELOW:

Addison frequently drew
careful copies of pieces
of furniture, along with
measurements. About the
chair (which ended up in
his office) he writes, "good
proportions." (COURTESY OF THE
KIM MIZNER HOLLINS FAMILY)

RIGHT: The scene at the opening of the Ritz Carlton Cloister at Boca Raton. Amongst the fashionable people in attendance are Wilson and Ysabel Chase (center), while Addison holds court at a careful distance (upper left). (COURTESY OF THE BOCA RATON HISTORICAL SOCIETY) BELOW: The house at 237 Worth Avenue that Addison designed for Wilson. (COURTESY OF THE KIM MIZNER HOLLINS FAMILY)

The door from which eggnog and

Christmas Greetings flow

LEFT: Addison always sent out amusing Christmas cards. This one shows his baronial front door, with the legend "The door from which eggnog and Christmas greetings flow." BELOW: A corner of the living room of the Villa Mizner after Addison's memorial service. One can almost imagine him still sitting in his well-worn oversized chair, near a photograph of his mother and a bound volume of his memoirs. On the arm of the chair is the sprig of orange blossoms pinned there in his memory by Mrs. Stotesbury.

(BOTH: COURTESY OF THE KIM MIZNER HOLLINS FAMILY)

The cover of a brochure for Addison's greatest dream and ultimate downfall—Boca Raton, Venice-on-the-Atlantic. (Courtesy of the Boca Raton Historical Society)

In addition to his personal critiques, he would write down the measurements of a corridor in a palace, or the width and height of a cornice of a church or cloister. He often made pencil sketches to accompany particular photographs, sometimes on tracing paper for a more accurate rendition. On occasion, when he was short of time, he would ask someone else to do a measured drawing for him of a piece he particularly favored, such as a carved walnut chest in the Museo Correr in Venice; it was sketched to scale by a draftsman friend, Lester Margon. Almost a century later, architects marvel at this attention to detail. Taking measurements of the great buildings of Europe is something no architect today has time for (and some of the buildings and artifacts no longer exist), so Mizner's meticulous and comprehensive records have now become a highly prized resource both for architectural students and practitioners.[8]

In 1905, after his first trip to Europe, Addison had a visit from his mother, now seventy years old, who stayed a couple of months and was entertained royally by her proud son. They went to the opera, to the theater, to dinners. He produced a piece of lace from Guatemala and cut down an old black dress of hers, inserting the lace into the back and front. "She looked too lovely, and I was delighted with my work, for I hadn't dressed anyone up since the old theatrical days in the barn at Benicia." Finally, Edgar arrived to take her back to California. "I was terribly sorry to see her go," Addison confessed. "The only thing the entire tribe agreed on was a love for mother. She was certainly a grand old lady."

Even Wilson made a few appearances during his mother's visit, to take her out to dinner. This was not as easy for Mama's Angel Birdie as it sounded. He always had important postdinner "engagements," which meant he had to flee the table very quickly after the meal. (Among their friends, the brothers were known as the "day" and "night" Mizners.) The other problem for Wilson was that his mother enjoyed her food and always ordered expensive courses of food and wine, which of course Wilson had to pay for. (Mama Mizner was not behaving thoughtlessly here. Wilson appeared to be flush with money, his usual posture.)

By 1906, however, Wilson's money problems seemed to be over. During the year since he had met Myra Yerkes, he had remained in close touch with the millionairess, spending time at her Fifth Avenue mansion and escorting her to entertainments. On December 29, 1905, Charles Yerkes died, and a month later, on January 30, 1906, Wilson married the widow. The press had a field day with the story. It was sensational enough that Wilson was twenty-nine years old and Mrs. Yerkes, forty-eight. But journalists soon uncovered some of the murkier sediment of Wilson's past. Stories surfaced of his Klondike adventures, his liaisons with call girls, even a totally unsubstantiated rumor that he had murdered a girl in Honolulu.

When Addison found out about the marriage, he rushed over to the Yerkes mansion, where he found his brother in bed. "Upon the dais, with two green velvet steps, stood the nuptial couch. It had been made for the 'crazy king' of Bavaria, and was of inlaid woods with bronze gilt appliques. At the head there was a swarm of gilt cupids covering up a semi-nude figure of 'Night' and at the foot they were tearing the covers off her. In the bed lay Wilson, with a woolen undershirt that had shrunk. A million dollars' worth of point-lace covered him to his middle and he was rolling a Bull Durham cigarette in a brown paper."

Addison demanded to know why on earth Wilson had got himself into this "messy alliance." After gallantly protesting that he found Mrs. Yerkes very beautiful and that she did not look her age, Wilson added, "Things are very comfortable here and the service is excellent."

Shortly after their marriage, Wilson got hold of Charles Yerkes's will. In this document Yerkes, who had been worth millions, had shown his feelings for his wife by leaving her the modest sum of $200,000 plus the New York house, "library, linens, horses, and other domestic animals," and articles for personal use. He specifically did not leave her his priceless art collection. Available to her for her lifetime, it was thereafter to be incorporated into an art gallery, generously endowed by the testator. (The gallery did not survive; his most lasting legacy was the Yerkes Observatory at the University of Chicago.)

Whether his wife's disappointing inheritance soured Wilson on the deal is not clear. Soon Myra suspected that her new husband was surreptitiously removing some of the art treasures from the house. Relations became tense. She refused to write any more checks for him. Wilson moved into a hotel, where he was harassed by policemen and Pinkerton's detectives. The marriage lasted all of one year. According to Addison, Wilson came out of the divorce with nothing but his freedom.

During this strange episode, a more serious matter demanded the Mizners' attention. On April 18, 1906, San Francisco suffered a devastating earthquake that practically destroyed the city. Addison first learned of it from Tessie Oelrichs, who called him over at once. "There were already a dozen Californians cluttering up her library. Some were in silent tears; others just dazed, whilst still others were hysterical." Addison's first thought was for his mother and brothers. "Everyone at Tessie's had relations there and her house became one of terror." The phone lines were jammed, and newspaper reports were horrifying—it was impossible to know what was really happening.

Two days later, on April 20, Addison received a terse telegram from his brother William: SF RAZED FAMILY ESCAPED OFFICE AND RESIDENCE COMPLETE LOSS.[9] Shortly afterward the Broadway actress Marie Dressler, who was organizing a relief drive for the earthquake victims, came to Addison for help, and together they collected more than $75,000 from generous New Yorkers.

While he was out raising money with Marie Dressler, other friends rallied to the cause of rebuilding the city. Stanford White offered his professional advice to Daniel Burnham in Chicago and Willis Polk in San Francisco, both of whom had been called in to consult. To guard against such damage ever occurring again, White suggested that the new structures be "hot riveted skeleton buildings, with columns or concrete bases . . . and cross-bracing as well as upright and horizontal bracing."[10] Mrs. William K. Vanderbilt, Jr. (Tessie Oelrichs's sister) consulted White on the rebuilding of one of her properties in the earthquake-devastated city. "The San Francisco disaster has added so much to my labors that I have hardly had time to think," he wrote to a friend.[11]

Shortly after the earthquake, Addison received a letter from his mother, describing how she survived. She had been sleeping at the Hotel Pleasanton on Sutter Street when the quake struck, and "fortunately, I had on one of my nicest nightgowns with hand embroidery, for in the halls people were running about in very common lingerie." Fire broke out in the hotel, but she got a lift on a fire truck and found safety with a neighbor. A day later, with Lansing's help, she boarded a steamer leaving the Presidio dock for Vallejo, and from there she went to Stag's Leap.

While she was worried about abandoning her "boys" (her oldest being by this time forty-six years old), leaving San Francisco was an emotional moment for her in other ways as well. "Many, many years ago I sailed into this beautiful bay without anything, after a great tragedy of the sea, and now I am leaving it in the same way, after a tragedy of fire. It was then only a little settlement and I have watched it grow into a great city and I know that I will live to see it arise from its ashes, greater and more beautiful than ever."

Another passage in this letter spoke more directly to Addison's tender heart. "Now, my dear son," she wrote, "I do not wish to distress you and I do not think we should think of it when everyone is suffering so, but we have lost everything we have." This was a call to action that Addison could not ignore. Over the years, he and his brother Henry had both promised her that she would have a home with them. But Henry was busy running St. Stephen's House, a missionary outpost of the Episcopal Church in a slum district of St. Louis, and was in no position to take on his aging mother. It was up to Addison to fulfill the promise.

CHAPTER 10

"ALL DOWN FIFTH AND MADISON, THEY LOVE OUR BABY ADDISON."

That Addison pursued such an active social life in New York may make him appear a trivial person, but like most architects then and now, he depended almost entirely on connections for his commissions. Even Stanford White worked tirelessly to stay on good terms with people who might become clients. Unlike his mentor, however, Addison was not prepared, for all his crossing of social lines, to transgress sexually. This is not to say that Addison had no sexual appetite, but his reserve on the matter, and the lack of any written evidence, indicates that whatever he was doing, he did very quietly.

Up to the death of Bertha Dolbeer, all his love affairs with women had been disappointing. He undoubtedly felt genuine affection for these women: his youthful journal, written at critical moments of desire and despair, reflects the authentic outpourings of a young man in the throes of unrequited passion for the opposite sex. They also contain no soul-searching about identity, nor any erotic references.

Bertha's tragic death and the ensuing trial help shed light on Addison's maturing sexual aspirations. Although he had supposedly been planning to marry Bertha, at the trial he did not behave like a grieving lover. The one extant letter from Bertha to Addison during that summer they were apart (which the Warren lawyers used at the trial to show her balanced state of mind) might kindly be described as chatty, offering details about the theater in London and the trip to Paris. She allowed as how she enjoyed reading his letters on the steamer: "As I was not seasick I could appreciate them." No romantic undercurrents are evident here.

Indeed, the couple were on such easy terms that she felt able to tell him candidly that she had left her fortune to Etta Warren, and Addison teased her about what she had bequeathed to him—"a pianola or a kitchen stove?" These are not the exchanges of a couple rapturously in love. He even spelled her name wrong in his memoir (not that that means much, knowing Addison's spelling). In short, there is no hint of anything more than a fond friendship between Addison and Bertha. She clearly trusted him enough to confide in him about her most personal affairs. Was Addison's role perhaps to be that of trusted confidant rather than lover?

By the time Addison moved to New York, he was thirty-three years old, and seen in hindsight, these romantic failures suggest that his heterosexuality was beginning to falter. There are other clues as to his true disposition. His friend Jack Baird, who had accompanied him down the California coast in his pursuit of Bertha Dolbeer, was more than just an amusing fellow with whom to ride in a new roadster. Baird was artistic, intelligent, and a collector of rare books. For a time during Addison's rootless years in San Francisco they shared an apartment, combining their steadily accumulating libraries and collections of objets d'art.

On December 12, 1905, Addison's birthday and over a year after he moved to New York, Jack Baird was killed—ironically in one of the sporty motors he so loved. Baird's companion in the car survived, a young woman of dubious background called Ruby Neil. In a scandalous aftermath of the tragedy, she announced that she and Baird had been engaged. Family and friends were incredulous, and Baird's large funeral was held without her.[1] (Addison did not attend either. There were no planes to fly him across the country in those days, and he never could have made the service in time by train.)

According to Alice DeLamar, one of Addison's closest friends during his later days in Palm Beach, the friendship between Baird and Mizner was so intense that they had written out wills bequeathing to each other their most precious possessions.[2] She reported that when Baird's sister found her brother's will leaving his treasures to Addison, she promptly burned it, declaring that Addison had been a decadent influence on her brother.[3] (Newspaper reports of the will simply said that he had devised his entire $300,000 estate to his mother.)

Alice DeLamar's account reflects what was recognized in Palm Beach fifteen years later as the truth of Addison's personal life. Perhaps the fey cartoons of him with the drooping lock of hair, and those black socks with their pink roses, which the onlookers at the swimming pool in Monterey accepted as part of Addie's "eccentricity," could be regarded even then as inferring a very different word. But since it was a word that dared not speak its name, in an era deeply hostile to its meaning, it was not likely that he would openly flaunt his sexual bias, at least not at this time.

Certainly Stanford White's circle of friends enjoyed homosexual pleasures in private. Architect Whitney Warren, Charles Freer (whose art collection was later donated to the Smithsonian), Nikola Tesla (an eccentric inventor), and Joseph Wells (a gifted draftsman for McKim, Mead & White) were all members of White's "bachelor" circle, and gossip abounded about their sexual tastes. Thomas Hastings remained single until he was forty, during which time his reputation was distinctly male-oriented, and his surprise marriage to Helen Benedict saw them more apart than together. Richard Harding Davis, the swashbuckling "man's man" of popular fiction, was singularly matched in a platonic marriage that lasted for more than twelve years.[4] (He later married a dancer when he was forty-eight and she was twenty-four.) No public comment was ever made about these unconventional liaisons, and the incidents that destroyed Oscar Wilde remained taboo on this side of the Atlantic.

Then in June 1906 Stanford White was shot to death in Madison Square Garden by Harry Thaw, a rich playboy, in a fit of jealousy. Several years earlier White had seduced a beautiful sixteen-year-old showgirl called Evelyn Nesbit, who later became Thaw's wife. Thaw was tried twice for murder, and the ensuing court cases, with their breathless accounts of orgies, drug addicts, and ravishments of pubescent girls, suddenly brought these issues into the open and scandalized a society still in the thrall of Victorian morality.

Many people who had known Stanford White for years distanced themselves from the murdered architect at this juncture and refused to defend his reputation publicly. One of the few who remained loyal was Richard Harding Davis, who rushed into print with a spirited defense in *Colliers* magazine. (The hostility to White was so intense that after the publication of this article, a public library in New Jersey pulled all Davis's books off the shelves.)[5] Curiously, although the murder and the trials of Harry Thaw dominated the New York press and dinner conversation for months if not years, Addison did not mention them in his memoir. Moreover, Thaw's leading defense attorney for his first trial was Delphin Michael Delmas from San Francisco, one of the most successful defense lawyers on the West Coast and a relative of Addison's old friend Paul Delmas. Possibly, like most of Stanford White's friends, Addison was embarrassed by the revelations of White's private life. But he carefully preserved in a scrapbook the cover of the catalog of the sale of White's possessions, "The Artistic Property Belonging to the Late Stanford White."

While avoiding the subject of Stanford White's death in his memoir, Addison did mention meeting Evelyn Nesbit. At one of Stanford's parties (which Addison claimed were very boring), the famous architect said to him, "I have discovered the beauty of the age. Now, Mizner, don't drag out any rough talk for she is only seventeen and a virgin." Addison went into White's studio and "almost dropped dead when I came face to face with Evelyn Nesbit. She gave me a frightened and then a pleading look and I said, 'not a word,' and passed on as though I had never seen her before and talked to some of the other guests." Later Addison saw White put Nesbit into a carriage and send her home.

Curiously, Addison's text strongly implies that he and Nesbit had already met—and that she was anxious to deny it. Perhaps Addison had seen her somewhere in a less savory context? Considering her B-level Broadway show-business career, the name Wilson Mizner comes to mind. In fact, she did know Wilson, but according to her, she met him only after Harry Thaw had gone to jail, when she encountered "the witty, brilliant Wilson Mizner" in an opium den with Jack Francis, a journalist who later sold to the newspapers the story that she had had an illegitimate child.[6] So the allusion to an earlier meeting between Addison and Nesbit remains unexplained.

Unfortunately, Addison did not record the date of this meeting: was it before or after Nesbit married Thaw? White first met and seduced Nesbit in 1901, when she was sixteen. Addison could not have met either of them until he came to New York in late 1904 and probably did not do so until 1905, when Nesbit was twenty and certainly no longer a virgin. She married Harry Thaw in April 1905. If Addison met her at White's studio after her marriage, this would have been an invaluable piece of evidence for the defense at the Thaw trial, who were intent on proving that Mrs. Thaw continued to see White after her marriage, thus further discredited the dead man's reputation and justifying Thaw's crime of passion. Newspaper accounts aver that after her marriage White and Nesbit met only once, in the street, but other evidence indicates they had several additional meetings. If the meeting that Addison recorded was one of them, that would explain her embarrassment at being seen in White's company.

Until his untimely death, Stanford White had successfully steered his way through the rapidly changing currents of New York society. As an architect, he had access to the new wealth inundating the Fifth Avenue salons. As a member of the Old Guard, he also socialized freely with the WASP establishment. They belonged to the same clubs, ate at the same restaurants, and bespoke their suits from the same London tailor. The scandal surrounding White's death revealed the fragility of this social structure. Edith Wharton, who knew the territory intimately, described in *The House of Mirth* the tragic efforts of Lily Bart to maintain her position in a society eager to destroy those who fell from grace. The story reflected the desperate struggle for position that arose during this period. Perhaps the fierce antipathy toward Stanford White provoked during the Harry Thaw trials was caused in part by the perception that he had betrayed his class.

The same social tension that brought down Lily Bart played into Addison Mizner's hands. As an outsider from California, he was able to enjoy the company of his eastern countrymen without having to align himself with any of them. With his extra-large stride and western dash, "Addie" found himself comfortably straddling the worlds of Fifth Avenue and Broadway. His social standing in San Francisco and his personal charm allowed him, albeit guardedly, into the inner circle. He was, after all, the frequent consort of Tessie Oelrichs, who was in the habit of giving dinner parties for two hundred people and wearing a lot of jewelry. For a fancy-dress ball at Sherry's, generously proportioned Tessie covered herself from head to foot in a costume of pearl-covered gold-and-blue fabric with a dangling gold headdress, representing Amneris. Not to be outdone, the well-upholstered Mrs. Stuyvesant Fish coolly appeared as Queen of the Fairies at the Mother Goose Ball she held in Newport two years later. What Addison came as on these glorious occasions is not recorded, but we can be sure it was competitive.

On the downtown side, Addison's friendship with Metropolitan

Opera regulars such as Lillian Nordica and Frances Alda, and musical comedy stars such as Marie Dressler, gave him entree to New York's racier night life. Membership in the Lambs' Club introduced him to the country's major stage actors and producers.[7] Around the Broadway bars, his rugged experiences in the Klondike and his exotic travels, combined with his *Cynic's Calendar* fame and winning ability to shock, produced a highly spiced cocktail eagerly downed by his audiences. To the new rich, he was a wit and bohemian with enough style to make them feel just a little better-connected for having him at their dinner tables.

Addison's two worlds collided when he arranged for Marie Dressler (then appearing in the musical *Tillie's Nightmare* on Broadway) to perform at one of Mrs. Fish's evening entertainments. Dressler arrived with her regular accompanist, Jerome Kern, who was just beginning his songwriting career. The performance was a huge success. But according to Addison, no places had been set for the "entertainers" at the dinner afterward, so he hauled up chairs at Tessie's table, "and the laughter brought first one and then another to our table." Thus was born café society. (Publisher Condé Nast later claimed the invention for himself, when he seated George Gershwin next to Mrs. Cornelius Vanderbilt at one of his famous dinner parties around 1922.)[8]

An unattributed poem written at about this time sums up Addison's double image:

> All down Fifth and Madison,
> They love our Baby Addison.
> And even, t'is surmised,
> On Broadway and the Bowery
> They trail his accents flowery.
> But that's not advertised.[9]

"Baby Addison" slipped remarkably easily in and out of his dual roles. Some evenings he would be at the theater, listening to Marie Dressler or Frances Alda sing. On other nights, he escorted his rich Fifth Avenue companions to parties, listened to their troubles, and arranged entertainments for them; in return he enjoyed their food and drink and luxurious surroundings. In this role, as observer and companion to the beau monde of the early 1900s, he was like Harry Lehr, one of the first accepted "walkers," not only as an escort of women like Caroline Astor and Alva Belmont but a walking gossip column, knowing everyone's names and everyone's secrets. In that preliberated era, Lehr was acceptable to husbands (and society) because he was married—but only just. (Author Margaret Hayden Rector, however, described Lehr, without giving a source, as an "announced and public homosexual.")[10] His wife, who was very rich and a Roman Catholic, rarely made appearances (and when she did, it was usually at costume parties in disguise), so Harry was free to do the honors at dinners, entertainments, and balls. He was quite a card. "The high spot of any evening came when Harry Lehr donned one of his fabulous gowns to do his bit in drag."[11] Addison's role with Mrs. Oelrichs and Mrs. Fish was more closeted, so to speak, and after his boyhood showstoppers one never hears of him in drag. But he was a useful replacement for Harry, who, wearying of the social circuit, retired with his wife to Paris.*

Only a few years earlier, Addison had been living in one of the roughest environments in the western world. Whatever the artistic merit of Robert Service's Yukon verses may be, they express in ruthlessly honest detail the hardships, isolation, and desperation suffered by the gold miners during the bitterly cold winters in the wilderness. In this almost exclusively male environment, nobody could have endured what Addison endured without gaining a level of toughness and self-discipline that strikingly counteracts the "accents flowery" attributed to him in the little ditty. The contrast between those harsh nights with the drunken Swedes in the stinking cabin and the gala soirées in perfumed Fifth Avenue mansions could hardly have been more extreme. He did not dwell on his Alaska experience, except to make good stories out of it, but as he "sachayed," as he put it, from Fifth Avenue to Broadway, that toughness was tucked away somewhere in his psyche and perhaps added a measure of wariness to his private life.

Where Addison went late at night, after his grand charges were safely tucked up in their Louis XVI beds, was probably not to the turn-of-the-century equivalent of the meat-packing district. He was too careful and fastidious for that—and perhaps not even sexually driven enough. Even

---

*The scuttlebutt was that he became insane there, but in fact he was diagnosed with a brain tumor and returned to die in his hometown, Baltimore, in 1929.

though he attended several of Stanford White's notorious parties, the fact that he made an effort to describe them as dull ("I never saw one that wouldn't bore a present day debutante to tears") indicates either protection for White (and himself) or a genuine lack of response to that sexually charged atmosphere. By 1905 White was already tired, depressed, and sick, and the parties must have lost some of their earlier fizz. In his later life in Florida, Addison had a series of young boys in tow, but wild decadent parties amid the palm trees was not to his taste then, and it is unlikely that it was in 1904–06, in his first years as a hungry architect trying to garner commissions in New York City.

CHAPTER 11

"FROM TIME TO TIME I HAD TO DIP INTO MY SAVINGS."

I n the spring of 1907, Addison visited his friends the Bourke Cockrans in Port Washington, a small, unpretentious village on Long Island Sound. Addison liked the place and found an old farmhouse called, variously, Old Cow Bay Manor and the Old Baxter Homestead, that was for rent. It overlooked the sound and was adjacent to a pond. For the next eleven years, Addison commuted to New York from this charming eighteenth-century house, the proud tenant of his first permanent grown-up home.

It was a smart move on Addison's part. Port Washington was one of the oldest communities in Nassau County, and when Addison moved there, it was experiencing the kind of explosion that comes to towns located in beautiful oceanfront positions within easy reach of the city. Nearby neighborhoods such as Sands Point had already been discovered. Not only the Bourke Cockrans but the Angier Dukes, the Joshua Cosdens, and later Condé Nast also built second homes there. Perhaps the most famous was Harbor Hill, a $6 million mansion with fifty rooms and a wing for 134 servants, built by Stanford White for Clarence Mackay, son of James Fair's partner and a close friend of Tessie Oelrichs, her sister Birdie Vanderbilt, and Addison. The unprecedented surge of millionaires buying up estates along Long Island's north shore created a concentration of wealth never before witnessed in America.[1] Addison found himself in the middle of a land boom right in his own backyard.

Like many country houses named for their prior owners, Mizner's house continued to be called the Old Baxter Homestead until he gave it a new, more amusing name: the Chateau Myscene.* In dramatic con-

---

*Could this strange name be Addison's typically erratic spelling of Mycenae? At least one local journalist thought so, reverting to the classical spelling in his reports of the place.

trast to the vast mansions in New York City and Newport where Addison had been spending so much time, the Old Baxter Homestead was small, with no central heating or plumbing, a modest central staircase, and equally modest living and sleeping quarters. He probably could not have afforded anything much bigger, but his home also had qualities that proved interesting. Unlike the new millionaires' houses he saw going up all around him, his little nest was steeped in history: the earliest part of the house dated from the 1670s, and the Hessian army had used the dining room as headquarters during the Battle of Long Island. For an architect, renovating a piece of the past presents a special challenge. Addison went to work almost immediately, and the results show his sensitivity to the task.

Respecting the sturdy simplicity of the white clapboard exterior, he focused on sprucing up the front porch, which faced Manhasset Bay, and moving the main entrance of the house to the back. He then extended the porch to three times its width, creating an eighteen-foot-wide terrace. He took down the existing railing and built in its place a low wall. He removed the wooden floor of the porch and replaced it with brick. With the pretty shutters on the front of the house, vines climbing over the roof, and a fountain set in the north wall (he created it from a Spanish stove), this new gardenlike terrace showed the architect's talent for glamorizing exterior space and exploiting the view. In other structural changes, he added two bathrooms and enlarged the entertaining space by removing a wall between two downstairs parlors, thus creating a large living room measuring 17 by 32 feet.

The interior decoration reflected Mizner's developing taste for contrast and texture. The hall was painted gray and white to look like marble, an effect accomplished, according to local lore, by rubbing gunpowder into the rough-finished plaster. Much of the furniture was of the dark Spanish kind he had brought back from Guatemala, including an ornate carved bishop's chair and a heavy burl-legged dining table. The rooms were packed with the eccentric antiques that formed the basic ingredients of his evolving decorative cuisine: a stuffed anaconda, an Aztec carved bowl, a two-hundred-year-old papal bier (with electric lamps replacing the four crucifixes at each corner), a thirteenth-century ivory statue of an archbishop, a set of Spanish pages' caps, an eighth-century Fu dog, a twelfth-century Moorish iron stirrup, an illuminated music manuscript dated 1551, a Japanese ceremonial banner, and a series of sixteenth-century wooden candlesticks and crucifixes.[2]

These antiques were treated with characteristic irreverence by their owner and his ever-expanding menagerie. Ever since his trip to China, Addison had loved chow dogs, and in Port Washington he lived with his treasured Ching and Ying and their various offspring, which, being a very rare and desirable breed, could be sold for large sums of money. Permanent residents of Chateau Myscene also included Mico the monkey, Krazy Kat the Maltese, 125 white leghorn chickens, and an Angora rabbit.[3]

Mico gained a moment of fame in 1911, when he escaped from Addison's New York apartment and fled up the fire escape to the top floor, which belonged to the actress Grace Studdiford. As she entered her apartment, the "ape," as the newspapers called him, swung on the chandeliers and generally created havoc with the actress's interior decoration. Miss Studdiford was not amused and sued Mico's owner for $5,000 in damages. This is the kind of fracas Addison loved, and he kept the newspaper reports of the episode in a scrapbook. Grace Studdiford was not the only person to resist Mico's charms. After the monkey escaped several times from his cage in Port Washington, Mama Mizner sighed, "I hope there will be no more monkeys."[4] (She hoped in vain. Addison kept monkeys to the end of his life.)

It was not only animals that ruled the roost at the Old Baxter Homestead. In 1907 a serious economic depression hit the United States. Banks closed, and the stock market took a nosedive. George Lee, a New York friend of Addison's, lost his fortune in the crash and found himself with four young sons and no place to live. Addison immediately suggested that the two oldest sons, Merwyn and Wybern, come and live with him in Port Washington. They stayed for eight years.

This characteristically generous offer from Addison reaped rewards. The boys were a lively addition to the household and helped out with chores. Along with the Lee brothers, the household included at various times an Irish housekeeper, a Spanish cook, a French maid, and an Italian butler. (His beloved New York maid, Louise Darry, would not leave the city, even for him. But like all those who worked for Addison, she never lost touch.)

During the week, Addison would stay in New York, where he had an office, first at 103 Park Avenue and later at 431 Fifth Avenue (while keeping his apartment), or on location as his work, or Mico, required. On the weekends, he would drive back to Port Washington in his Buick, where people and parties would inevitably follow. The local newspaper, *Plain Talk,* liked to record the goings-on at Chateau Myscene, faithfully reporting the visits of Mrs. Hermann Oelrichs, Mr. Merrit Lund of Chicago (who wrote musicals), the Shane Leslies, and other luminaries. Close by in Sands Point lived Ethel Watts Mumford, Addison's collaborator on the *Cynic's Calendar.* In 1912, as befitted an increasingly grown-up resort, the Anchorage Hotel opened in Port Washington, advertising itself as an "attractive summer home for refined people," bringing many new and important guests to the region.

During this time, with San Francisco rebuilding after the earthquake and fire, Mama Mizner abandoned Stag's Leap as soon as she could and returned to the city, where she rented a small apartment. She regularly regaled Addison with complaints about the expense, observing pointedly that Lanny and Edgar were out "trying to mortgage something so that I may live a few months." Distressed, Addison urged her to come east and join him, but Mama suddenly became coy. In a letter written on Valentine's Day 1912, she said, "You write as though you would enjoy really to have me with you, this in itself is a joy, but I fear you forget that I am quite deaf and no earthly use to anyone."[5] Addison prevailed (to nobody's surprise), and in 1913 Mama Mizner, at the age of seventy-eight, finally achieved her dream of living with one of her beloved sons.

Mama Mizner had expensive tastes, but Addison was at last in the position to be a willing and faithful provider. "From time to time I had to dip into my savings," he conceded. She took a great interest in his work and friends, and her handsome appearance and quick mind contributed to the merriment at Chateau Myscene. Thanks to the Lee brothers' presence, she was never lonely, although she managed to make Addison feel guilty when he left her for long periods; a "little hurt look" would appear in her face.

During her years at Port Washington, she wrote regularly to her family about her amusing new life with Addison, and on one memorable occasion her three sisters, Mary (the only married one), Isadora, and Elsie, all in their eighties, decided to leave the home they shared in Erie, Pennsylvania, to visit her. The other Watson sisters were high-minded, old-fashioned, and fervent Christians, and Ella Mizner's up-to-date ways shocked them. She provoked her sisters by pretending she smoked (which she didn't) and drank (which she didn't) and generally teasing them about their stuffy ways.

In contrast to the respectability of Ella's long-lived Watson relatives, the themes of poverty and failed promise haunted her as she contemplated the fates of her daughter and six sons. Minnie and her mother were not allies; competitiveness and two overbearing natures had soured their relationship. But at least Minnie had married well and produced two children, Ysabel and Horace. Ysabel by this time was becoming as successful a debutante in San Francisco as her mother had been, with her name in the newspapers at fancy-dress balls and horse shows. But Minnie and Horace had for a long time lived beyond their means, and in 1912 they were forced to give up Stag's Leap (which later became a hotel, then was restored to a vineyard in 1953). The Chases moved to Burlingame, where Minnie died in 1923.

Lansing, thrust into the pole position after the early death of his much-admired elder brother Murray, faded in the stretch. His mother sensed his vulnerabilities early and counseled him in 1890, when he was thirty-two, "You have the ability to make of yourself a distinguished man if you were only more self-reliant and would persevere."[6] Lan did not persevere. He never fulfilled his early potential as a lawyer; nor did he attempt to step into his father's shoes as a diplomat. He never married or had a home of his own, living mostly at the University Club in San Francisco.

Sometime in his mid-fifties, Lansing visited Addison in Port Washington. Addison was struck by his brother's premature old age and withdrawal from the world. One night, while they were sitting before the fire, he asked Lansing why he never practiced law. Lansing "twisted the stump of his cigar to the other side of his mouth and contemplated the dying embers. 'I do not think it a very honorable profession. If a man has a good case, he does not need a lawyer, and if he hasn't one would be party to his crime if he should take the case.' " What a futile, wasted life, Addison thought. "He was the most beautifully educated, well informed, and the wittiest man it has ever been my fortune to know." The leader of the Mizner tribe during the champagne days of San Francisco at the turn of the century, now he sat, a tragic, lonely man, all passion spent.

His death was equally futile. At the beginning of 1920, he was suffering from chronic gastric and kidney problems. He holed up in a San
Francisco hotel room without food, not leaving it for days on end. His
brother William urged him to come and stay with him and his wife,
Frances, at their house in Oakland. When he arrived, he was in seriously
weakened condition. Frances tried to tempt him to eat, but after a few
weeks he refused all food, and after being rushed to the Wakefield Hospital in San Francisco, he died, as William put it to Henry, of "starvation," in August.[7]

Edgar, after a promising start as an entrepreneur, had also failed to
achieve anything substantial. (His obituary writer came up with
"prospector, athlete, adventurer and clubman.")[8] His mother had praised
his ability to make money, but she could not help twanging the old note
about the family ambitions: "You can do so much now with your life, not
having to contend with poverty—Do impress upon your brothers the
necessity of making the most of their opportunities—not to fritter away
their time in nonsense." Edgar toyed with business, with mixed results,
but like Lansing he never married or had a home of his own, instead living at the Bohemian Club or the Alexander Hotel. He died at the hotel
in December 1918, of pneumonia, brought on, according to a newspaper
report, after a strenuous visit to a disused mine in Arizona, but more
specifically from complications from the influenza epidemic that was
sweeping the country.[9]

William sustained a modest practice as a doctor, and in 1901 he married Frances Marion Taylor, who was not interested in his career—she
refused, for instance, to allow him to get involved in medical relief
efforts after the San Francisco earthquake. Keeping him on a protective
rein, she encouraged her husband's tendency toward invalidism. William
had had knee trouble for much of his adult life. (Bearing in mind Addison's permanently damaged leg, their mother once commented, "It is too
bad the Mizners should have trouble with their legs and knees.")[10]
When Addison saw William in 1923, after a long absence, as with Lansing, he was shocked by the similar deterioration of his once handsome,
upright brother, who was "now a fat, old man, on crutches." Perhaps
William's finest hour was when he nursed poor Lansing in his last days.
William died in 1926, his wife surviving him until 1940. There were no
children.

Henry continued to give luster to the Mizner name. He was a charismatic cleric to his mission and an enthusiastic storyteller to his St. Louis friends, particularly about his wild and crazy brothers, who reminded listeners of the saying about Irish families: "One's a priest, one's a criminal, and one's a cop."[11] In 1912 at the age of forty-four, after an engagement of twelve years, he married Margot Alice Postlethwaite. Margot's aunt and guardian, Mrs. Castleman, had until then refused to allow her to marry a clergyman whose parish was in the slums and not in a fashionable neighborhood uptown. The wedding finally took place at Christ Church Cathedral on November 12, 1912. Addison was best man—and almost came to blows with the dreaded Mrs. Castleman after she made insulting remarks about the bridegroom.

When Margot became pregnant, her mother-in-law was in a frenzy of excitement. "I shall rejoice with you, in a few days, over the arrival of a dear baby," she wrote to Henry in September 1914, adding, "I hope a son."[12] But it was not to be. The baby was a girl, and with her, the Mizner name came to an end. "I guess it's just as well," said Addison.

As for Wilson, he pulled off a surprising coup. He had knocked around the city, at one time running a sleazy hotel called the Rand on West Forty-ninth Street (for which Addison designed the bar and a fountain in the lobby), where dope and girls were trafficked freely. (His instructions tacked up in the elevator for visitors to the hotel, "No opium-smoking in the elevators" and "Guests must carry out their own dead," were much quoted.) A devotee himself of opium (known fondly as the Hong Kong Flute), Wilson was a familiar sight in court on assault charges and evasion of bill collectors. After giving up his dubious career as a hotelier, he became the manager of the boxer Stanley Ketchel (a profession he knew well), before finally acquiring legitimacy as a playwright. Never having written so much as a postcard in his life, as Addison dryly noted, Wilson sat down and wrote a play in collaboration with established author George Bronson-Howard about chorus girls and gigolos. It was entitled *The Only Law,* and it opened, to dismal notices, at the Hackett Theatre on August 2, 1909.

In spite of this failure, Wilson proceeded to write two more plays with the help of another well-established playwright, Paul Armstrong. The first and most successful was *The Deep Purple,* a play about con men and New York City's underworld. Its slangy, streetwise dialogue and urban situations were quite new to Broadway, and the reviews were very favorable. When it opened as a benefit in San Francisco in 1912, Mama Mizner and William showed up for the first night, beaming with pride.

Thanks to this play and its follow-up, *The Greyhound,* Wilson's name became known far beyond Broadway. His sayings and actions were reverently chronicled by the popular newspaper columnists of the day, Walter Winchell, Karl Kitchen, and Damon Runyon, spreading his name to a mass readership. Dubbed "the Beau Brummell of Nome and Broadway," he became so famous that now when Addison appeared in the newspapers, he was identified as the brother of Wilson Mizner.[13] The younger sibling had finally trumped his brother.

It was a mixed blessing. The more successful Wilson became, the more the spotlight revealed his true character. Jim Tully, a contemporary profile-writer of America's lowlifes, described Wilson in harsh terms: "Six feet four: a quick-moving two hundred and seventy pound man, his hands and feet were too small for his body. . . . Affable and adroit, his smile was never from the heart. . . . he was in reality a vast and grandiloquent pimp to whom all life was a house of prostitution."[14]

In 1912 George Bronson-Howard published a vicious story in *The Smart Set* called "The Parasite," in which he heaped vitriol on his former collaborator. Named Milton Lazard in the story, Wilson was easily identifiable with his "huge head shaped like a coal scuttle, a heavy round stomach, and the thinnest legs and smallest of feet, which, in one more than 6 feet tall, made him something of a monstrosity." Lazard, the "court jester," injected himself with morphine, sold girls to rich clients, practiced blackmail, and even defrauded his mother by getting a friend to tell her that her son was dead and asking her to send money for the burial.[15] According to Walter Winchell, Wilson merely laughed at the book, considering it comical: "The irony of the feud was that Bronson-Howard, who threatened to ruin Mizner, committed suicide in Hollywood in 1922 in his 38th year. . . . Curiously, Mizner always spoke handsomely of him."[16]

What Addison felt about his brother's reputation he kept to himself. When Wilson made one of his rare visits to Port Washington (thinking, naturally enough, of moving in on his brother's patch if it suited him), the local paper made much of his presence: "Wilson Mizner, the noted playwright, spent a few days with his brother Addison, recently, while looking about for a country place. He thinks Port Washington all right."[17] ("All right" was about the highest praise Port Washington could extract from Wilson. He did not stay long.)

Wilson's success was of course pleasing to his mother. But he never visited her, not even after she moved east and was easily reachable, and not even after she became increasingly bedridden. "Wilson has not been to see me yet," she said bitterly in an Easter 1913 letter to Henry. "I can never forget his neglect."[18]

Mama Mizner's last days passed in the shadow of the First World War. While the mood abroad was grim, she was cheerful and patient, celebrating her seventy-ninth birthday in February 1915 in good spirits. Later that spring her heart began to fail, and her doctor asked Addison if any other family members should be notified. Furious with Wilson for having abandoned his mother, Addison for a moment felt resentful enough to keep the news from Mama's Angel Birdie. But his good nature prevailed, and he called Wilson: "I knew that he adored mother as much as I did; that he was careless and a little thoughtless; and that he would be broken-hearted if anything did happen and he hadn't known."

Rushing into the house, Wilson explained that he had been sick for the last ten days—"Never felt worse in my life." He got no further, Addison reported, for their mother laughed till she cried. "For forty odd years she had backed up her 'Angel Birdie,' and now, for the first time, she let us know that she had been on to him all the time. He hadn't asked her how she felt; just the same old stall and for the first time he hadn't gotten away with it."

Ella Watson Mizner died on Easter Tuesday, April 6, 1915, at the age of seventy-nine. She had had a colorful childhood and a happy marriage (though marred by Lansing's later years of depression). She had adored her children, although all had disappointed her. Addison was the only son who was achieving any commercial success (apart from Wilson's flash-in-the-pan writing hits), and although a committed bachelor, he was the only one to provide a home for her. She clung tenaciously to these small mercies. At least her wish, expressed to Addison all those years ago when he was exiled in Alaska, of "a dear little house somewhere with you, my beloved son," had been granted.

Excessively high maternal expectations, a remote, authoritative father who faded fast, a large family construct tending toward neglect—to these general conditions can be attributed some of the flaws in the Mizner children's character, in particular their failure to make lasting relationships. But in the end, nature and nurture must battle it out in the evolutionary pit. Whatever Mama Mizner's faults—and one does not need to consult the Freudians to recognize that she had many—Addison's reaction to the loss of his mother was unequivocal. "The greatest spirit in the world had slipped away to keep a love tryst with Papa Mizner," he wrote in a touching epitaph.

A few days after Ella's death, Addison wrote to his sister, describing their mother's last days and explaining that it was her wish to be cremated and the ashes shipped to California to be placed alongside her husband in the family plot in Benicia. But it turns out that there is no family plot in Benicia. The only Mizner with a gravestone there is Murray, the firstborn son who died in 1874. Lansing Mizner, U.S. ambassador, lawyer, and distinguished Benicia citizen, did not get a proper marker when he died, or a place where his wife might join him. Was there no money even then to pay for one? Implicit in this dishonor was the Mizner children's recognition that their father was a loser. Addison as much as said so when he wrote that his father was "always on the wrong side of a bet."[19] But the omission also reflects a basic tenet of the Mizner culture: to avoid emotional confrontation. For all its size and bravado, the Mizner family was consistently vulnerable to meltdown at times of crisis, and with Mama Mizner distraught at her husband's death, no one else in the family was prepared to grapple with the issue of a gravestone.

In 1921 the subject surfaced again. Wishing finally to correct the iniquity, Minnie and William proposed commissioning an inexpensive marker shaped like an open book with their parents' names inscribed on the pages. Henry was horrified at the design and wrote an urgent letter to Addison saying he thought this a cheap solution and "entirely out of keeping with the personal dignity and prominence of our parents." He urged that his brother sketch a much plainer stone, which would probably cost more but be more appropriate.[20] Nothing came of either proposal.

After Mama Mizner's cremation, Addison wrote Minnie that he was too much of a nervous wreck to accompany his mother's remains to California. Wilson found himself also unable to make the trip. Addison signed the letter in his and Wilson's name, probably in an effort, as usual, to improve Wilson's reputation in the eyes of his sister. So with two of her beloved offspring absent, in the pretty hillside cemetery over-looking Benicia, her old hometown, Ella Watson Mizner's remains were committed to the anonymous earth.

CHAPTER 12

"HOW RICH YOU AMERICANS ARE."

In spite of all his elaborate homework and increasingly impressive connections, after five years in New York Addison Mizner had yet to build a house. The assignments he did manage to acquire apart from "bungalows and warehouses" were for interior decoration rather than architecture. One of his early scrapbooks, for instance, contains several pages of notes on fabrics (with the manufacturers' numbers, such as "Schu[macher] 15285—50") for curtains and bedspreads for Mrs. William Sewall in Bath, Maine. For another client in Bath, John H. Hyde, Addison decorated the whole house, including den, music room, and billiard room, itemizing fabrics, wallpapers, valances, and fringes.

He continued to do interiors even after his architectural work took off, indicating that he was originally regarded primarily as an interior designer. He did a series of rooms for William H. Earhardt, including a library with Gothic bookcases, and a sitting room with a pillow-covered daybed, cushions, and wicker chair that the pioneer of American decorating, Elsie de Wolfe, would not have scoffed at. For another client, he produced a classic English Georgian dining room with Adam mantel and moldings, Hepplewhite furniture, and a huge mirror over the sideboard. In 1917 he began experimenting with a different style of decorating, more in tune with his evolving architectural style: a paneled library, with a coffered ceiling, a heavy carved desk and chairs, and above the fireplace an elaborate dark velvet valance swagged with tassels as a lambrequin (smoke valance).[1]

In these early years, he had two commissions to do the interiors of yachts, one for George W. Landers of New London, Connecticut, and the other for financier Morton F. Plant, also of New London. (Word of mouth must have been positive.) Although these jobs sound somewhat unimpressive, in fact yachts were becoming a favorite expression of status, and the crowned heads of Europe, along with the Vanderbilts, Goulds, and their rich friends, flaunted bigger and grander yachts each year at the European regattas. Addison's client Morton Plant was one of the most ambitious. In 1904 Kaiser Wilhelm visited Plant's current floating palace, the *Ingomar,* and was deeply impressed. He particularly noticed Plant's silver-covered visitor's book. "Dear, dear, even a silver book. How rich you Americans are," the Kaiser reportedly remarked.[2] Plant's choice of Addison Mizner to decorate his next yacht, the *Kanawha,* was a major assignment for the architect.

Addison had enjoyed decorating the rooms in the Martins' house in Palm Springs, and the fact that he continued to accept decorating assignments throughout his architectural career in New York indicates the importance that he attached to interior design. The photographic record of his New York interiors indicates that, while eclectic, he was constantly experimenting with antique woods, fabrics, and textures. Working on yachts presented special problems in the use of space as well as materials. He would use what he had learned from these experiences when he finally came to design the interiors of his Florida houses.

He came a little closer to architecture in late 1908, thanks to the opera singer Emma Eames, whom he had known in San Francisco. She introduced him to Mrs. Stephen Howland Brown, a well-known hostess whose husband had a fine collection of medieval art. She was building a house at 154 East Seventieth Street and had just fired her architect. Addison took over the project. The exterior design, in the style of an Italian palazzo, remained the former architect's work. Addison did the interior decoration. There is no record of what it looked like, but it was probably grand, because the house became a showplace for Stephen Brown's art and his wife's parties, the first of which, a *bal masqué,* celebrated the opening of the house in February 1909.[3]

As well as doing interiors, Addison found an outlet in designing gardens, in which he had always been very interested. (His library contained a huge number of books on gardens.) His first major landscaping job was in 1910, for comedian Raymond Hitchcock at Sands Point, Long Island, which was populated not only by Guggenheims, Pulitzers, Astors, and Goulds but also by many theater people. (Hitchcock's house stood between Eddie Cantor's and Leslie Howard's.)

For William Bourke Cockran, the colorful congressman and orator who had first introduced Addison to Port Washington, the architect designed a terrace with thirty grass-lined steps down to a miniature Greek amphitheater, built over a dry lake. He removed a high privet hedge, then replanted and pruned it to act as low-cut wings for the grass-covered stage. An opening in the center revealed the natural scenery beyond. In this inviting theater, the ambitious politician could happily hone campaign speeches in his ringing Irish brogue.[4]

Discussing this garden, Addison offered his manifesto of landscape design: "The day of gardens planted helter-skelter, without any preconcerted idea of the ultimate result, is over. We are no longer building the useless towers and minarets which formerly served only to horrify the eye. Things that have merit must also have a reason or some one idea to hold the many trees, shrubs and flowers in pleasing combination." In other words, garden design should have an underlying aesthetic—an unassailable principle that served him well throughout his later career in Florida.

Gradually, as Addison spent more time in Port Washington, he became part of the cocktail circuit where, as Stanford White had done, he met many of his future clients. But business did not come easily. While being in the center of a country-house-building boom had its advantages for him, his architectural portfolio was still alarmingly slim, and he was up against top-level competition. Most of the architects working in this part of Long Island already had major reputations, such as McKim, Mead & White, Delano & Aldrich, C. P. H. Gilbert, Carrère & Hastings, John Russell Pope, Hunt & Hunt, Horace Trumbauer, and Charles A. Platt. The majority of these men had been hatched in the Beaux-Arts incubator, and their houses were built in traditional styles, which, as Delano once admitted, were what their clients wanted. The question for Addison was not only would he find clients, but would he follow in his competitors' wake and produce these kinds of houses?

In 1910 Addison helped complete the design for an Adirondack camp in upstate New York. The camp was the brainchild of Archibald S. White, the Cincinnati-based president of the Columbia Gas Company, who wanted the camp to contain a rustic guest compound along with a main cabin. White had previously hired another architect, William G. Massarene, to design the camp, but the relationship had gone bad, and White asked Addison to help extricate him from the awkward commitment. Addison's tact in the situation was exemplary, and White, complimenting him for "the intelligent manner you have displayed in handling matters," obviously felt confident placing the assignment in the hands of the less-experienced architect.[5]

Addison let his imagination run riot. Massarene had already built a cluster of cabins, but Addison went further, envisioning a "typical mining town" with a series of Tudor-style cottages along a narrow main street with a grocery store, post office, blacksmith shop, and saloon. The complex was given unity by the use of green siding on all the buildings, which produced a rustic effect. Still, it is a stretch to assume that Dawson, in the Yukon, was his model for this "typical mining town," particularly since at the end of the street was a tennis court.[6] (The camp was later used as President Calvin Coolidge's summer White House and later still, a center for Paul Smith's College. Thereafter its cost became prohibitive, and it was abandoned.)

Addison used the Tudor model again a year later for a double-winged tennis house on the Sands Point estate of his good friend Ralph Hill Thomas. According to the architect, the right-hand wing of the tennis house was similar to that of the Norman inn where William the Conqueror had stayed while collecting his troops for the invasion of England in 1066. It had a refreshment room on the ground floor with copper sinks and dressing rooms and racket lockers upstairs. The left-hand wing had a tea room with sliding doors fronting the tennis court, and a sitting room with a brick open fireplace 6½ feet high and 7 feet wide. The floors were of red brick, the walls were stained chestnut brown, and the ceiling had exposed rafters. All the beams were attached by wooden dowels rather than nails. Casement windows, antique hammered-copper candlesticks, and a sign bearing the legend "Sandhurst Inn" were other novelettish flourishes for what was really a glorified locker room, where sweating tennis players changed, showered, and stored their rackets.[7]

In short, Addison was out of control. It was time he built a real house.

In 1911, while working on Thomas's tennis house, he was invited to design a house and garden in Huntington, Long Island, for Sarah Cowen

Monson. Mrs. Monson had traveled extensively in the East, bringing back fine examples of Japanese art, rugs, furniture, and screens. These collections dictated the style of the house and garden, which Addison welcomed. He had studied Japanese garden design and greatly admired Japanese principles relating to the connection of indoor and outdoor space.

He proposed a series of pavilions 150 feet long, each topped by a green roof with the shingles turned up at the ends in the oriental manner. The exterior walls were white stucco with half timbering; the central court at the front of the house was made of brick, laid in a mosaic pattern. The interior, which had a thirty-foot central hall and a gallery reached by a stairway, reflected Mizner's taste for wood paneling and large fireplaces—at 7 feet wide and 6⅓ feet high, this one was almost as big as the one he had designed for Ralph Hill Thomas. Addison's decor included silvered paper for the walls, along with Mrs. Monson's Japanese furniture and furnishings. Recognizing the importance of modern conveniences, however, he also installed glass windows instead of more authentically Japanese sliding paper panels, plus modern plumbing and heating. The garden was laid out with stepping stones, Japanese lanterns, and a bronze fountain from Kyoto.[8] (The house has been demolished.)

During this year, Addison also designed a residence for William A. Prime, called Warburton Hall, in Brookville, Long Island. (The Primes wintered in Palm Beach, where Addison would later see them.) Nothing remains of the original facade, but the ground-floor plan prefigures much of Mizner's mature work. The house was designed around a rear courtyard, 20 by 49 feet. The reception hall was 27 by 40 feet, like the Great Hall of an Elizabethan house in England. Its paneling, seven-foot-wide fireplace, and cathedral ceiling with exposed beams show Addison's increasing comfort working with a very large central space. Today it is the only remaining room of the original house, which was absorbed in the 1920s into a huge Tudor mansion renamed Hillwood, for E. F. Hutton and his wife, Marjorie (later Merriweather Post), and is now part of the C. W. Post College of Long Island University. A north and south wing contained bedrooms, a dining room, and kitchen areas.

In 1911 Jerome Alexandre, scion of a prominent New York family, hired Addison to build a country house in Colebrook, near Winsted,

Connecticut. The budget was estimated at $150,000. The architecture of the house, Rock Hall, might be called Mizner Uncertain. The plan is H-shaped, with two gabled wings of three stories and a central section of two stories. The ground-floor exterior, including a porch with a stone pediment, is constructed of huge boulderlike gray Connecticut rock; above the string course, the facade is stucco. Dormer windows, decorated with gable frames, are set into the roof of the central section. The roof is red tile.

Inside, the visitor is greeted by a thirty-two-foot-long reception room, a slightly smaller version of the Primes'. Leading off it, in the south wing, are a library and porch. The north wing contains a dining room, a pantry, and kitchen quarters. Some of the interior detailing repeats that of the Primes' central hall; the interior walls are exposed, showing the same dark gray stone as on the exterior facade, with windows set into the boulders (several with stained glass), giving a Gothic effect. As in the Prime house, there is a massive fireplace in the great hall, oak paneling, and a fine staircase.

The interior ground-floor space is pleasing, and some of the landscaping, with a terraced lawn, stone walls, and entry posts designed like Japanese lanterns, is charming. But the jarring juxtaposition of monumental gray stone and light stucco on Rock Hall's facade creates an unsettling effect. The windows are too austere; the wood-framed gables seem awkward. This was perhaps Addison's first house without a consistent stylistic vision, and it was not very successful.

For Alfred E. Dieterich in Millbrook, New York (not far from the Alexandre estate), he built a stone bungalow, with a huge loggia leading to a forty-five-foot-long living room opening onto a porch. Two symmetrical wings contained a library, dressing room, dining room, and breakfast room, with an added wing for bedrooms. Dubbed the "Million Dollar Bungalow," it reflected Addison's growing interest in Spanish forms, and its huge, elaborately detailed interiors retain some of his most elegant work from this time in his career.

In February 1912 *Plain Talk*, the Port Washington monthly newspaper, announced that John Alley Parker, who owned thirty acres on Sands Point Road, was going to build a "handsome villa thereon, after the Spanish style of architecture, with inside court, etc. Mr. Mizner is the architect, and that means it will have some style about it."[9] (The editor of

Plain Talk, H. K. Landis, was a great admirer of Addison's work, and for the three years the newspaper was in print, he chronicled the architect's commissions with enthusiasm.)

This is the first specific request for the "Spanish style" that would make Mizner's fortune. Addison committed himself wholeheartedly to the Spanish theme by giving Parker's house a huge (75 by 90 feet) courtyard, around which the living quarters were arranged. A fifty-foot living room was placed next to a library along the south side of the courtyard, with a porch to the west, a dining room to the east, and bedrooms and bathrooms upstairs. Perhaps for the first time, he also designed a tile roof with a bracketed cornice.

I. Townsend Burden, Jr., in Greenvale, New York, was another client for whom Addison created one of his U-shaped floor plans, with living rooms surrounding a huge central courtyard, and a large terrace off the living and dining rooms. While much of the facade was Georgian, with long rectangular windows and a classically columned entrance, Mizner left his by-now-familiar trail of breadcrumbs: a tile wall fountain, a projecting roof with wood brackets, a heavy paneled door, and a quatrefoil fountain at the front entrance.

In 1917 his old clients Mr. and Mrs. Stephen H. Brown asked him to design a Spanish-style house for them in Locust Valley. This time Addison found more freedom of expression, devising for Solana a central three-story tower, from which three wings extended outward. The forty-foot living room and dining room opened onto a huge courtyard, which contained a fountain and a trellised pergola. Historian Donald W. Curl noted the small windows and understated arched entry, which "gave little hint of the great expanse of glass that opened the house to the patio, a device Mizner often used in Palm Beach."[10]

Sadly, Stephen Brown died suddenly in July 1917, while the house was still being built. It was sold and remodeled, and four years later it looked like an Italian farmhouse, with stucco and gray slate roofs, flagstone floors, and a wrought-iron door. In a *House & Garden* article describing the house, pictures show traces of Mizner's work, such as cement steps leading from the terrace to the garden, punctuated by mature cedars that look like cypress trees. Spanish furniture is used throughout. (The most entertaining part of the article is the caption stating, "Wilson Mizner was the original architect of the house." Game, set, and match to Mama's Angel Birdie.)[11]

Addison's busiest years in New York were 1912 to 1916. He was soon making enough money to purchase Chateau Myscene outright and make a $5,000 kitchen addition, as well as continue supporting his mother, the two Lee brothers, a housekeeper, a menagerie, and a constant stream of weekend guests. For most of the first year of *Plain Talk's* monthly publication, starting in September 1911, Addison had put his own advertisement in the newspaper ("Addison Mizner, Architect; New York and Port Washington"). But after May 1912, it no longer appeared, presumably because he had no need for the publicity. By the end of 1916 he had built at least six houses in or around Nassau County, where wealthy New Yorkers continued to build summer homes.

While few of these houses were completely Spanish, Addison was clearly finding his "voice" in that idiom, and as is evident from the *Plain Talk* item, he was beginning to be identified with it. While a few West Coast architects, such as Wallace Neff, were working in the Spanish style back in southern California, Mizner embraced it more eagerly than most. San Diego architect Irving Gill, for instance, was building houses at the same time as Mizner; he was a student of Louis Sullivan, Frank Lloyd Wright, and the Chicago School. His houses rejected ornamentation and color in favor of a cubist purity of line. But taking into account Addison's California background, combined with his love and knowledge of Central and South American culture, perhaps he was destined to be identified with Spanish rather than any other style of architecture. His Long Island work simply brought this latent artistic seed to fruition.

While Gill worked with new fireproof materials—concrete, cement, and stone—for a very simple, modernistic group of houses in California, and Addison refined his Spanish-style designs in the East, their contemporaries continued to work in the familiar European genres that still provided the terra firma of American architecture. Between 1917 and 1919, Albert Kahn built an urban Italian mansion in Grosse Pointe, Michigan; Walter Burley Griffin produced a native-style stone house in Mason City, Iowa; W. Lawrence Bottomley created a Federal farmhouse with shingles, shutters, and rectangular chimneys in Mill Neck, Long Island; Henry G. Morse chose a Tudor-style half-timbered cottage in New Rochelle; John Russell Pope designed an Elizabethan manor copied from Compton Wynyate's in Tarrytown; and Slee & Bryson devised a brick Colonial house with Georgian detailing in Brooklyn.[12]

Of all the houses built along the north shore of Long Island between

1890 and 1918, only one—other than those built by Mizner—was Spanish-influenced, and that was by a little-known architect, J. Clinton Mackenzie, who built it for himself.[13] In 1899 Carrère & Hastings surprised people by designing a Mediterranean-style villa for Henry R. Kunhardt in Bernardsville, New Jersey, and in 1928, long after Mizner had departed for Florida, Warren & Wetmore designed a fanciful Spanish-style mansion for William K. Vanderbilt, Jr. (who was by then divorced from Addison's old friend Birdie Fair and remarried), at Centerport. The design was immediately pounced on as "exotic" and "personal." The Vanderbilt house was also accused of being "without stylistic precedent."[14]

Yet during those years in Long Island, Addison Mizner carved out an architectural identity that clearly diverged from the English Georgian, Jacobean, Colonial Revival, French Gothic, Italian Renaissance, and other eclectic orthodoxies of his more established colleagues. While modern architecture was slowly seeping its way into the American consciousness (not until 1922, with Eliel Saarinen's design for the Chicago Tribune Tower, could a building safely be said to "show no trace of historical precedent"), and most successful architects were still dedicated to historicism, Addison found his own architectural language— backward-looking perhaps, but culturally and aesthetically unique, as Warren & Wetmore's version was later targeted.[15] It suited Addison well enough to be a maverick. His California background made him comfortable in the role. But it was professionally risky, since acquiring clients depended to a large extent on inspiring confidence. Moreover, was being identified with one particular style going to limit his options?

Mrs. Oliver H. Belmont answered this question by giving him a commission. Nationally known as a fearless promoter of women's rights, Alva Belmont had also become equally passionate about building, in recognition of which she was invited to be a member of the American Institute of Architects. Addison knew "Miss Alva" well in and around New York; his friend Birdie Fair had for a time been her daughter-in-law, and he had visited Marble House in Newport several times. Mrs. Belmont sometimes came to call on Addison and his growing menagerie while she was staying at Brookholt, the property she had built with her husband in the 1890s in Hempstead. She admired Addison's chows and in December 1911 adopted one of his puppies.

In 1911 the indomitable suffragist started a farm for women on her

Hempstead estate, which required several additions, garage conversions, and the like, to house the land-girls. "The house they will live in is really very attractive," she announced. "I went over the plans very carefully with the architect when it was put up and more care and thought was given it than is usually the case."[16] She did not, however, mention the name of the architect.

One likes to think it was Addison. The French landscape architect Henri Duchène worked on the gardens of the original estate. Duchène was a very popular promoter of the Versailles look and, according to Mrs. Belmont, "the greatest authority in France on landscape gardening."[17] It is unlikely, however, that Duchène would have been called in again after so long. Alva probably got her unidentified neighbor to go over the plans of the extension with her during her visits to Chateau Myscene.[18] (The women's farm was not a success and closed in 1913.)

For her major building projects, Mrs. Belmont had always been loyal to Richard Morris Hunt—the creator of her French Renaissance mansion on Fifth Avenue and Marble House in Newport—and after his death in 1895, she maintained her loyalty to his two sons, who took over the business. After the death of her second husband, Oliver Belmont, in 1908, the Hunt brothers built the family mausoleum at Woodlawn Cemetery. She also used the Hunts to design a Chinese teahouse on the cliff-top grounds of Marble House in 1912.

Considering her commitment to the Hunt family, Alva Belmont paid Addison a major compliment in 1912 by inviting him to design for her yet another Long Island house on waterfront land she had bought in Sands Point. In both financial and publicity terms, this was by far Addison's most significant commission, the high point of his career so far. But she asked, not for one of Mizner's trademark Spanish mansions, but for a "small French château." Surprisingly, he dropped the ball.

In his sketches, to be sure, he gave his client what she asked for. He gave her towers, a 76-by-78-foot *cour d'honneur,* a 22-by-76-foot open cloister, a great hall, a dining room, a 30-by-60-foot living room, south-, west-, and north-facing terraces, and a formal garden. But Alva Belmont was disappointed by the sketches, in spite of his enlargement of several of the rooms. She turned again instead to the trusty Hunts, who completed for her, instead of a small French chateau, an astounding Scottish fortress five stories high, with battlements, balconies, turrets, towers, and gables. Addison had failed. Perhaps he should have gone ahead and designed one of his Spanish castles. In any case, he had misread his client's signals—a mistake he rarely made again. (Called Beacon Hill, the Scottish fortress was torn down in 1945.)

But Mrs. Belmont did accept Addison's design for a small teahouse on the beach at Beacon Hill. The Hunts had already created her successful Chinese teahouse in Newport, so the fact that she gave Addison another commission, in spite of the Beacon Hill fiasco, shows her fondness for him.[19] In October 1915 Addison sketched for her a charming little one-story cottage sited on a steep, terraced gradient with landings leading down to the beach. Its pitched roof had subtle Chinese curlicues (to reflect the one at Newport?), shutters, and a wall fountain. The interior included a 16-by-20-foot living room, with French windows looking out toward the water. Alva also gave him a second, equally modest commission, for a beach house in Newport. (The grounds of Marble House were getting quite crowded.) Nothing is known about the project except for an attractive watercolor sketch of the proposal found in Addison's papers. (It is not clear that either house was ever built.)

However modest Addison's architectural work was for her, their friendship was secure, so much so that in January 1916 San Francisco gossip-mongers were delighted to announce that Addison Mizner had become engaged to Mrs. Belmont. Addison's brother William reportedly confirmed the happy news of the marriage, saying that the golden ripening of this friendship into a more lasting attachment had begun when Addison designed Mrs. Belmont's home for women in New York.[20] (Alva Belmont had opened an office of the National American Woman Suffrage Association in New York in 1910, which Addison may have remodeled, but more likely William confused this work with the farm designs for Hempstead.)

On February 18, 1916, Addison performed in a one-night theatrical project called *Melinda and Her Sisters*. Described as a "suffrage operetta," it was organized by Alva Belmont to raise money for the Women's Party. The show was written by Mrs. Belmont and the well-known New York hostess Elsa Maxwell. Marie Dressler and Frances Alda took leading roles in the entertainment, along with appearances by Tessie Oelrichs and Otto Kahn's daughter, Maud. The event raised $8,000.[21] Addison played a butler.

Melinda and her Sisters was the architect's first and last appearance on the New York stage. Those starry nights soon clouded over. His marriage to Alva Belmont was never more than a journalist's dream. The mood was growing increasingly somber in the face of the carnage taking place overseas. While a world war is raging, people are not eager to give splashy parties or build lavish private residences. Addison's contributions to the New York social world were radically curtailed, and by 1917 his architectural practice was almost at a standstill. The Port Washington idyll was coming to an end.

As a carrier of one of the most prevalent but useless Mizner genes, Addison was never able to save money, and with little or no income, his financial situation quickly became so serious that he could no longer pay for Chateau Myscene. A lawyer friend of Wilson's, Phelan Beale, arranged for a corporation consisting of Alva Belmont, Jules Bache, and other friends of Addison's to buy it, raising about $12,000 in cash. (The house was later sold again at a profit, fortunately for the investors.)

Once again Addison had turned a corner in his career, only to be stopped in his tracks by a mixture of bad luck and bad business management. Having finally achieved recognition as an architect, and accumulating important clients who could bring him equally well-connected friends, he now found many of them abandoning the city as the fighting raged on in Europe, leaving him without his practice and incapable of adapting his work to a wartime world. Having accomplished so much, he was now as useless as his discarded blueprints, his future as an architect once again in the wastebasket.

But his ability to inspire loyalty and affection was never more clearly proven than at this moment. Just as Andrew Martin, fifteen years earlier, had given a major architectural commission to his inexperienced friend, now his New York friends rallied to save him from humiliation. His remarkable temperament accomplished the rest. The energy of the western pioneers and their taste for adventure, combined with his natural optimism and willingness to pick up and move on, stood him in good stead at this turning point in his life.

PART THREE
FLORIDA
CASTLES IN THE AIR

THE UNTOUCHED CANVAS OF FLORIDA'S GOLD COAST.
(Courtesy of the Kim Mizner Hollins family)

CHAPTER 13

"STRANGE TO SAY,
WE HIT IT OFF AT ONCE."

Addison Mizner, for all his social distractions, had the sense to take notice of the people he respected and say, "I can learn from you." They were not mentors, for that word bears too self-conscious a meaning, but they opened doors for him, offering him by their example possibilities and opportunities that he was quick to grasp. California in the 1870s threw up few academic or artistic giants, but Willis Polk in San Francisco challenged Addison's intellect, conveying to him some of the excitement and satisfaction of an architectural career. Once in New York, Stanford White's influence was also critical, even though he knew the older architect for little over a year.

Now, at forty-five years old, facing one of his regular career crises, Addison was fortunate once again to meet two men who were to carve out of the half-formed stone the final shape of his life and work. Henry Morrison Flagler had been dead for five years when Addison arrived in Palm Beach in 1918, but his legacy was incalculable. Paris Singer was a solitary visionary, whose energy and enthusiasm mirrored Addison's, and whose money allowed the architect to fulfill his promise a thousand times over.[1]

Henry Flagler, a millionaire from his partnership in the Standard Oil Company with John D. Rockefeller, made his first trip to Florida in 1876, hoping that the warm winter climate would help cure his ailing wife. It was a long journey—the only way to get even as far south as Jacksonville was by steamboat from Savannah. His wife died anyway, but Flagler's love for Florida was born, and by 1894 he had bought up four local railroads stretching to Daytona and consolidated them in a company called the Florida East Coast Railway, with standard-gauge tracks ultimately reaching as far south as Palm Beach.

Without Henry Flagler, there would have been no Palm Beach for Addison to invent. Flagler almost single-handedly took on the "rainy and mosquito-ridden labyrinth of mangrove islands and dark tidal rivers," as Peter Matthiessen describes the strange, uncharted state of Florida. In the late nineteenth century, fewer than 250,000 people lived in the entire state and only a handful in the south, where the dangerous wildlife, unhealthy swamps, and erratic weather systems made it unappealing for pioneer homesteaders. Its local inhabitants, mostly unbridled outlaws or Spanish Indians from Cuba, were further deterrents to Anglo exploration.

Flagler, like the California speculators on the other coast, was undeterred by nature's obstacles. What he saw was a golden opportunity to wrest a profit out of the virgin landscape. Between the eighteenth and twentieth centuries, white Americans often had this kind of confidence in Manifest Destiny, assured that God and Science were on their side. Like the western mining prospectors, Flagler took risks, gambling on luck and the promise of power and prosperity. But it was the American way. As Tocqueville observed, "Those who live in the midst of democratic fluctuations have always before their eyes the image of chance; and they end by liking all undertakings in which chance plays a part." Taking a chance often means disappointment. Henry Flagler on the whole succeeded in fulfilling his grandiloquent dreams.

As Flagler's railway expanded, railroad magnate Henry Bradley Plant developed the western part of the state, building the Belleview Hotel in Clearwater in 1896 and moving south toward Boca Grande. Flagler, like Plant, saw that hotels were the way to lure people to the area. In 1885 he hired Carrère & Hastings to design the 540-room Ponce de Leon in St. Augustine. The result, a hotel combining the styles of Moorish, Renaissance, and Spanish architecture, was described by contemporary critic Claude Bragdon as "a building so original, so beautiful, so rational, so suited in every way to its environment and purpose that it may truly be called a masterpiece."[2]

Happy with his architects' results, Flagler, traveling down the coast, hired the team to repeat their success in Palm Beach. In 1894, on the narrow strip of land between Lake Worth and the Atlantic Ocean, the Royal Poinciana Hotel went up. This time Carrère & Hastings abandoned their Spanish theme and built a vast, 1,300-room Colonial-style wooden structure, painted yellow with green trim. It was a triumph not only of construction but of population redistribution. When George W. Vanderbilt III hired Richard Morris Hunt to design for him the largest private house in the country—Biltmore, in Asheville, North Carolina— a village sprang up nearby in order to house the huge number of construction workers and craftsmen imported to work on the mansion. Similarly, Flagler created a working-class community in West Palm Beach to work on his hotels, with its own city hall, fire station, courthouse, Catholic church, and hospital.

Flagler wanted another hotel on the ocean side of the island, and a year after the Royal Poinciana was completed, the smaller Palm Beach Inn opened, which in 1901 was greatly expanded and renamed the Breakers. Carrère & Hastings again did the job. (Another wooden structure, it burned down twice and was rebuilt in its current guise in 1926.) Near the Poinciana, Flagler then built a wedding present for himself and his third bride, Mary Lily Kenan, who, at thirty-four, was thirty-seven years his junior. Carrère & Hastings were brought in for what was to be their final work for their great patron. They gave him Whitehall, a palace with a neoclassical facade and a French Renaissance interior that was completed in eighteen months at a cost of $4 million. Flagler's consuming energy gave out only after he had managed to extend his Florida East Coast Railway all the way to Key West. A nightmare task slowed by hurricanes and other obstacles, it was dubbed "Flagler's Folly," but the track was completed in 1912, the year before Flagler died at the age of eighty-three.

Flagler's hotels were very popular. In 1916 the New York society columnists listed in breathless detail the names of the families making their way to Palm Beach for the winter season. Many, like Flagler himself, saw the advantages of this benign winter climate for anyone with health problems. Addison's own reason for making southern Florida his destination derived in part from this compelling reputation.

His own ailment stemmed from an ordinary mugging. In the spring of 1917, while driving back to Port Washington late at night, he gave a lift in his open roadster to three young men. As he was about to let them out at Lynbrook, one of the men grabbed him by the throat and another hit him in the face. Staggering out of the car, with typical Mizner bravado he took them all on. Although big and strong, he could not beat off all three attackers, and when one of them gave him a terrific kick in the leg, he fell like a stone. They took what money they could find on him (which was not much) and ran off.

The kick landed precisely on the fragile bone where Addison had suffered his injury as a teenager. In agony, he managed to drive himself back home, where he promptly fainted. When he woke up, his swollen leg was throbbing with pain, and once again he faced the prospect of amputation. Once again he was required to lie flat on his back, this time in his mortgaged house in Port Washington, while doctors wondered how to remedy what they called necrosis of the bone and his continuing pain. "I was sick all over with that terrible agony in my left leg that ran clear to the hip." Friends came to cheer him up, including Alva Belmont, who arrived clutching yellow chrysanthemums and told him, "If the doctors want your darned old leg, they are going to get it." Wilson arrived with a song-and-dance man who jumped about madly, trying to entertain him so earnestly that Addison could not bear to tell him to stop, although the performer's hopping and stamping were jarring the wound in an excruciating fashion. It turned out that the dancer had a wooden leg. This was Wilson's way of showing his brother that losing a leg was not so bad.

By the end of 1917, Addison had managed to keep his leg, but the house was freezing cold (there was a coal strike) and lonely. Mrs. Townsend Burden, for whom Addison had built a house, would visit in her Rolls-Royce with firewood and sacks of coal. He spent his forty-fifth birthday that December in Port Washington with an English friend of his, Lady Colebrook, who took pity on him and decided that he should be moved to New York. She found him rooms in her apartment house on Madison Avenue and Forty-eighth Street, which was run by a couple of Cockneys. "I felt I had suddenly been transported to Piccadilly," he later said. Another ex-London resident of the apartment building was Syrie Maugham, novelist Somerset Maugham's ex-wife, who had become a successful interior designer like Addison and whose sharp wit was a welcome distraction to the invalid. Able now to move around on crutches, he had many amusing visitors, including Elsa Maxwell, the well-known hostess and fellow Californian (she claimed she was born in a box at the San Francisco Opera). Elsa Maxwell was a very large woman, and one day she came to see him with a grand piano in tow that she had "borrowed" from the apartment upstairs. "For a moment, I couldn't tell which was which," Addison noted mischievously.

Thus he whiled away the days, waiting for the pain to diminish and the leg to heal. As his own home in Port Washington was now in the hands of a corporation and his financial plight remained bleak, he had little incentive to rise from his bed and walk.

But out of this ordeal emerged a friendship that, of all Addison's many friendships, proved most critical to his future life and work. A six-foot-three, thin, elegant, fair-haired, naturalized Englishman called Paris Singer was brought by Lady Colebrook to the invalid's room one afternoon in early 1918. The meeting changed Addison's life.

Paris Singer was the second youngest of twenty-four children sired by Isaac Singer, inventor of the sewing machine. Paris's mother, Isabella, Singer's third wife, was Scottish, and with names running out, two of their six children were named after the places where they were born—Washington and Paris. Paris's father liked England, and the family moved there when Paris was three, growing up in Oldway, a huge Victorian mansion built by his father near Torquay. The house was nicknamed "The Wigwam," and its French formal gardens were designed by the same Henri Duchène who worked for Alva Belmont. Isaac Singer died there in 1875, five years after the move, leaving a fortune of approximately $15 million, which, vast though it seemed, was considerably diluted when divided up among the many offspring.[3]

Paris left home early, and when he was nineteen, he married a Scottish girl like his mother, who bore him five children. Living mostly in Paris, in 1903 Singer met Isadora Duncan at his brother-in-law Prince Edward de Polignac's funeral, and by 1909 the two were locked in an electrifying romance. Isadora was an internationally renowned artist of the dance, and her career was greatly helped during this period by Singer's financial and emotional support. She also became the mother of Singer's two children, who both tragically died by drowning when the car they were in lost control and rolled into the river Seine.

Singer's relationship with Duncan was tempestuous, with Duncan constantly unfaithful and the loss of their children a permanent wound. There were repeated breakups and reconciliations. A typical scene took place at Sherry's in New York sometime in 1916, witnessed by Arnold Genthe, the San Francisco photographer who had once photographed

Ella Watson Mizner, and who had since moved to New York and become famous for his portraits of artists like Isadora. "To please Singer," Genthe recalled, "she wore an exquisite white chiffon frock and diamond necklace which he had just given her." All went well until Isadora fixed her attention on a man who was said to be the most famous tango dancer in Argentina. They proceeded to dance a tango that went well beyond dancing. Singer stood furiously watching them until they were halfway through. "Then he strode into the middle of the floor, took the Argentine by the scruff of the neck, and slithered him out of the room. Isadora turned pale, and . . . called out, 'If you treat my friends like that, I won't wear your jewelry.' Then she defiantly tore the necklace from her throat, the diamonds scattering all over the floor." As she swept from the room, she passed Genthe in the doorway. Without looking at him, she whispered, "Pick them up."[4]

Singer's ultimate humiliation took place in early 1917, when he took an option on Madison Square Garden for Isadora to use as a performance space. When he eagerly told her about it, she mocked him: "Do you mean to tell me that you expect me to direct a school at Madison Square Garden? I suppose you want me to advertise prizefights with my dancing?" Singer turned livid, and with hands shaking he left the room. He took her to Palm Beach later that year in one last hope of building a winter school for her there, but she left in a rage and this time there was no reconciliation.[5]

This was the man who appeared in Addison's bedroom in December 1917. Scarred by tragedy and ill health, he had just emerged from eight years of emotional turmoil. Now he was meeting a crippled, out-of-work architect without a future. "Strange to say, we hit it off at once," Addison declared. And so they did.

Singer and Mizner started a conversation at that meeting that lasted for almost fifteen years. From the first, Paris, who had briefly practiced architecture himself, was fascinated by Addison's wide-ranging knowledge, wit, and worldliness. When he realized the state of Addison's leg, he immediately summoned his own personal nurse, Joan Balsh, who was visiting relatives in the United States.[6] "It shouldn't take such a time to heal," Paris observed correctly. Addison feared another dragon lady, like his current nurse, but Joan was an attractive, single young woman of English and Irish background, and very efficient. She started unwrapping the dressings on his leg so delicately that he said, "You're doing it like you were unpacking a rare bit of Greek glass; that stevedore I've had just throws me on the wharf and handles me as though I were a crate of rocks." Joan Balsh gave him a quick glance out of her clear Irish blue eyes, and as Addison said, "there was a wonderful twinkle in them that made us pals for life."

Joan had a sensible suggestion for her new patient: to expose the wound to a dose of sunshine. Singer, whose admiration for his nurse was increasing by leaps and bounds, was quick to agree. A year earlier, when he had visited Palm Beach, not liking the accommodations offered, he had purchased a small villa next to the beach. "Let's go there." He asked Joan if she would like to take care of the patient for a month, adding, "I think the sunshine would do us all good."

With typical Singer dispatch, on January 3, 1918, they all boarded Flagler's train bound for Florida. Arriving two days later in West Palm Beach, they found waiting for them a big Buick touring car. Paris had bought it by wire. "We rattled over a rickety wooden toll bridge and into a jungle and on to Peruvian Avenue. There was the great Atlantic looking like a millpond swish-swashing on miles of perfect beach." This "jungle" was the place that Addison and Paris were to transform, in only five years, into the most desirable resort in the country.

Like Singer, Addison had visited Palm Beach once before, on a trip from New York in 1905. His recollection of this first sighting was dismissive—"nothing but two old wooden Flagler hotels." (One of his companions on that trip was a widow, Florence Martin, who, in another piece of serendipity for Addison, later married Preston Satterwhite and became one of his most important Palm Beach clients.) In fact, Palm Beach was not quite the desert Addison later liked to have people believe. In 1898 Colonel Edward R. Bradley had set up Bradley's Beach Club, a gambling institution so successful that in 1908 editor and bon vivant Frank Crowninshield rated Palm Beach number one among eastern resorts: "not exclusive, but merry, sumptuous, and expensive. Chance to meet many men in the gambling rooms."[7] Nor were the accommodations altogether as unsatisfactory as Paris Singer made out— Flagler had never stinted on amenities for his guests.

But apart from the two Flagler hotels and Bradley's casino, the island in early 1918 was still a landscape waiting to be designed. Singer's "villa," for instance, was part of a depressing development along Peruvian Avenue that, as Addison remarked, was spoiling as much of the natural beauty of the place as possible. Sand lots had been cut raggedly into the lush vegetation, leaving bare holes. The main attraction was Joe's Alligator Farm, a swampy spot where the intrepid Joe wrestled alligators and other reptiles to the delighted horror of tourists.

On the block next to Singer's house was what was probably the state's first beach club, called Gus' Bath, with a sign in front that said, "Welcome to our ocean." Here one could buy a bathing suit and dance to an electric piano on the "best picnic ground on the East Coast." Advertisements encouraged visitors (who were not yet in the soothing lap of air conditioning): "Night bathing is becoming more popular every day. It is good for your health to cool off and get this excellent form of relaxation before retiring."[8]

Paris knew that his villa was not going to win any architecture prizes, and immediately he found his new friend paper, pencils, and watercolors and urged him to suggest improvements. Although Addison had been bedridden since his arrival, he had a photographic eye and instinctively understood every angle of the house, so he amused himself by adding a Chinese roof (with decorative fish), putting in a Japanese railing, giving the shingles bright colors, and inserting all sorts of posts and panels. (It was a sort of pastiche of his work on Sarah Cowen Monson's Long Island house.)

When Paris looked at the sketch, he said, "Quite splendid—I like a bit of color." Addison didn't find out for years that his friend was color-blind. But he also hadn't reckoned with the qualities that made Paris Singer so exceptional—his unbounded energy and ability to get things done. By the very next day, Singer had organized builders, painters, and carpenters to start transforming the house according to Addison's impulsive and fanciful sketch. The house became known as the Chinese Villa, and Singer retained it until 1924, although he stopped living in it in 1919 when the Everglades Club was completed.

Paris and Joan (who were beginning to spend a lot of time together) installed Addison in a bed on the porch, and within a few days, he felt strong enough to move around on his crutches. But the architect was never again going to be the sturdy young ox who had lifted equipment over the Chilkoot Pass or heaved buckets up from the icy ground in Alaska: he was overweight to the tune of three hundred pounds and never thought twice about eating astronomically large and calorific meals. Within two weeks of arriving in Palm Beach, he had another health scare. He suffered a sudden heart attack, which led to pneumonia, and for a while it was thought he would die.

Addison's health had been an issue ever since childhood, and considering his weight and careless habits, it is remarkable that he always managed to rally. On this occasion, while he was still very sick, he overheard Paris and Joan discussing funeral arrangements, including the problem of producing a casket big enough for Addison's huge frame. The patient immediately summoned them to his bedside and announced, "Don't you think the Mizners are well enough brought up to know it's rude to die in somebody else's house? I'll be all right in a day or two."

And he was. Within days Addison was up and walking, and he and Paris reverted to discussing their favorite topic, architecture. The two men were inseparable. Both over six feet tall, they must have looked madly dashing as they made their daily promenades together—Paris skinny and irascible, with a bristly mustache and piercing gaze, Addison large, affable, and mellow: the wolfhound and the Labrador scouting the empty landscape in pursuit of glory.

Exploring a stretch of deserted beach along the south shore of the island, Paris observed that it would make a beautiful site for a house. He asked his friend what he envisaged there. Addison closed his eyes and murmured, "A Moorish tower, like on the South Coast of Spain, with an open loggia at one side facing the sea, and on this side a cool court with a dripping fountain in the shade of these beautiful palms." Paris said nothing, but the next day he told Addison he had bought the site (now 1200 South Ocean Boulevard), and was eager to see sketches for the Moorish tower. On a subsequent trip, the friends drove to Lake Worth and watched as the mullet jumped in the sunset and hundreds of egrets flew home to Cabbage Island. Again, Paris asked, "What do you see on this site?" Again, Addison responded without hesitation. "It's so beautiful that it ought to be something religious—a nunnery, with a chapel built into the lake, with great cool cloisters and a court of oranges; a landing stage, where the stern old abbess [ever the terrible speller, Addison wrote this word as "abyss"] could barter with boatmen bringing their fruit and vegetables for sale; a great gate over there on the road, where the faithful could leave their offerings and receive largesse."

Two days later Paris bought that property as well, nearly a half-mile wide and running from the ocean to the lake. Thus did the architect first articulate the themes of his work, in the language of fantasy, at his impresario's prompting. And thus, on this beautiful strip of land between the ocean and lake, thanks to Paris Singer's vision, was born the first and perhaps the finest building that Addison Mizner created in Palm Beach.

The first letterhead of the Everglades Club stationery read "For Convalescent Officers of the United States and Allied Nations."[9] It was Paris Singer's idea to add to the string of hospitals he had already built in England and France for the war-wounded, on the site that had so appealed to him. To this end, he founded the Ocean and Lake Realty Company, making Addison its first president and designating the newly purchased property as the first product of this collaboration.

It was now March 1918, and the season was rapidly winding down. While flattered by his new position, Addison had no thought of staying on in Palm Beach and was making plans to return to Port Washington and try to revive his stalled career. But Singer urged Addison to stay and build the convalescent home. He sweetened the offer with the promise of a regular paycheck. There was no contest. Addison went back to Port Washington, sorted out his debt on the house, packed up his furniture, and returned to Palm Beach, this time for good.

His timing proved for the second time to be impeccable. He had arrived in New York in the first decade of the twentieth century, when hundreds of newly hatched millionaires were flocking into the city to build, to breed, and to bring bright new noise to the faded chorus of fin-de-siècle society. As in most economic booms, architecture was the profession of the hour, as people demanded apartments in the city and houses in the country; money was no object, the only criterion being that they be bigger and more luxurious than any that had existed before. Addison's work in Connecticut and Long Island had been a direct consequence of this building frenzy.

Ten years later, with New York in the throes of postwar social and political upheaval, a deep yearning for stability drove the war-weary rich to look for new places to settle and achieve security by building lasting monuments for themselves. After four years of death and destruction, they were intent upon devoting serious time to leisure. Addison again was positioned to reap the benefits. He was leaving a city already becoming mature, old even, to help found a new one, a paradise that would be impervious to global angst, one that could be designed as a utopian environment for its fortunate residents.

One must marvel at Addison's good fortune, while once again on the brink of disaster, to have found his salvation. Paris Singer's offer was a promise of a working future that was given in the nick of time. Even slowed down by his heart attack and leg injury, there was never any question that Addison would accept the gift.

Addison Mizner was lucky, yes, but he was also the right man for it. His California spirit responded brilliantly to the enigma of this tropical Alaska to which his friend had brought him, with its crocodile-infested, palmetto-fronded horizon. From an architectural point of view, the landscape was tabula rasa, the kind of challenge that Addison embraced wholeheartedly, however crazy or improbable it seemed. While Paris Singer traveled to and from his perches in New York, England, and the French Riviera, Addison enthusiastically laid down the foundations of a new, permanent base in Palm Beach, finding there the source of his most productive years.

CHAPTER 14

"THE PLACE TOOK
THE TOWN BY STORM."

Summer 1918 found Addison hard at work on his first building in Palm Beach. It turned out that Paris Singer's involvement with the hospital was closely allied to his friendship with Mary Fanton Roberts, founder of the New York magazine *Touchstone,* devoted to the cause of democratic institutions. Both Mrs. Roberts and her husband were frequent guests of Singer's in Palm Beach, and they took a great interest in his philanthropic venture, so much so that Addison's original plans were titled "The Touchstone Convalescents' Club." The magazine's readers, exposed to a long article about the club in July 1918, were assured that the project was entirely nonprofit.

The plans for the convalescent home revealed a vision far more ambitious than anything the architect had yet produced. The main building included a Court of Orange Blossoms; a salon; a living room (44 by 85 feet), sporting one of his six-and-a-half-foot-high fireplaces; and a dining room seating four hundred (40 by 70 feet). These public rooms fronted a huge terrace and lawn with views of Lake Worth. A tower contained apartments for Addison and Paris. According to the plan, the south side of the building was to remain surrounded by jungle. (Alligator Joe and his friends had to be moved—although some said the alligators lingered.) The north end, running alongside Worth Avenue, had service rooms, kitchens, pantries, and bathrooms. Beside the clubhouse, the architect designed ten villas, each with seven large, airy bedrooms, and a medical building.

Singer approved the floor plan and then disappeared to New York with the Robertses, leaving Addison to break ground on his grand enterprise alone. He immediately saw that the prospect of building anything at all was laughable. Most ablebodied men were still away at war. Flagler's workmen had long retired or been dispersed. The rest had little experience in any kind of construction work. The use of brick as a building material was unknown to them. "What the hell are these things for?" Addison's "mason" asked him.

In short order, Addison got the men to work. As well as bricklayers, he needed carpenters, tile makers, blacksmiths, stonecutters, and gardeners to put together the exceptionally elaborate building he had designed. Finding and training these people, most of whom would rather spend their time out of the heat and swatting mosquitoes, was a herculean task.

Joe Earman, editor of the *Palm Beach Post,* had become very excited about this new local venture and its architect, and he devoted a whole column to Addison, greatly increasing his visibility in town:

> Like all celebrities, he likes to SMOKE CIGARETTES, DREAM, and TALK. His conversation is as a rule, trivial, until pinned down and then he has a world of interesting information or conversation good to hear. He has an observing turn and this is the secret of his ability as an architect.
>
> He is the best PUDDING for mosquitoes that I ever saw. They work on him fast and vicious. He walks around the various projects with a bottle of Mosquito Chaser and a small sprayer. His office on Gardenia Street is carefully screened and this is where he does what he calls "HIS SKETCHING."
>
> He is what I call a REGULAR TEMPERAMENTAL NUT, but like all others that excel in their profession he is one of the very best and Palm Beach County should be pleased beyond measure that this great Architect is drawing plans for the alleviation of our wounded sailors and soldiers, which will also add renown to Palm Beach County.[1]

This boosterism eased Addison's complicated labor relations. An enormous amount of energy, commitment, and persuasiveness was required to do so, but this strange out-of-town giant of an architect succeeded in forging a working relationship with an inexperienced band of odd-job men. He built kilns and imported clay from Georgia and taught his men to make the Spanish roof tiles he specified. Singer was more fortunate than he knew in hiring his gimpy-legged friend from New York to build his club; without Addison's charm or his experience of manual labor in Alaska and San Francisco, the project would never have gotten off the ground.

Ten years later, after the project was completed, Singer gave unstinting praise to his friend's extraordinary talents: "When he could find no one to carry out his orders, he set to work with his own hands and made the thing he wanted. He could do this for he is like the architects of the Middle Ages, a master of all the crafts that serve his profession. He paints, carves wood and works in metals, knows all about the making of glazed pottery and his wrought iron is second to none in Old Spain."[2]

On August 1, just as the architect was beginning to get things going, most of the carpenters employed in West Palm Beach went on strike. Addison quickly telegraphed the news to Singer in New York, who returned to Palm Beach. Between them, they talked their men back to work, pointing out that the job was for the good of their fellow men, that Singer was paying above the disputed hourly rate, and that their employment in the region would be guaranteed for ten years.

Joe Earman reported the results of the union decision with elation, giving Addison much of the credit. "They all shook hands with him so much and so often that he can't write his name today. Addison is a big man RIGHT NOW. He can control votes. He doesn't know his own power. Mister Politician, DON'T FORGET ADDISON."[3]

The armistice was declared in November, and Addison thought his Palm Beach work was over—a hospital for the war-wounded would no longer be needed. But Singer was not diverted. People will be coming home, he argued, and we shall make them come to Palm Beach, the greatest resort in the world. Quickly he rethought the project as a private club, and a friend of his, Mrs. George W. Jonas, came up with an appropriate name for it. Before the end of 1918, locals had come to accept the fact that the convalescent home was now the Everglades Club.[4]

Work continued. By Christmas, the visiting rich could see for themselves what was going up on the shores of Lake Worth. Their enthusiasm was muted. They thought the site—at the southernmost end of Worth Avenue—was too far out of town. Their favorite watering holes, the Royal Poinciana, the Breakers, and Colonel Bradley's casino, were all close to each other in town. How could the wicker tricycles pedaled by a driver, the preferred mode of transport in town prior to the motorcar, make such a long trip? Moreover, the "jungle" specified on Addison's floor plan was far too close to the real thing for comfort. And what about the alligators? For the visiting rich, the standard for architecture was the Breakers, Flagler's wooden hotel with its signature yellow-and-green paint. Mizner's building looked nothing like it. In fact, Mizner's building looked like nothing most of them had ever seen.

But the *Palm Beach Post* was quick to see the point of Addison's design: "Instead of repeating the common and hideous mistake that has been perpetrated all through Florida of using a style of architecture adapted to northern surroundings and a bleak and repellent climate," the newspaper declared, "he has searched Italy, Spain and Northern Africa for a model, and has used a blended, softened type of color and line that will prove a revelation."

The Everglades Club was due to open on February 4, 1919. But in the middle of January, the terrace was still nonexistent. A collection of mature royal palms had still to be dug in place. Orange trees were waiting to be planted. Calamitously, at the last minute the dredge that was to pour the concrete for the terrace broke down, and Addison in desperation bribed a tugboat with a dredge to stall in front of the clubhouse, so that he could borrow the dredge and finish the job. The day before the opening, Addison bought a dozen crates of oranges and as many boxes of hairpins, and "by morning the trees were hanging heavy with fruit." The club opened as planned.

The architectural impact of the Everglades Club building cannot be overestimated. As the *Palm Beach Post* had said, it proved a revelation. While visitors to St. Augustine in northeastern Florida might previously have seen Flagler's Ponce de Leon and Alcazar Hotels, nothing could have prepared them for Addison's gorgeous pink stucco palace, with arcades, wrought-iron balconies, and terra-cotta-tile roofs, shimmering like a fairy-tale castle along the shore of Lake Worth. No real estate development they had ever seen was comparable to the charming cluster of Moorish-style villas, each painted a different pastel shade of pink, blue, and green, that stretched away from the clubhouse.

Signs of Addison's passionate interest in garden design were also in abundance. The royal palms and Australian pines (transplanted fully grown, to the astonishment of observers) gave vertical elegance to the flat Florida terrain. Hibiscus, bougainvillea, and crotons softened the harsh line of the buildings' sandy foundations. Clusters of shade trees, palms, and ferns offered relief from the sun-baked landscape.

Nothing had prepared visitors for the elegant wrought-iron grillwork at the arched entryway to the clubhouse, or the heavy paneled wooden doors that gave no hint of what lay within. People were amazed at the vast and lofty interiors, with their painted beams, gleaming tiled floors, and arched French doors letting in the light and views of the lake's sparkling blue waters. No detail had escaped Addison's attention; in every room the eye feasted on jewellike panels of tile, exotically carved Spanish antique furniture, embroidered gold, blue, and red velvet and damask furnishings and tasseled hangings, and antique brass hardware, all glowing in the light of wrought-iron chandeliers and sconces.

Many of the artifacts were rare antiques, including a pair of four-hundred-year-old doors, carved with the heads of saints; Spanish and Portuguese chairs of equal antiquity; and some sixteenth- and seventeenth-century paintings of a kind hitherto seen only in European museums. The living room incorporated a collection of superb two-thousand-year-old tiles, purported to have come from Troy and acquired by Paris Singer.[5]

This was by far the largest and most complex commission Addison Mizner had ever undertaken. He had never built a public building. None of the houses he had designed in Long Island or Connecticut even came close to it in scale. He had never had to train from scratch a crew of workmen to fulfill his requirements for Spanish and Moorish detailing, let alone meet the exacting standards of craftsmanship he had set for himself. He had to accommodate plumbing, kitchens, coat rooms, barber shops, gardens, and tennis courts, not for a small family, as in his previous commissions, but for very large numbers of guests. He had never had to dredge a lake before.

Did he falter? Did he have sleepless nights? Did he reduce his grand design to something less ambitious? It seems not. From June 1918, through the terrible hot, humid, and mosquito-ridden summer months, to February the following year—only eight months—he worked non-stop, never leaving the site, doing much of the work himself, until it was finished. Even today it would be an astonishing accomplishment. (It is remarkable, given the magnitude of the job, that only one major flaw could be found in its design: the Everglades Club kitchen was unequipped to feed a large number of people. But this problem was easily fixed.)

According to the club's formal history, the official opening was on January 24, 1919, with twenty-five charter members and Paris Singer as president. Singer wanted to make his club truly exclusive, which meant that he personally chose the (all-male) members and limited their membership to a year only, subject to renewal. This guaranteed him total control, which was how he liked it. Members who planned to give a party in the club even had to submit their guest list to him for approval.[6] Naturally, many clamored to become members. For the first year, Singer allowed 350 memberships (at an annual fee of $275 per couple), and in 1920 the elite list closed at five hundred, with E. Clarence Jones and Edward T. Stotesbury as officers, and Joshua Cosden, James Deering, Joseph P. Kennedy, Edward S. Moore, Henry C. Phipps, Percy Pyne, Rodney Thayer, and George D. Widener as charter members. The club was a runaway success.

"The place took the town by storm," Paris Singer recalled ten years later, "so remarkable was the sense of proportion, composition and color shown in the buildings, the gardens and patios."

The Everglades Club was Addison Mizner's masterpiece. It was also his architectural passport to a new sunshine-filled world. Probably he had not thought about it when drafting those elegant floor plans, but his stunning design galvanized a generation of wealthy winter visitors to come to Palm Beach, who, on seeing his work, immediately knew that this man's architecture was precisely what they wanted for their own pleasure palaces. Addison Mizner, totally eclipsing the competition at the time the Everglades Club opened, was perceived as the one architect who could fulfill these millionaires' dreams.

On February 20, 1919, just after the completion of the Everglades, Addison was invited to speak before the Women's Club in West Palm Beach. The report of the evening gives a striking picture of the man and his work at this critical moment in his life: "He sauntered on to the stage in an offhand manner with his hat in his hand and a quizzical smile on his face, and made himself quite at home by leaning up against the piano and saying he wished he was at home for this was the most terrifying moment of his life."

Addison then proceeded to give his women listeners an uncompro-
mising lecture about design and architecture: "The most important thing
in a home is simplicity. Decoration can come along later and disfigure it,
but original simplicity will always stand: any cook can make a cake with
a bridegroom on top of it and sugar-plum kisses all around it but that
isn't architecture.

"Ladies, architecture is a development. It rose from the tombs, rolling
up through the ages. . . . An architect must know everything. He must be
a plumber and an electrician, a brick mason and a tile-layer—the latter
I know because I had to teach my men over on the island to make tiles."
In conclusion, he ventured that an architect, if he manages to get on
with his women clients, "might be an artist."[7]

Addison himself was put to the test almost immediately. The first
client to secure his services was also one of the richest—Mrs. Edward
T. Stotesbury from Philadelphia. "Oh, Mr. Mizner," she said to him one
day on the terrace of the Everglades Club, "you have made me so dis-
contented with the plans I have for El Mirasol. I don't think I will ever
be content with them after seeing this."

Eva Stotesbury was the second wife of the Philadelphia banker
Edward T. Stotesbury. They lived most of the year at their huge estate in
Philadelphia, Whitemarsh Hall, which had been built by the well-
respected architect Horace Trumbauer. But like many "snowbirds," the
Stotesburys found the winter climate of Palm Beach very much to their
liking. Eva particularly appreciated the open society of southern Florida;
as a New Yorker, she realized that her attempts to become a serious contender within Philadelphia's famously exclusive Main Line were doomed
to failure. In Palm Beach, she found a level playing field; and with her
fabulous hats, fabulous dinner parties, and fabulous royal connections,
the field soon tipped in her direction.

As Tessie Oelrichs had known, building the biggest house around
was the most direct way to elevate one's status. Whitemarsh Hall, Trumbauer's neoclassical mansion, was Eva Stotesbury's first foray into the
Vanderbilt style of building. It had 147 rooms and a resident organist
who played concerts every afternoon; it was ranked one of the top five
largest homes in America. In 1918 Eva Stotesbury had hired F. Burnham
Chapman to trump Trumbauer's Philadelphia achievement by designing
for her an equally magnificent palace in Palm Beach.[8] There is no record

of the drawings he came up with, but they clearly faded into insignificance after the revelation of Addison's Everglades Club. Eva Stotesbury did not hesitate.

By early 1919 Addison's version of El Mirasol had been approved. In a floor plan even more elaborate than that of the Everglades Club, he gave his new client a multilevel Spanish-style mansion with *rejas* (window grilles), loggias, patios, cloisters, tiled roofs, and courtyards. The entry hall was a vast sweep of flagstone, arches, and exposed ceiling beams, lined with heavy oak pews and tall wrought-iron candlesticks. The rooms had twenty-foot ceilings, paneled or pale plaster walls, tile floors, and antique Moorish roofs. The sunken living room had a huge stone fireplace and high arched windows. The main staircase was made of stone, with sculpted decoration in relief, and a wrought-iron balustrade on the landing. There were niches with double columns, beds with heavy canopies, dressing rooms with painted wall-panels, and bathrooms modeled in marble and tile. The entertainment spaces were decorated with Spanish and Moorish tiles, furniture, and rugs. On the walls were religious ornaments and tapestries, antique paintings in elaborate gold frames, and beaten silver and marble medallions. Even the kitchen had a tiled sink and a colorful tile panel inset into the wall.

The architect had thought out the exterior details equally brilliantly. Every patio or loggia corner was washed by the sun, with containers of palms, ferns, and crotons, a tiled bench tucked into a wall niche, and flagstone steps shaded by rows of coconut palms and cypress trees. Tunisian tiles formed a walkway punctuated by a small pool. A plain octagonal fountain surrounded by a brick path in the main patio echoed another on the other side of the loggia; the second fountain was enriched by a gorgeous covering of tiles acquired by the newest convert to this form of decoration, Mrs. Stotesbury herself. Throughout the gardens, palms, orange trees, scented flowers, and Spanish stonework provided an atmosphere of tropical magic.

There was a Moorish teahouse with a square-tile entrance and pediment, with its own patio and small octagonal pool. There was a garage for twenty cars, a movie theater, and forty-two acres of landscaped grounds with mature palms, hibiscus, and—a status symbol beyond price in Palm Beach—a juicy green lawn.

Not only was this commission far greater and more expensive than the Everglades Club (reports assessed the price at over $1 million, or over $9 million in today's currency), Mizner had to learn how to get along with a client who had more money than anyone he had ever worked for. This was not easy. As he himself said, Eva Stotesbury "was accustomed to great wealth and thought nothing of a few little changes." As a client, Paris Singer had been absent much of the time, and he had paid his bills without question, trusting completely in Addison's taste and skill. Eva Stotesbury was not so compliant. With regard to her own bathroom, for instance, she was typically difficult. "There are only three pieces of furniture that must go in [to a bathroom]," Addison argued. "We made several different arrangements of these before things looked right, then she decided to move her sitting room over to where her bathroom was and make the sitting room the bath."

Eva Stotesbury liked to complain later that she had a beautiful house with fifteenth-century plumbing and no bells.[9] But these were light-hearted criticisms and did not prevent architect and client from becoming good friends. He called her Mrs. Simon Legree, after the famous taskmaster in *Uncle Tom's Cabin*. Eva was amused by this nickname, and she and Addison both used it in their affectionate correspondence over the years.

Marjorie Merriweather Post said later that she thought her friend Eva enjoyed El Mirasol more than any of her other houses: "From her upstairs porch Mrs. Stotesbury could see the ocean most beautifully, and I must say she spent many hours there attending to her mail or reading."[10]

If there were any doubts about Addison Mizner's talent after the opening of the Everglades Club, they vanished for good when spectacular antique furnishings and furniture finally put the finishing touches to El Mirasol. For this aspect of Mizner's creative contribution was perhaps the most unexpected—his personal involvement with interior design. During his early years in New York, he had honed his skills as a decorator of rooms, and by the time he arrived in Palm Beach, he knew that interior decoration was an essential part of his architecture. "With all my houses, I made a stipulation that I must be consulted about the furnishing of the first floor," he said later. ("I didn't care what people did in their bedrooms," he added.)

This requirement was extremely unusual. Very few architects of the day could, or wanted to, work on the interiors of their houses. Stanford

White, for instance, generally left the interior details to others (although he did the decor of the dining room at Kingscote in Newport). J. Allard et Fils did most of Rosecliff's interior work. One would have to look to the Adam brothers in eighteenth-century England, A. W. N. Pugin a century later, or Frank Lloyd Wright in Mizner's time, to find an architect whose interiors were so integral to the overall architecture. Moreover, most architects hired landscape architects to do their gardens. (For instance, Marion Sims Wyeth brought in E. L. Olmsted, Jr., son of the designer of New York's Central Park, to landscape one of his major Palm Beach houses, Casa Alejandro.) But as Singer so astutely observed, Addison was that rare combination of architect, interior decorator, and landscape designer, and he wore all three hats with panache.

With El Mirasol, Addison completed the architectural journey he had embarked upon when he designed the Spanish-style houses for Jerome Alexandre and Stephen Brown on Long Island. With the building of Eva Stotesbury's Moorish paradise, he cemented the design idiom that was to be his trademark for the rest of his career. These artistic and decorative innovations appeared in all the houses that followed. El Mirasol was the blueprint for his future work, the original cast from which everything else was formed, the experimental model that became the patented work of art.

CHAPTER 15

"ONCE I HAVE MY STORY, THEN THE PLANS TAKE PLACE EASILY."

After Eva Stotesbury gave Addison her imprimatur, the Palm Beach colony scrambled to climb onto the Mizner bandwagon. By the end of 1920, his list of clients read like a combination of the hundred richest men in America and the Social Register: E. Clarence Jones, Charles A. Munn, Gurnee Munn, John S. Phipps, Barclay H. Warburton, Anthony Drexel Biddle, Joshua Cosden, Angier Buchanan Duke, Edward Shearson, Rodman Wanamaker II, Edward Moore, Paul Moore, and William Gray Warden.

From 1919 to 1924, Addison Mizner designed approximately thirty-eight houses for the Palm Beach winter colony. His first clients after Mrs. Stotesbury were two brothers, Gurnee and Charles Munn, for whom he completed adjacent Spanish-style family houses in late 1919. Both residences were situated on the ocean, facing north. Louwana, Gurnee Munn's house, was the larger of the two. Its minimally embellished exterior gave little hint of the gloriously designed interior courtyard, with its soaring loggia, punctuated by fig trees, palms, and climbing shrubs. Two first-floor wings were connected by a covered veranda with a carved wooden balustrade, and two stories of arcades led to bedrooms and nurseries, with wrought-iron railings protecting an exterior staircase. Amado, Charles Munn's house, had a more ornamented exterior, with similarly designed wings and interior patios.

In 1920 Mizner built a house for Willey Lyon Kingsley, a New York banker, who had bought a site on the southern end of town. Similar to Louwana but bigger, Kingsley's La Bellucia had several roof levels, a simple exterior with an enclosed patio, a tile loggia, and covered walkways. This house featured the "open" staircase Addison liked—showing the form of the steps without boxing them in.

The other commissions during these years followed roughly the specifications first devised for the Munns. The architecture was harmonious, of a piece. The houses were large, mostly with pink, terra-cotta, or white stucco facades and tile roofs. Casa Bendita, John S. Phipps's house, was one of Addison's most elaborate designs, with an octagonal tower, an open staircase, and a colonnaded swimming pool. Wishing to vary the Moorish look, Mizner turned to Venice for the design of Leonard Thomas's Casa Leoni, which arose like a palace on the Grand Canal from the shores of Lake Worth. For Edward Shearson's Villa Flora, Mizner chose Byzantine windows and tiled cloisters reminiscent of the Palace of the Doges in St. Mark's Square. Those for Joseph Cudahy, Alice DeLamar, Barclay Warburton, Arthur Claflin, and Preston and Florence Satterwhite were variations on the same theme. In five years, rather than five centuries, Addison Mizner created a Mediterranean village.

He also took on a large nonresidential project, the Gulf Stream Golf Club south of Palm Beach (now Delray Beach), planned as a private male enclave with an exclusive membership of two hundred persons looking to play golf somewhere besides the increasingly crowded Everglades Club. (Paris Singer was the new club's first acting chairman, with William Warden, Edward Stotesbury, and Edward Shearson on the board.) The clubhouse was much smaller than the Everglades, but it was immensely graceful, with an abbreviated H-shaped floor plan, a sinuous double staircase leading up to a long colonnaded veranda, and second-floor windows with balustrades. Addison later said he had done the sketches in six hours.

The Gulf Stream Golf Club was completed in 1923. By that time he had built roughly thirty-four private houses. It is almost impossible to comprehend the speed and precipitousness of his rise to prominence in Palm Beach. Only five years earlier he had been flat on his back with a leg injury in a borrowed New York apartment, his house foreclosed, his career a shambles, his financial prospects dim. When he arrived in Florida, he was on crutches and suffering from pneumonia, and apart from Paris Singer, he knew hardly a soul. When he first started building in Palm Beach, his name was unknown—his houses on Long Island and Connecticut warranted only marginal recognition. For such a physically large person, he was a pygmy beside the towering figures in the field of architecture to which most Palm Beach clients were accustomed: such as Delano & Aldrich's French chateaux, and Horace Trumbauer's red-brick Colonials. Indeed, some anxious voices were raised at the beginning of Mizner's reign. "The Spanish atmosphere of Palm Beach may be considered at first blush as the expression of too 'foreign' a spirit," one anxious reporter wrote, concluding that "this, however, is just what it is not!"[1] Yes, Mizner's designs were refreshingly different, the Everglades Club in all its glory was a testament to his ability, and Mrs. Stotesbury had fallen for him. But some very tough-minded businessmen, investing a great deal of money in a house they would use for only about three months of the year, still had to be convinced that Mizner, with his "foreign" spirit, could do the job.

How did he pull it off? Darling Addie had a shameless way with clients, which is why some of them became so fond of him. He himself tells how he built the William Gray Warden house in 1922: "Mrs. Warden wanted a nice, comfortable, big house. Bill wanted something small, as he hates ostentation, something that would not overshadow the houses next to his." How to reconcile these two positions? The site was on North Ocean Boulevard. Across the street were two houses, one a small clapboard Colonial, and the other made of stucco. "I took my sketch block up and drew in these two houses in a large and important manner and then went back to the office and designed the Warden house one-half the scale of the others. It looked rather long, but truly insignificant. As I had told Mrs. Warden the trick, everybody was satisfied."

William Warden, a Standard Oil millionaire, took a great interest in the building of his house, and early in the autumn of 1922, to Addison's surprise, he came down to look at it. Addison managed to distract him from the fact that the house ran the whole length of the block and had a huge central patio and a large garden. "I never left his side, and stepped with all my might on the charm pedal," Addison reported. Finally, as Warden was leaving, he asked the architect if he could take the elevations, to show his friends back home.

"Elevations? Why, Bill, you look intelligent at times; how could I send you elevations when the house isn't finished yet?" The befuddled client went quietly home without them. "Thank God," Addison added artlessly. "I haven't seen my own elevations since I passed the two hundred and fifty–pound mark."

This anecdote shows Addison at his most mischievous. Warden in fact came down in June and went over the house with Addison, so there were few surprises for him in October. But Addison enjoyed a good story, and it sounded better in this more dramatic form. It is absurd to suppose he never drew elevations or floor plans. He drew hundreds of them, and many of them survive. But Addison liked to play the amateur, and myths like this one became the received wisdom.

The only client with whom he almost came to blows was E. Clarence Jones, a difficult man who had come from modest beginnings and was very reluctant to spend money. (He may have been especially difficult in his dealings with Mizner, since gossip had it that he had wanted to marry Myra Yerkes!)[2] Jones instructed Addison to build him a house, complete with furniture and gardens, for $10,000. "It couldn't be done," Mizner recalled, "so I put in three thousand of my own to make good. There were no specifications as to furniture and I must say the house was not a museum, but it was comfortable and rather attractive for the price."

Jones appeared satisfied and asked Addison to order a few more pieces of furniture from Giles, a store in West Palm Beach, for $2,400. Shortly afterward, Addison was visiting Mrs. Stotesbury when a deputy sheriff arrived and served him with a subpoena. With the support of Clarence Jones, Giles was suing Mizner for the price of the furniture. Jones, hoping to humiliate the architect, had promised the sheriff twenty-five dollars if he would serve the subpoena in front of Mrs. Stotesbury. Furious, Addison went to Giles and paid the bill for "Swillcan" Jones, as he called him, adding, "I hope you drop dead right where you stand." Louise Munn phoned him a few days later and told him that that was precisely what had happened: Giles had dropped dead at his desk.

Addison used to say that a doctor has an advantage over an architect, because a doctor can chloroform his patient and then do what he likes. His own formula, and that of senior executives everywhere, was never to disagree with a client but always to pretend you think his ideas are excellent. Addison would say, "Yes, I like that idea very much"—pause—"but do you know, I think I like your first idea best." He would then suggest an idea of his own and fool them into thinking it was theirs. "Most people know that they can't paint a portrait, cut off a leg, or build up a law case," was his wry observation, "but everyone thinks they are a better architect than you are."

Addison was a canny negotiator. His straight, unvarnished language, free of the obfuscating jargon employed by so many architects, pleased his clients. In the best of cases, they would agree to his plans and then disappear for eight months, leaving him to get on with the job without breathing heavily down his neck. Certainly many architects would envy this arrangement. Yet his astonishing number of commissions obviously did not depend solely upon his seductive way with clients. He had to be a salesman and an artist. And his houses had to stand up, architecturally speaking. A prospective client had only to drop in on one of these new Spanish castles sprouting up everywhere to react either favorably or unfavorably. In a tiny town like Palm Beach, word of mouth could create or kill a reputation in no time.

The success of Mizner's Florida houses rested on his shrewd adaptation of Spanish, Moorish, and Mediterranean styles to contemporary requirements. His goal was to exploit the local climate and vegetation while modifying its excesses, to utilize local materials, and to reflect the ambitions of people who had abandoned chilly northern winters to spend three months mostly outdoors, entertaining constantly, and enjoying both security and privacy under a clear blue sky. (Mosquitoes were a problem that even Addison found difficult to solve. One possible solution came from James Murdock Marrs, a Jacksonville attorney who, after being taken around the Everglades Club by Addison, suggested shooting poison down the holes of land crabs, where it was believed millions of mosquitoes lived. Whether the architect took this advice is not recorded.)

"What I really did was to turn the Spanish inside out like a glove," Addison explained later. "Instead of making all the openings face a patio or courtyard, I made every room face two or three ways." Medieval Spanish castles were designed with interior courtyards and balconies and were heavily fortified on the outside with barred windows, or *rejas,* and narrow entryways, to protect the inhabitants from attack. Addison's adaptations eliminated the fortressed and minimally fenestrated exterior and replaced it with breathtakingly long loggias and cloisters, giving a feeling of infinite lightness. Windows were often small and placed close to the roofline so that the widely overhanging eaves cast as much shadow as possible. To allow light and air to pass through the house, he used wrought-iron gates instead of doors, and railings instead of walls as space-dividers. These porous spaces acted as connecting links between the exterior and the interior, opening up the core of the building to sun, breezes, and views of the ocean and landscape. The interior courtyards, as in the Spanish manner, were both open to the air and completely private. His exterior plans—with trees, shrubs, waterworks, and terraces—were equally important. "The landscape gives you no help in Florida," he remarked. "You must make your own."

Addison criticized the derivativeness practiced by so many of his contemporaries. "Most modern architects have spent their lives carrying out a period to the last letter and producing a characterless copybook effect," he explained. "My ambition has been to take the reverse stand—to make a building look traditional and as though it had fought its way from a small unimportant structure to a great rambling house that took centuries of different needs and ups and downs of wealth to accomplish. I sometimes start a house with a Romanesque corner, pretend that it has fallen into disrepair and been added to in the Gothic spirit, when suddenly the great wealth of the New World has poured in and the owner had added a very rich Renaissance tradition."[3]

This "storytelling" was very much a Mizner characteristic. "I never begin to design a home without first imagining some sort of romance about it," he used to say. "Once I have my story, then the plans take place easily."[4] If the grand mansions of the Gilded Age embodied "the wish of turn-of-the-century American millionaires to relate their lives to those of European aristocracy," then Addison Mizner's Spanish confections offered his clients the romantic notion that they were fairy-tale princes and princesses carrying on affairs of courtly love beneath the arches of the loggias, or perhaps that they were medieval priests and "abysses," floating their souls up to God in the scented cloisters, an illusion of self-improvement that no doubt many of them found delightfully satisfying.[5]

But his buildings, while mythic in some sense, were often simpler than they first appeared. As early as 1919, he had urged the ladies of West Palm Beach to devote themselves to simplicity in design. Over the years he often expressed his distaste for overly ornate decoration, which, in his typically salty language, he described as "like a whore at a christening." He subscribed to the doctrine promulgated by Elsie de Wolfe, his feisty contemporary: "Simplicity, Suitability, and Proportion."

There are two famous canards about Addison Mizner. One is that he could not draw, which is easily disproved by examination of his many scrapbooks and sketches. The better-disseminated one is that he forgot to include a staircase in Casa Nana, the house he built for the Rasmussens in 1926, and hastily added a circular one onto the exterior of the house only after discovering his error. It is not clear who originated this story, but Alva Johnston picked it up somewhere and reported it as truth in *The Legendary Mizners,* and subsequent writers have continued to repeat it. Enjoyable as it is, the legend is not true. Addison's associate, Lester Geisler, described precisely how the circular staircase evolved. "I remember Mizner's sketch," he recalled. "He started with a big circle. Why he did, I don't know. Maybe he had talked with Mrs. Rasmussen and sold her the big stair. But he started with a circle. Then he worked his rooms around it. The workmen who put up the stair were afraid it would fall down. It hasn't yet. There is no central support. You don't need it. You build around in a circle. It's like building an arch, every step holds every other step. It's confined with concrete and steel or it would fly out. Your reinforcement is a spiral."[6]

The plain fact is that seventy years after they were built, most Mizner houses are still standing. Not one has succumbed to the hurricanes, floods, or other natural disasters that have destroyed so many residential buildings over the same period. In the devastating hurricane of 1926, the worst that El Mirasol suffered was water damage and a tile falling off the roof.[7] Some Mizner houses have been demolished, and many others have been added to or restored almost beyond recognition. But that so many are still standing, with their structural bones intact, is testament to the architect's practical genius. If he wished to build a circular staircase onto the exterior of a house, he would draw it, and it would work.

The visitor to Palm Beach today sees the familiar landscape of a high-maintenance resort—manicured lawns, tall, obsessively trimmed ficus hedges, and houses glimpsed through huge stone or wrought-iron gates. But the similarity of the architecture of these great mansions sets Palm Beach apart from most American playgrounds. Santa Fe, New Mexico, is one of the few other resorts that has effectively restricted building to conform to the style, size, and shape of the city's historical architecture. Thanks to Mizner's original and consistent vision, the town of Palm Beach has survived for over eighty years without being desecrated by the massive condominium and hotel construction that other coastal regions have suffered. As development runs rampant through these precious enclaves, new building vernaculars may appear, but thanks to Mizner's taste and practicality, Palm Beach emerged from its jungle origins to become a showcase of Mediterranean architecture that is unique in America.

CHAPTER 16

"WE'RE GOING ON A BUYING TRIP TO SPAIN."

When Addison built the Everglades Club, he had managed to produce the effects he wanted with a lot of personal involvement and patient training of craftsmen. But as new commissions flooded in, he had to organize his workforce more efficiently, delegate responsibility for overseeing products and materials, and, perhaps most important, gain immediate access to the supplies and materials he needed. Since Palm Beach lacked any industry except sailing, fishing, tourism, and—after Prohibition in 1919—rum-running, this was a major challenge. Addison Mizner, who had never organized anything in his life except a few good parties, was about to become the head of a huge production company.

If you can't find it, make it. This was Addison's policy as he started his great building program, and it paid off handsomely. His first venture into the manufacturing business was Los Manos Potteries, formed with the craftsmen he had assembled to produce the handmade roof tiles for the Everglades Club. When Addison first started work, Singer had financed the creation of kilns and workrooms, but afterward, in a jealous fit over his friend's success, he threatened to close them down. So Addison borrowed some money and bought him out. Los Manos Potteries became the foundation of Mizner Industries, Inc., which also consisted of La Puerta, a full-scale supplier of authentic period furnishings, paneled rooms, chimney pieces, and other antiques, with reproduction Spanish-style furniture, candlesticks, lanterns, locks, hinges, shields, mirrors, and fabrics; and the Mizner Cut Cast Stone Company, makers of ornamental building stone, stone fountains, balustrades, plaques, and garden furniture. Thus Addison's modest venture into the marketing of Guatemalan treasures blossomed into a mighty business.

Mizner experimented extensively with materials to produce the precise effects he wanted. His experience with Willis Polk in San Francisco served him well as he worked with stonecutters and masons to find the best mixtures of cement and limestone to create the carved columns for his cloisters and loggias. Later he was one of the first to see the possibilities of coquina, a beautiful, pockmarked coral stone that has now been banned as being too rare for use as a building material. For the vast amounts of wood needed to make his Moorish ceiling beams, he used pecky cypress, a soft, heavily streaked and knotted wood that most people had dismissed as being ugly and impractical. In his view, it aged wonderfully under the soft color washes he specified for the interiors. It was also impervious to termites.

Addison used pecky cypress in almost all his houses. It was often treated with a coat of lime whitewash, over which was applied creosote. The lime bled through the creosote, and the natural oils of the wood bled through both, creating a streaked effect that looked like driftwood from the beach. He also used regular cypress, which he sandblasted to bring out a weathered look or treated with acid and brushed with wire to bring out the grain.[1] Another Mizner invention, "woodite," a light but tough mixture of wood shavings, plaster of Paris, and fibers, reproduced the look of distressed wood. Poured into plaster molds, it was very useful for paneling.

Addison called upon his innate sense of color to create a wide-ranging palette for his pottery. The glazing material, which was imported from Italy, came in a variety of distinctive shades: Mizner blue (a luminous turquoise), light blue, Valencia blue, green, neutral green, yellow, orange, red, brown, blue, blue black, and so on. The Los Manos catalog offered pottery of all shapes and sizes: Ali Baba jars, Moorish handbasins, Seville and Salamanca jars, fern bowls, lion's head pots, Alhambra and Granada pots, and huge Guadalupe jars with handles. Addison himself taught the workmen how to apply the colors. He even designed the kilns, which were intentionally built to give out uneven heat, thus creating variations of tone and color in the terra-cotta.

To obtain antiques, he traveled to Spain and shipped back large quantities of furniture, tapestries, religious items, grillwork, fabrics, and decorative objects. He also went into business with Ward and Ruth Wickwire, importers of antiques based in Buffalo, New York, splitting the profits from the sales. Nearly all his clients had accounts with the

Wickwires, whose prices were set at Addison's direction according to the bank account of the particular client.

An inventory of his European acquisitions between 1923 and 1925 reveals the extent of his purchases during those years: hundreds of lanterns, chains, doors, pedestals, knockers, lock plates, fountains, brackets, and scrolls were shipped to Palm Beach. But however many he acquired, there were never enough to fill the ever-increasing number of houses he was building. His solution was simple: he trained local crafts-men to reproduce the heavy, elaborately carved furniture and ironwork required by his architecture. He taught them many tricks of the trade. To soften the sharp corners of the wood, for instance, the workmen beat the edges with heavy glass bottles. To make the wood look old, they used chains to carve indentations. Wilson, who later joined his brother in Palm Beach, once suggested shooting fake wormholes into the wood with a BB gun, but Addison said that wormholes would indicate decay.[2]

Mizner's reproductions were made to look old, stressed, and worn because he believed that they blended better into the Spanish environ-ments he created than did brightly polished, hard-edged new furniture. But the furniture he designed also had to withstand the humidity that cursed southern Florida most of the year. His heavy, solidly made pieces, using wooden dowels rather than metal, for instance, resisted the blight of warp, rust, and mildew endemic to the climate. Critics tend to dis-parage "distressed" furniture, which interior decorators today still use. Jokes abound about the oxymoronic phrase "authentic reproduction." But Mizner, whose only concern was that the reproductions be of good and enduring quality, never pretended that his factory products were original, never concealed the tricks he used to achieve his effects, and would never have stooped to fuzzy promotional locutions in order to deceive his clients.

Addison employed similar techniques to make the exteriors harmo-nize with the interiors. To this end, he performed what seemed to his astonished workforce like acts of vandalism. A stoneworker who had just finished some pieces recalled the experience: "He [Mizner] said the job was good. 'Do you have a hatchet?' I thought that he was kidding me, so I went and got a hatchet. He knocked corners off my pieces here and there. Then he told me to patch them on again but so that the patches were noticeable from 25 feet away. I couldn't believe it."[3]

All the procedures Addison introduced had to be learned by unskilled workmen. His patience, enthusiasm, sense of humor, and ribald language helped win and maintain their loyalty. Many of the workers were black or Hispanic, and Addison worked alongside them, showing them how to set plaster, lay a brick, or fix a pipe. In those early years, he was still so strong that when some laborers were having trouble moving a bathtub from a truck into a house, he simply picked up the tub and carried it in himself.[4] But perhaps the most useful weapon in Addison's arsenal was his fluency in Spanish. Explaining how to fire a piece of pottery or paint layers of different washes on a piece of wood was time-consuming enough in English, but for an architect to be able to speak colloquial (and often scatological) Spanish to his workers was an incalculable advantage.

He also found time to educate them about architecture and design. He would explain how the Greeks had learned, through trial and error, to slightly thicken the shaft of a column to make it look stronger. He would go to the drawing board and sketch the preliminary design for a stairway, then ask an apprentice to draw in stone balusters and a handrail for it. On examining the results, he would point out how and why the proportions were wrong. He would go so far as to make wooden mock-ups of the balusters and rails so that the student could see his mistakes for himself.[5] A seventeen-year-old junior draftsman hired by Addison in 1925 later described the architect's charismatic effect this way: "I was such a worshiper of his talents. He did so much for me."[6]

Addison also learned how to delegate. When he designed a house for his niece Ysabel Chase in Pebble Beach, the general contractor said that the architect "just walked out on me, after sticking a roll of wrapping paper [on which the plans were drawn] and a list of timber, plumbing, and things in my hand, and expected me to put them together. All he said was, 'You'd better make a good job of it or I'll wear it out on you.'" Contractors tend to appreciate this freedom from the architect's scrutiny, and in Addison's experience, projects done this way worked very well.

By the early 1920s, much of West Palm Beach, which Flagler's army of railroad and hotel workers had earlier transformed from a tiny outpost of small farming and fishing shacks, once again hummed with activity as Mizner's factories, stores, warehouses, and construction crews took over the little town. Just as he had imprinted his vision on every house in the elegant resort across the intracoastal waterway, so West Palm Beach too became an emblem of Addison's astonishing success.

As his architectural work exploded, he staffed his office with more designers, draftsmen, and architectural students. But for a business to run smoothly, suitable administrative personnel are essential. Addison was spending most of his time at the drafting table or on site. Who would run the potteries and the antique shops? In an odd reversal of Mizner lore, his family resurfaced at this juncture. Maybe the news had spread over the Mizner telegraph that Addie had finally struck it rich.

Minnie Chase, true to Mizner form, had not communicated with her brother since their mother's death. She now wrote to Addison asking if he would look up her son, Horace, who had just come back from the war after two years in the Canadian Flying Service and was living in New York. Addison, the good uncle, took the train north and found his nephew working as a mechanic in a garage. Since Addison had just purchased Los Manos Potteries from Paris Singer, he immediately saw a role for his young nephew. So in late 1919 the charming, flamboyant Horace came to Palm Beach and took up residence as an employee of his uncle; his job was to run the Potteries and put it on a sound business footing.

Two years later an Englishman called Alex Waugh (no relation to Evelyn) arrived in Palm Beach as the young and handsome protégé of a wealthy winter resident, Joseph Riter. Riter's house, Al Ponienti, which overlooked Lake Worth, had originally been built in 1903 by George Bywater Cluett. Riter was a talented organist, and in 1920 he added a music room complete with an organ and a movable stage, designed by Francis Burrall Hoffman, Jr., who, like Mizner, often worked in the Mediterranean idiom of architecture.*

Not surprisingly, Addison Mizner was often invited to Riter's house, and so one night he got to meet the new favorite. Waugh had a background in history and antiques, and while listening during the dinner to one of Mizner's colorful stories about Spain, he had the temerity to correct a mistaken date tossed out by the famous architect. Instead of being

*Hoffman had built several houses in Palm Beach before Addison's arrival and, with Paul Chalfin, produced the Italianate masterpiece Villa Vizcaya in Miami in 1916, one of the few local houses and gardens that competed with Mizner's in beauty and grandeur.[7] Al Ponienti was later demolished.

offended, the next day Mizner invited the young Englishman to lunch, and they soon discovered a shared passion for antiques and the decorative arts.

In 1922, shortly after this meeting, Waugh decided to leave Palm Beach and his generous patron Joseph Riter, so he accompanied Riter to Paris with the intention of going on alone to England. As he was walking disconsolately down a Paris street, uncertain about his future, by an extraordinary coincidence he ran into Addison Mizner. He told the architect he was going to London to try to find a job. "Like hell you are," Mizner said. "You meet me on the Madrid Express tomorrow morning. We're going on a buying trip to Spain."

Thanks to this chance encounter, Waugh got involved in a journey that could hardly have been more improbable. The architect's goal was to buy as much furniture, linens, glass, fabrics, and furnishings as possible to fill the houses under construction back in Palm Beach. On the train from Paris to Madrid, he dictated to Waugh a list of what he wanted (which was extensive). Waugh noticed the architect's physical problems: he was overweight, his leg was very painful, and he suffered from stomach ulcers. ("I feel as if I'm about to give birth to a litter of horned toads," Addison complained to his surprised companion.) Waugh wondered how Addison could possibly complete the trip.

Waugh did not know his man. Addison swept his young assistant through Madrid, Seville, Burgos, Ávila, Salamanca, and Granada, buying furiously—wrought iron, tapestries, furniture, grillwork, even whole staircases. In each city, Mizner would discourse on its history, telling Waugh the secrets of ancient Spanish culture with such passionate eloquence that the young man was astonished. "All doors seemed to open to him; and for me never more memorably so than when we were allowed entry to the Alhambra and the Generalife in Granada in the evenings, when tourists were not permitted." The two men wandered through the great palaces, courts, and water gardens of the Alhambra, flooded with moonlight, while for three hours Addison poured out a living, breathing narrative of the ancient Islamic civilization that had created that magical acropolis and that contributed so much to science, literature, medicine, and astronomy.[8]

If Waugh fell under the spell of this capacious figure spinning tales in the moonlight, a more mercenary crowd found Addison's presence equally attractive. The huge, baby-faced American was already legendary for making a vast number of extravagant, outrageous purchases, and antique dealers who heard he was in town clamored for an audience. Of course his fluency in Spanish added to his fascination. He accumulated so many hangers-on that back in Madrid, he told the concierge he could not see anyone else. One man was so persistent that finally Addison opened the door. It was Alfonso, the king of Spain. "Well, you old son of a bitch," roared Addison, "why didn't you say it was you!"

At the end of the trip, the architect turned to Waugh and said, "Get everything together and have it packed and shipped. I'm off to meet Nell Cosden in Florence." Waugh's task was daunting. He had to sort out hundreds of scraps of receipts written in Spanish, a language he did not speak. He had to fill out thousands of customs forms, oversee the packing of all the valuable pieces that Mizner had airily picked up, and arrange to ship them all to the United States.

Being a resourceful Englishman, he accomplished this—only to discover that when the packing cases were opened at customs in New York, all the objects had been put in the wrong cases. No invoices matched the contents. Thus when everything finally arrived in Palm Beach—absurdly late, of course—there was total chaos. The decorators, such as Lillias Piper, who finished up much of Addison's interior work, were desperate to get their hands on the furniture and art objects. The seamstresses, who were making the curtains and upholstery, were equally frantic for the bolts of velvet, damask, and silk. Clients crowded around the packing cases looking for chairs or tables that they had been promised would arrive in time for the start of the season. After much scrambling and hair-tearing, Waugh managed to divide up the furniture and fabrics that were earmarked for staff and clients and deliver the rest to Mizner's antiques showrooms.

The Spanish trip of 1922 cemented the friendship between the two men and created a working relationship that lasted almost until the end of the decade. Mizner, with his usual mixture of intuitiveness and good luck, had found just the person he needed in this bright, rootless Englishman, and making him manager of the antiques and reproduction furniture store for Mizner Industries was a masterstroke. Waugh's extensive knowledge of interior design and, it must be said, his English accent, gave the clients confidence and added a great deal of class to the business. Moreover, he got along extremely well with young Horace Chase. The two of them set up house together in Horace's tumbledown shack on the beach, which had virtually no amenities except a large iron tub where, thanks to Prohibition, they hid their generous supplies of gin and rum. Later the two young men moved into a houseboat on Lake Worth, where their bootlegging exploits and wild parties were the subject of much local gossip. Whether they applied themselves to their work with similar commitment is debatable, but easygoing Addison was not about to complain. Things were going too well.

As we have seen, when things were going well in Addison Mizner's life, something would surely go wrong. In 1922, just when Addison's reputation was skyrocketing, Wilson Mizner hove into view. Like a retriever roused by a rabbit, Wilson scented success, money, and fun in Palm Beach, and he started out for it, wagging his mangy tail.

To be fair to Wilson, it didn't happen quite as directly as that. In 1922, the year Addison went to Spain with Alex Waugh, he learned that Wilson was very ill in a New York hospital. Wilson himself said that for over a year he "had had every square inch of the posterior on the toboggan."[9] In fact it seems to have been heart trouble, a family pathology. Addison took the train to New York and rescued him from the "gut garage" (Wilson's term), inviting him to recuperate, just as he himself had recuperated four years earlier, in the healing climate of Palm Beach. Of course Wilson accepted. And as soon as he saw the luxurious way people lived in this Lotusland (so much more agreeable than Port Washington), he decided to stay.

In the years since the production of the plays that had made him famous, Wilson's career had become somewhat desultory. Unable to repeat his theatrical success, he became among other things a producer, an artists' manager, and a screenwriter, traveling through the United States and Europe picking up jobs, girls, and cocaine. He arrived in Florida in late 1922 and moved in with Addison. (Later Addison built him his own house on Worth Avenue.) Almost immediately the inveterate flimflam artist announced that he and his brother were going to start a moving-picture company called Palm Beach Pictures. Soon Wilson, like Horace and Alex, was playing a role in Addison's booming creative empire. The business side was completed by a good-looking young man called John F. Roy, who became Addison's office manager.

While Horace Chase and his friends were running rum and avoiding the law, another member of the family turned up to see what the excitement was about. Minnie's only daughter, Ysabel, Horace's elder sister, first showed up in Palm Beach in November 1920. For Addison, it was one of the happiest moments of the season. "She is the one I really love best in all the world," he confessed. She wasn't a beauty, but she was a true Mizner, "the funniest white woman I have ever known," he said. "She is the only human being in the world with whom I would be willing to be shipwrecked on a desert island."

His favorite Ysabel story concerned a visit to Palm Beach from one of the less favorite Mizner cousins, the Edgar Floyd-Joneses from St. Louis, who brought with them their twenty-one-month-old son. The spoiled brat spent most of his time attacking Addison's precious furniture and furnishings and throwing butter balls at everyone. When Edgar remarked to a disgusted Ysabel, "Dear cousin, isn't he adorable?" Ysabel retorted, "You aren't any relation of mine. I'm illegitimate."

One of the many pleasures shared between Addison and Ysabel was a love of animals. Ysabel was a fine horsewoman, and as a young girl, during the prosperous years at Stag's Leap, she had owned several polo ponies. She also loved dogs, and when Ching, Addison's favorite chow, had puppies during Ysabel's first visit, she took one of them home to California with her. After this trip, she was to return many times, enjoying her besotted uncle's generosity and giving him enormous pleasure.

For in spite of Addison's jokes about the Mizners, and although he rarely saw any of his siblings, his friend Alice DeLamar always felt he missed the family side of life. He was happy to act as father-protector to Horace and Ysabel, although Alice wondered if they weren't exploiting his hospitality. Henry, the steadiest Mizner, also managed to keep in touch, and in 1923 the brothers met in Venice with Henry's wife, Margot, and their daughter, Alice. It was an affectionate meeting.

Also in 1923, three years after Ysabel's first visit, Addison went to see his old friend Paris Singer in St. Jean Cap Ferrat. Singer had married Joan, the nurse who had coaxed Addison back to life in 1918, and was building a strange, medieval fortress for her on the French Riviera. During this visit, Addison received a cable from San Francisco telling him that his sister, Minnie, had died, at the age of sixty-three.

The following year, perhaps in recognition of his sister's death and his concern for Ysabel, Addison forwent his usual European trip and returned to California for the first time in twenty years. He was excited by seeing Benicia again, remembering the last time he had seen it, through his tears, when at sixteen he had left for Guatemala. But instead of the broad streets, green fields, and pretty houses of his childhood memories, he was greeted by "the dirtiest, stinking little town I had ever seen." This shock was compounded by the bitter realization that the Mizner name, once so important in the rowdy living rooms of San Francisco, was now totally forgotten. The concierge at the St. Francis Hotel couldn't even pronounce it correctly.

These disappointments were assuaged by the drive he took with Ysabel up the coast to the spectacular Monterey Peninsula. Arriving in Pebble Beach, Ysabel told him she would rather live there than anywhere else. Calling on a friend of Addison's, the famous golfer Marion Hollins, who was involved in real estate in the area, they came upon a beautiful piece of land on a steep site overlooking the ocean. Addison bought it on the spot for his beloved niece. Hastily drawing up some plans on wrapping paper, he thrust the paper into the hands of a local contractor and left for Florida. Three years later, he returned to find the house built as planned.

It remains one of Addison's most appealing designs. Poised on a steep hillside, the yellow-washed stucco walls and terra-cotta-tile roofs are first glimpsed through the tall Monterey pines that cluster around the site. A monumental stone-trimmed arched entrance seems to emerge naturally from the rocks, like the doorway to a cave. Inside, an arcaded cloister with graceful double columns leads to a sunlit patio, its irregular flagstone floor sprouting flowering plants. The interiors are simply furnished, with tiled floors and beamed ceilings. The house is small, as befits a single owner, but as always, the scale and proportion of both interior and exterior were perfectly executed. Evidence of the architect's attention to detail was the fact that, in spite of the house being built at long distance, the pattern of tiles of the garden fountain was meticulously laid out by Mizner himself.

Addison returned to Florida with another appendage: a kinkajou, purchased, with Ysabel's encouragement, at a pet shop in California. Soft-hearted Addison could not resist the little creature, whom he called Neuter (later adapted to Nettie). As he said, his greatest loves were animals and trees—and perhaps, though he would not admit it, his family.

CHAPTER 17

"EACH HOUSE ADDISON BUILDS IS MORE BEAUTIFUL THAN THE ONE BEFORE."

Addison's success in Palm Beach happened so fast that he hardly had time to make a home for himself. His first living quarters were next to Paris Singer's in the tower at the top of the Everglades Club. Although happy with it, it soon became untenable, thanks to the club's board of governors and in particular its master of protocol, E. Clarence Jones.

Ever since Addison had lived in Port Washington, he had always owned chows. In Palm Beach, he had two. Around this time he also acquired a monkey, Johnnie Brown, who was just as mischievous as the infamous Mico, and to whom Nettie was later to be introduced. At a meeting one day in early 1919, "Swillcan" Jones and his colleagues ruled that dogs were not permitted in the Everglades Club. As an added insult, they declared that ladies were not admitted above the first floor. Since popular Addie's apartment was on the fifth floor, these two regulations rang the death knell for his own social life and that of his pets.

So in 1919 Mizner, architect of fine residences, was homeless. Undaunted, he quickly rented a place while he started work on a small two-bedroom house for himself called El Solano, with a modest Spanish facade. It stood on land a mile south of Gus' Bath, at 720 South Ocean Boulevard. At that time, Palm Beach was still essentially undeveloped, and people thought him crazy to move so far out into the untamed jungle, but Addison's instinct was sure, and almost as soon as the house was finished, it was snapped up by Harold S. Vanderbilt. (Addison said he sold it because he was financially strapped after buying the Los Manos Potteries and losing money in his argument with "Swillcan" Jones.) Vanderbilt immediately had it enlarged, with a new living room and one of the first private swimming pools in Palm Beach.

Once more homeless, Addison started over. He rented an old mule shed on County Road that had not been used since the building of the Royal Poinciana Hotel, and there he began another small house called Concha Marina, on the corner of South Ocean Boulevard and the aptly named Jungle Road. Concha Marina had an L-shaped floor plan, with one wing overlooking the ocean and the other facing the jungle. A path led from the road through a patio and under a fine arched entrance into an inner courtyard. But he couldn't hang on to this house either, selling it in 1921 to George and Isabel Dodge Sloane. (The house has since been greatly enlarged.)

Building houses for himself was becoming a habit. The next time Addison took a site five miles outside town, supposedly to discourage any more buyers. At this far end of South Ocean Boulevard, he built another of his little gems, with a loggia, four bedrooms, and ocean views, called Sin Cuidado. To go with this little villa, he carved out a pictur-esque landscape with a terraced garden and a flight of stone steps, dec-orated with his Los Manos Alhambra and Ali Baba jars, leading down to a marble fountain. It was irresistible—and hardly had he slept in it when Edward S. Moore bought it, requesting that Mizner add more bedrooms and staff quarters to suit his family.

Thus, contrary to later perceptions, not all of Addison's houses were on the huge scale of El Mirasol and La Bellucia. He felt just as com-fortable designing houses with two bedrooms as with twenty. Later, when the smaller houses were purchased by grander clients, they were given major exterior and interior additions. (Since he got a lot of extra work when the new buyers demanded extensions, one wonders if he cunningly kept his own houses small so that more work would be nec-essary!) This building and selling became so much a pattern that when Paris Singer, who lived at the Everglades Club, was asked why he did not get Mizner to build him a house, he replied, "Each house Addison builds is more beautiful than the one before, and I intend to someday live in the most beautiful of all of them."[1] In this accretive fashion, Addison pushed out the frontiers of Palm Beach; his houses and gardens reached into the palmetto-and-scrub terrain, bringing fertility to the arid mead-ows and form to the sun-baked brush.

But he still had nowhere to live. The site he finally found changed the face of Palm Beach forever and saw him through to the end of his life.

Worth Avenue was a small residential street opposite the Everglades Club, where Alligator Joe had once promenaded his alligators and where visitors now drove in their novelty motorcars, which were fast replacing the old wicker tricycles. Addison, eager for more office space for his expanding staff and for showcases for his growing collections of antiques, pottery, and reproductions, decided to build a three-story office tower on Worth Avenue opposite the club. The first floor contained a showroom for his artifacts. Above it was a large studio for his architects and draftsmen, and on the top floor was a small apartment. But as he observed the relationship of his new office block to the street, he was overtaken by a larger vision. Medieval Spanish castles had contained within their fortified walls what might be called "inner cities," where the soldiers and castle employees lived and worked. These walled urban areas were later transformed into commercial spaces. "They usually faced on small winding streets and were entirely open to the people who traversed the narrow pathways," he explained.[2]

This was the inspiration for Via Mizner, which Addison single-handedly brought to fruition. It was a street within a street, entered through archways, revealing narrow winding flagstone passageways, or vias, that meandered past fountains, lush green foliage, and a series of small shops and apartments. Shortly afterward he created a similar streetscape on the west side of Via Mizner. Since his old friend and patron Paris Singer had invested in both these new projects, Addison called the second one Via Parigi.

People were enchanted. The idea of taking the air and going shopping in such delightful surroundings was almost unknown at that time in the United States. Nobody had ever heard of a mall, let alone a theme park. Moreover, the timing was serendipitous. As Addison pointed out when mentioning that a friend was coming to Palm Beach to take charge of a small shop, "It was quite the chic thing now for girls of the very best families who didn't have a lot of money to do this sort of thing; everywhere you turned you ran into a grand duchess selling drawers, or a prince selling caviar." What could be nicer than to become a working girl in such classy surroundings? With their architectural flourishes and the Mediterranean atmosphere, the galleries in the Via Mizner and Via Parigi hardly seemed like shops at all.

With these two brilliantly conceived open-air arcades, Addison Mizner became, in a modest way, a town planner. While his arcades were changing the look of Palm Beach yet again, assuring its reputation as the most desirable resort in Florida, Addison thought more and more in terms of designing whole communities, whole cities even, an ambition that would ultimately lead to his downfall.

Within his beautiful new complex, incorporated into the Worth Avenue side of his office building, he built a majestic residence for himself. Villa Mizner was five stories high—it was one of the first houses in the area to have an elevator. There were shops on the ground floor. Upstairs were his private apartments: on the lower floor, a living room, dining room, and kitchens, and above it two floors each with two bedrooms and bathrooms. On the top floor was a studio with spectacular views across the island.

Addison's villa, much of which remains intact today, represents the architect in his most confident phase. Both the layout and the interior design reflect his talent for perspective, space, and romance. The street entrance is an elegant wrought-iron gate. Up the stone steps a heavy wooden door, with a carved stone portal, opens into the second-floor foyer. The long corridor has a vaulted ceiling, with arches on one side opening onto a terrace. An arched doorway at the end of the foyer leads to the living room, a vast 35-by-40-foot space with carved Moorish windows, a pecky cypress ceiling, and a dark terra-cotta-tile floor, with a central oak panel for dancing. One side of the room is dominated by a huge stone floor-to-ceiling chimneypiece. The doors from the living room to the dining room are of Gothic origin, and above them is an arrangement of fourteenth-century Moorish tiles in blues, reds, and yellows, framed in a border of gold and black tile-chips. The dining-room paneling was taken from the private apartments of King Ferdinand and Queen Isabella of Spain in Salamanca (a gift to Addison from King Alfonso), the dark wood lightened with whitewash (just as Stanford White had whitewashed the paneling at Rosecliff). The hexagonal tiles on the floor came from Los Manos Potteries.

The two bedrooms on the third and fourth floors are modest in size, with practical rather than grand bathrooms. (The architect admitted his lack of interest in these spaces.) The top floor contains his most virtuoso work. Called the Mirador (or "beautiful view"), it was his studio. Reached by elevator, it is a spacious room, 25 by 33 feet, with fifteen plain glass windows on three sides, exposing views over charmingly irregular tile roofs to the ocean and the lake. The beamed cathedral ceiling is of pecky cypress, and the floor is covered in hexagonal- and rectangular-patterned terra-cotta tiles. To house his impressive library (he had more than 450 volumes), he installed an ingenious triangular bookcase to fit in a corner, as well as floor-to-ceiling shelving between the east-facing windows. The furniture was spare: apart from his drafting table, there was a damask-covered daybed and a few Gothic chairs.

A contemporary description of the Villa Mizner's decorating scheme enhances the now-faded image with stunning color. The dining room, with its whitewashed paneling, was muted, with a salmon-pink-tile floor and a smoky brown ceiling. The ceiling in the living room was originally painted deep ochre, with beams polychromed in dull reds, black, and white. A cabinet that was encrusted with gold and inlaid with ivory and ebony, one of his most precious pieces of furniture, stood in the entrance hall on a refectory table under a large tapestry. The Gothic and early Renaissance furniture was upholstered in green, red, and yellow velvet. Richly embroidered tapestries hung from the walls. With pale pink, blue, and green light washing the room through the panes of leaded stained-glass windows, the effect was like a jewel box under water.

Taking into account Addison's menagerie (the chows, the occasional bird, and a changing cast of monkeys), the main disadvantage of the villa was its lack of a garden. Addison compensated by designing an L-shaped terrace opening through the arcade parallel to the second-floor foyer, with a terra-cotta-tile floor laid in hexagons and squares and decorated with palms, crotons, and his Los Manos jars and urns. A delicate wrought-iron staircase spiraled up to the third floor. The terrace, also accessible from the dining room, overlooked Worth Avenue. (The monkeys were said to enjoy throwing peanut shells down onto the pedestrians below.)

Perhaps the most significant element of this bravura piece of architecture is its proportion. Although the living room and the Mirador studio are huge, one does not feel overwhelmed in any way. Even while the fireplace claims to hold ten men, nobody feels dwarfed. This is true of all Mizner's houses. Even in El Mirasol, one of Addison's most grandiose mansions, the human scale is never threatened. Edith Eglin, great-granddaughter of Edward Stotesbury, remembers El Mirasol as a little girl, before it was demolished: "Playing there, I never felt intimidated."[3]

In this villa, Addison spent some of his happiest years. With his new employees, however inexperienced, to help him run his empire, he was able to put in place an efficient yearly routine. The life of an architect is generally a test of stamina and flexibility. To build a building, one must travel to the site, evaluate it, make drawings, meet with the client, make presentations, return to the site, revisit the client, go back to the site, and so on, every day, every month, every year, with the old clients replaced by new ones in different places all over the world. Addison was liberated from this grueling routine. He lived in the same place as both the sites and the clients. The sites retained the same immutable characteristics—sandy soil, flat terrain, proximity to the ocean, sun, humidity, and threat of hurricanes.

Unlike most architects, who are at the mercy of clients' whims and commands, Addison was free to come and go for a large part of the year. Prior to the invention of air conditioning, Palm Beach was a seasonal destination. During the winter season, Addison would get his clients to sign off on plans for their houses. By the end of March, the "cottage colony" would disappear, leaving the locals to pick up the napkins and champagne glasses and sweep away the detritus of hundreds of vacationing millionaires. Addison would finalize the specifications and materials. Having hired several trained assistants, he found he could afford to leave the sites for longer and longer periods over the summer, freeing him up to do what he loved, travel abroad.

He went to England and took a firsthand look at Bowood, Harewood House, Knole, and Wilton, the great houses and gardens that had inspired so much American architecture. He went to France, to visit Paris Singer at St. Jean Cap Ferrat. But his most important visits were to Spain, his major supplier, where his clients followed his progress with the greatest interest. A typical communication was this cable sent in June 1923 to Mizner at the Ritz in Madrid: IF PANELLING SUITABLE HEIGHT FOR TAPESTRIES PLEASE PURCHASE — VANDERBILT.

Addison was such a popular traveling companion that many of his clients clamored to go on trips with him, picking him up in their Rolls-Royces and traveling through Europe together. When Nell Cosden heard of one of Addison's trips to Spain, she proposed that she and her husband, Joshua, go with him to buy furniture for their new house, Playa Riente. At the last minute Joshua couldn't go, so Nell and Addison went on alone. On the way, Nell introduced Addison to Peggy Thayer, a young Philadelphian, who developed a serious crush on the architect. The group, with Louise Munn joining them, spent several weeks in Spain, scouring the antique shops and ending up at a bullfight. They would sit spellbound as Addison evoked vivid histories for a Spanish pot, a wrought-iron grille, or a carved bench, caressing them lovingly as he conjured up their past. (Later, Addison said this was "the happiest two months of his life.") When the women left him to go to Florence, Peggy wrote to him, saying that "we really do miss our Addie *horribly*! I hope you are suffering a quarter as much as your heartbroken 'women' are!"

Many of his female clients became deeply involved in their architect's work. Nell Cosden learned about blueprints and floor plans, "even to the plumbing chases and electric conduits," and she spent many happy hours with Addison working on the plans for Playa Riente. During the summer and fall months, letters flew between the architect and his eager acolytes. "Would it be a terrible nuisance now if I asked you whoever is doing my bathroom if they could make the walls imitation dark blue marble and I would like the inside of the bath-tub to be light blue enamel" was one of Aggie Munn's requests.[4] Mrs. Simon Legree, aka Eva Stotesbury, continued to cable him with her thoughts, for example: IF YOU BELIEVE THE CRYPT WINDOW SHOULD BE REDUCED IN WIDTH FROM THE ORIGINAL OPENING I TRUST YOUR TASTE SO COMPLETELY THAT I AM WILLING FOR YOU TO MAKE THE CHANGE.[5]

These ladies became far more than Addison's clients. Nell Cosden used to confide in him about her son, asking Addie not to go to bat for the problem boy, "for you are in no way responsible for him nor under any sort of obligation to us in regard to him." Addison's "devoted" Aggie Munn wrote him what sound almost like love letters: "I would give anything to have you here so that we could have a long talk together—you know the kind that I mean!" Adele Robinson was even more passionate: "What joy sublime it was for me to have seen and heard you again and been able to breathe in that inspiring atmosphere of the glorious architect and artist." Even Eva Stotesbury was driven to a little coyness: "It is dreadful inconvenient to have a multimillionaire architect. What possible interest can an Empire builder feel in poor Mrs. Legree's 'Ocean Loggia'? Naturally none whatever!"

In December 1924, Addison was given a surprise birthday party by Willey Kingsley. The guests greeted him with a poem, composed by winter resident Dr. J. J. O'Brian of Philadelphia, inscribed in fifteenth-century lettering on embossed parchment. It ran as follows:

> *You have painted us a city,*
> *Your pigments stone and tile,*
> *Which has made the ocean happier,*
> *And the sunshine brighter smile.*
> *So pass in peace when your birthdays cease.*
> *There is nothing more to reach.*
> *Your biography, just beauty,*
> *And your monument, Palm Beach.*

Present at the celebration were most of his clients, including the Cosdens, the Satterwhites, Lytle Hull, the Warburtons, the Kingsleys, and the Shearsons. How many architects could inspire such a demonstration of affection from their clients?

By this time, Addison had become more than an architect. He was a commercial name, a designer label, a corporation. Palm Beach is a very small town, and everyone knew the very large Addison Mizner. He was instantly recognizable walking down the street, with his enormous height and weight, his slight limp, his nimble hands and feet, and his favorite monkey, Johnnie Brown, perched on his shoulder. (He hated wearing formal clothes, but Alex Waugh's story that he was the first to wear his shirt outside his trousers was never proven in photographs and was emphatically denied by Alice DeLamar.)

The stream of visitors to Villa Mizner was constant. Addison started each season with a traditional eggnog party on New Year's Day, playing his favorite game: putting High Society and Bohemia together. Thus in Addison's glowing living room, the grandes dames of Palm Beach would rub shoulders with young ladies from the Broadway stage, and if enough champagne was flowing, all was well. Addison had arrived in Palm Beach at the beginning of Prohibition, and with the enforcement of the Volstead Act in 1919, paradoxically, much more liquor tended to flow at social gatherings. "Now, no-one seems to be welcome unless they have their legs braided around their hat before they get to a party," he commented in the locution of the day. He himself "dipped the beak" sparely, having seen its ravages on friends and family, and after a bad experience with cocaine, he never took it again. Bedford, his valet, served the drinks at the Mizner parties, usually rum cocktails served in antique silver mugs, and seldom two to any one guest. "They came there for talk and friendship, not for booze," Alex Waugh observed.

Addison was on everyone else's invitation list. He was on committees welcoming visiting royalty; he was an essential participant in fancy-dress balls. The winter colony, whether they were his clients or not, loved having darling Addie to dinner and listening to his outrageous stories or encouraging him to make a wicked quip at some poor dumbbell's expense.

While many new friends found their way to the gala evenings at Villa Mizner, among his old friends there were some notable absences. Tessie Oelrichs came to Palm Beach during the winter season of 1918–19 to organize a building fund for a hospital (reports of her visit do not mention Paris Singer's plans, but presumably there was a connection) and succeeded in raising $5,000 at a large benefit dinner. But a year or so later, increasingly vulnerable to "the curse of the Fairs" (i.e., alcohol), she went to Paris, supposedly to avoid Prohibition. Returning to Newport as a recluse, she shut herself up in Rosecliff behind barred windows and died there in 1926.[6] Alva Belmont also gave Palm Beach a wide berth. She continued her women's suffrage activities in New York and then in 1924 also moved to France, where she bought and began restoring an old chateau near Fontainebleau, a project that absorbed her until her death in 1933.

When he had lived in New York among these wealthy philistines, Addison was in the habit of masking his artistic and musical sensibilities, disliking pretension and preferring his image as a roughneck Californian. But now at his soirées he began to let down his guard. One year his old friend the Metropolitan Opera star Frances Alda sang for him in front of three hundred guests. Alda was just the kind of person who appealed to Addison. She could sing beautifully. She was also witty, iconoclastic, and sharp-tongued (once calling Kirsten Flagstad "that Norwegian peasant").

Unhappily married to the Met's director, Giulio Gatti-Casazza, the singer had known the Stotesburys in New York and sung at a benefit concert at the Met for them during World War I. She was also a friend of the great soprano Mary Garden, who, according to Addison, once came to Villa Mizner and sang for him alone.

Addison's love of music was allowed free rein during these halcyon years. One season he had the New York String Quartet play every afternoon for two weeks. He later wrote about the concerts with uncharacteristic emotion. "They sat in the middle of the great Gothic room, with the lights on their music stands as the only illumination, and played divinely, as daylight died through the soft tints of the colored glass. People came in quietly, without greetings, and sank into big chairs, and one felt medieval as the footman stole about lighting great cathedral candles here and there." This was the atmosphere he most enjoyed evoking, and he worked to achieve it both for himself and for his clients. It was the ultimate justification, the apotheosis of his architecture.

But some evenings were not so poetic. On one occasion, after a performer called in sick, Addison arranged through an agent for an unknown Argentine tenor to perform. As usual, on the appointed evening his room was filled with music lovers, including Frances Alda and Jerome Kern. The tenor was to sing some Argentine folk songs, but as soon as he opened his mouth, he let out a yap "that no amount of bicarbonate of soda could sweeten," Addison recalled. "It was probably the most horrible sound I had ever heard." He managed to stop the concert by telling everyone the place was on fire.

Popular music also had a fond place in Addison's world. Jerome Kern was one of his inner circle. Kern was often a guest of the Donahues (of the Woolworth fortune) and liked to gamble at Bradley's while working on his musicals.[7] Addison also became friendly with the popular novelist Arthur Somers Roche, many of whose stories were made into movies in the 1920s and 1930s, one of the most famous being *Star of Midnight* (1935), starring Ginger Rogers and William Powell. Roche, whose ribald, bon-vivant personality was very close to Addison's heart, had first come to Palm Beach in 1919 with his wife, singer Ethel Pettit, at the invitation of Florenz Ziegfeld, who was taking a working vacation. (Roche spent much of his time in Palm Beach and died there in 1935.) Addison's old friend from New York, Marie Dressler, first invited down by Joe Riter, was also a fixture of the Palm Beach season.

But the most famous musical artist who descended on Palm Beach in the 1920s was Irving Berlin. He felt he could relax there. On one occasion, in 1924, when he came with Dorothy Parker, artist Neysa McMein, and producer Sam Harris, he was inspired to write the song "Lazy," about the dubious pleasures of idleness.[8] Berlin, like the others, was drawn to Addison's society. Addison claimed, no doubt wrongly, that Berlin composed two or three hits at the Villa Mizner piano.

Palm Beach was Irving Berlin's favorite vacation place as a bachelor, according to his daughter, Mary Ellin Barrett. But after he married Ellin Mackay in a scandalous elopement, things changed. Ellin had visited Palm Beach before the marriage, and she came back with Berlin afterward. She and Addison got along, helped by a San Francisco connection: she was the granddaughter of John Mackay, the mining partner of Tessie Oelrichs's father, James G. Fair. (Ellin's father, Clarence Mackay, who forbade the marriage, lived at Harbor Hill, twenty minutes from Addison's house in Port Washington.) But having married a Jew, she (and her husband) came up against the ugly fact that they were not welcome at the Everglades Club.* Moreover, even without the anti-Semitism, Clarence Mackay's supporters in town froze out the couple. After the first few visits with his young bride, Irving Berlin came back occasionally by himself to work, but never with his family.[9]

While Addison was a friend of Berlin's in Palm Beach, Wilson had known him in New York since at least 1909, when Berlin was writing songs for a music publisher, the Ted Snyder Company. Wilson once told Berlin a story about a man who wrote a strange will to imaginary lovers and children—which inspired the Berlin song "When I Leave the World Behind."[10] In 1913 the two men collaborated on a spoof performance of the Great American Drama, *The Get-Away, by Gorge Broadthirst*. When Wilson introduced Irving Berlin to Alex Waugh in Palm Beach, Wilson said, "Hey Limey" (the name he always called Waugh), "this is Irving Berlin, and I've just been telling him that if he ever writes music as well as he slung hash, we'll make something of him yet." Wilson's allusion to Berlin's early days as a waiter in New York delighted the songwriter. Wil-

---

*It is interesting to note, in this context, that Paris Singer's father was Jewish. The fact that the founder of the Everglades Club had Jewish blood is an irony that seems to have escaped most of the members.

son took Irving and Ellin Berlin to Gus' Bath, which had no exclusionary policies, along with Marie Dressler, Anita Loos (author of *Gentlemen Prefer Blondes*), her husband, John Emerson, Eleanor Chase (no relation to Ysabel), and his usual motley group of musicians, actresses, pickpockets, and jailbirds, who gathered there every night for drinks and gossip.[11] (Addison did not appear at these get-togethers, perhaps anxious to preserve his standing in the community.)

Again to be fair, Mama's Angel Birdie to some extent reformed after his arrival in Palm Beach. His first priority was to give up his cocaine habit. He got in touch with a doctor and nurse in New York, who sent him to a treatment expert. He came home after a week, looking a little the worse for wear, but clean. Addison was deeply impressed by his brother's reformation: "He did the most extraordinary thing, and my admiration is top for his grit." That Wilson stayed off cocaine completely is doubtful, but he certainly heeded Addison's threat that if he were ever found with drugs, he would be banished from Palm Beach.

Wilson also seemed willing to settle down to a job. Having moved into Addison's house on Worth Avenue, he started work as manager of the Los Manos Potteries. In Addison's biased recollection, Wilson did a fine job and made a marvelous success of it. A more jaundiced view was offered by Alex Waugh, who, *faute de mieux,* saw a lot of Wilson. He recalled a typical Wilson episode: Coming into the store one day, Alex found Wilson hard at work selling a rather ordinary Spanish table to his favorite customer—a sucker. He assured the buyer that the table was so rare that Addison would not want to sell it, for, according to Wilson, it had belonged to El Cid, and a scion of the house had been forced to sell it secretly to pay off debts, and that was why there was no authentication. Needless to say, the sucker bought the table at far above its market price.

In 1923 Wilson came back from a trip to California with a woman called Florence, whom he introduced to the community as his wife. If the notion of Wilson getting married seemed somewhat unlikely, nobody said anything. Couples, then as now, undoubtedly get invited out much more often than singles, and "Mr. and Mrs. Wilson Mizner" were soon seen together at the Everglades Club and other desirable destinations.

While Wilson frolicked and gambled the nights away, Addison somehow managed to keep his social engagements under control. He could not have continued his massive building program if he had been "dipping the beak" at musicales every night. He rose before six every morning, so he could get work done before office hours and before the endless stream of people pestered him for advice, decisions, revised plans, and so on. He would visit sites during the day and get home at five-thirty or later in the afternoon. Alex Waugh was awed by his self-discipline. "Those who knew him may find it difficult to believe that he was ever subject to discipline at all, still less discipline self-imposed," he wrote. "Bodily discipline, it is true, he never attempted. He could and did eat vastly too much, aiming to quell for a brief spell his raging ulcers. But, with things of the mind it was different indeed; the disciplines came into play and one could see them working in orderly progression on tried and proven principles, in architecture and in art."[12]

Although he was gregarious to a fault, Addison often claimed he could do with less social life. What he dreaded most was being stuck at a large seated dinner: "Once out of ten times you got someone amusing, but the other nine were like the dentist's chair to me." Of course, if one is in Palm Beach during the season, it is difficult to stay home, particularly a single man with as much charm and intelligence as Addison Mizner. "At a quarter to eight," he said, "when Bedford came in to tell me I was dining out, and where, I was always rebellious and dragged myself into the elevator about to die." But like all truly social animals, once he got to the party, he enjoyed it.

Addison had a tender heart. One day Wendell Weed, a rotund old man with a white beard, appeared out of the blue at the architect's house, destitute and, as some thought, mentally unhinged. Addison had known him once, a long time before, when the poor man was a respectable figure. The architect immediately took Weed under his protection, inventing a job for him as guard for the Via Mizner. Carrying a green golf umbrella, his wide girth swathed in a red cummerbund, and a fez on his head, Weed became an eccentric but endearing figure to Palm Beach residents.

Addison's generosity of spirit inspired intense devotion in those who were exposed to it. Weed would have gone to the North Pole for him. Louise Darry, the housekeeper who had worked for him in New York, wrote to him after seeing a photograph of him with his grand clients: "I trust this will find you looking as well and cheerful as you did when standing by Mrs. Munn in one of our dailies. . . . You deserve all the good that has come into your life, for one who has such a good heart as yours towards all."[13] His valet in Palm Beach, Arthur Bedford, was equally loyal and protective but kept a stern eye on his master. On one occasion, when they were on a trip together, Addison signed a hotel register for them both. Looking over Mizner's shoulder, Bedford said coolly, "There is only one 'l' in valet."

With social obligations, clients, family, and workers all clamoring for his attention, how did Addison have time for a private life? He had always been discreet, but now that he had become so successful, his love affairs, like his love of music, attracted notice. In his own writing, he mentions only the odd female liaison, such as his admiration for Peggy Thayer. The gossip columnists, tactful then as they would never be now, reported only on his architecture, his parties, and occasionally his monkeys. (Wilson was the easier mark; stories about his fistfights, entanglements with the law, and witticisms in the face of adversity had frequently entertained newspaper readers over the years.) Addison's public image as a tough-talking, earthy bon vivant was of a piece with his wish to remain undiscovered.

His mature sexual taste was for very young men. Not "rough trade" or sailors but pretty boys with pretensions, well dressed and well spoken, who could be fitted into his entourage and perform adequately at Palm Beach parties. The type is familiar; they come on to males for exploitation purposes, but ultimately they prefer females, having a basically conservative, not to say commercial, approach to life. Addison was highly susceptible to these creatures, and over the years a series of them sauntered into his heart, and he accorded them positions in the firm with titles like "secretary" and "office manager." They were mostly incompetent and caused numerous problems in the office, but over and over again Addison's emotions clouded his judgment and he paid the price. The relationships never lasted, and they caused him much private pain.

While the locals and his clients may have known something about these problematic romances, one friend was particularly sympathetic. Alice DeLamar was a philanthropist and patroness of the arts for whom Addison had built a house in 1922. Her father, a mining millionaire, had left her $10 million on his death in 1918, and she moved to Palm Beach to start an arts community and to support other artistic and theatrical causes. Very shy, she kept her philanthropy a secret and did not play much of a role in the social goings-on of the colony, but she developed a close friendship with Horace Chase, whose dashing high spirits appealed to her. Through him she saw a great deal of Addison during his years in Florida.

Alice loved women and had an intimate friend for many years called Lucia Davidova, a Russian emigré singer and dancer. But Alice's deepest feelings were for the actress Eva Le Gallienne. Le Gallienne had affairs with many women, but she did not find Alice sexually compelling; she allowed her pale, serious young admirer to pay her bills, fund her plays, and generally act as her patroness but did not physically return the favor. Alice was resigned to this chilly treatment from her beloved and never wavered in her devotion. When she died in 1983, she left Le Gallienne a handsome legacy.[14] Perhaps Alice's situation made her particularly sensitive to Addison's fate. "Addison wore his heart on his sleeve," she said. "He was extremely vulnerable and his emotional adjustments were not happy ones, and he was taken for some rides in this respect. He often laid himself wide open to it."[15]

One of the most notorious of Addison's "pocket-sized Adonises," as Alice called them, was Jack Roy, whom Addison had hired in the early 1920s as "secretary" and "office manager." In 1922, when Wilson showed up and concocted the short-lived moving-picture industry, Roy was made secretary of the company. "I trusted Roy about as far as I could throw a cat," Alice said, "but he was tolerably well-mannered and exceedingly well-dressed and dapper, and in a seasonal resort like this an 'extra man' can always fill the ranks on any party."

Alice thought better of Wilson's wife, Florence: "A rather passably pleasant and good looking woman, somewhat indolent perhaps, but nobody's fool. She was cooperative about the project of getting Wilson pulled together and rehabilitated as he was already something of a legend as a 'grand old ruin.'" But after two years in Palm Beach, during the off-season doldrums, Florence became restless. Her eye settled on twenty-three-year-old Achille Angeli, one of two Italian brothers whom Addison had brought from Italy to paint Renaissance-style frescoes in his houses. They had worked on the restoration of the Davanzati Palace in Florence and were skilled copiers of fine art. Achille Angeli was also very handsome. It was not only Florence's eye but also Addison's that rested fondly on Achille's slender form. According to Alice, all the male decorators in Palm Beach pursued Achille, "but they were barking up wrong trees."

So, indeed, was Florence. Frustrated, she looked around for a more kindred spirit—then suddenly vanished from Palm Beach, leaving no forwarding address. The disappearance of Addison's "secretary," Jack Roy, was noted shortly afterward. A few weeks later it was learned that they had married in Jacksonville. The most shocking conclusion that the Palm Beach colony had to digest was that Florence and Wilson had never been married at all!

Whether Addison was distressed at the loss of Jack Roy is not recorded. Since he was the last person to indulge in self-pity, he no doubt took the long view and worried more about the effect of the scandal on his business. Florence Atkinson (her real name) had been an old girlfriend of Wilson's, and Addison may have known all along that they were not man and wife. As for Wilson, he was already happily distracted by other women in town, including Anita Loos and Eleanor Chase, both of whom were seriously in love with him. Anita Loos (who never met Florence Atkinson in Palm Beach) found Wilson irresistible.[16] She openly flirted with him and later wrote a lyrical description of the "aging reprobate" in her book *Kiss Hollywood Goodbye*. She confessed she found everything about him exciting: "the aura of his reckless past; the challenge of his being a highly unsuitable companion: his air of tranquil assurance, which, as a rule, exists only in men of genius."[17] Later, when Wilson moved to Hollywood, Loos spent almost all her time with him until his death. Eleanor Chase, who shared Loos's adulation, kept trying to reform Wilson and so was not so popular with him. (She later deserted the Mizner camp and married the competition—Maurice Fatio, an elegant Swiss-born architect who followed in Addison's footsteps and became the leading house-builder in Palm Beach.)

Anita Loos was no slouch when it came to men, so perhaps there was more to Wilson Mizner than his rather off-color behavior and cruel humor imply; his qualities may have simply become murky with the passage of time. Writer Jim Tully believed that Wilson had had an experience in Alaska that had traumatized him. (Could the murder-suicide in Dawson have been the basis for this theory?) Certainly Wilson's bitterness about his gold-rush years sometimes spilled out into the open. For instance, he was enraged by Jack London's success, calling him a "damned romantic liar." He always aggressively asserted that there were no heroes, only cowards, in those days in the Klondike. Tully concluded that beneath Wilson's nonchalant, wisecracking exterior lay a lonely, angry man.[18]

Today Wilson's repartee, for which he was most acclaimed, seems very dated. Admittedly, what in a bar seems hilarious can look very labored on the page. Like Addison's, Wilson's wit was ephemeral, and its slangy vulgarity now seems deeply unfunny. Typical lines on Hollywood: "A ride through a sewer in a glass-bottomed boat"; and the more famous "Never give a sucker an even break." On the writing game: "If you steal from one author, it's plagiarism; if you steal from many, it's research." One of his funnier remarks was, on hearing of the death of Stanley Ketchel, the boxer whom he had once managed, "Count ten over him, then he'll get up." Bennett Cerf called Wilson "a genuinely tough hombre—with a magnificent sense of humor." Damon Runyon described him as "the greatest man-about-town any town ever had." We'll have to take their word for it.

For Addison, Wilson's presence in Palm Beach presented the usual mixture of vexation and affection. Yet despite Wilson's increasingly corrupt activities, in some ways the two aging bachelor-brothers remained strikingly compatible. Their shared background, their debunking wit, and their ironic sense of humor created an intense bond between them that they could not replicate with others. They loved to talk about old times in what Paris Singer called "Tavern English," feeding each other lines, in competition for the Most Profane Language prize. Wilson was a little taller than his brother, and a lot thinner. The two of them together must have looked like a magnified version of Laurel and Hardy. Alice DeLamar saw how much Addison protected his brother and was proud of his achievements. But she felt Wilson was an unsavory character. "I can see [him] as though it were yesterday," she wrote, "leaning over the iron balcony of the house where he lived on Worth Avenue, in bare feet and a preposterous wrinkled night shirt that hung to his hairy knees, a four day growth of unshaven beard adorning his chin, and obviously nurturing a devastating hangover."[19]

Addison and Wilson, Wilson and Addison. Sooner or later the pair of Mizner sluggers were destined to try some new lark, some new scheme that would hit the jackpot. But their final show together ended in disaster. A melodrama with amateur gangsters and incompetent felons, like characters out of Wilson's plays, it played out in the sun and heat of southern Florida.

CHAPTER 18

"THE GENIUS OF PLANNERS, POET OF ARCHITECTS, FOREMOST THINKER OF THE FUTURE."

If Addison's early masterpiece was the Stotesburys' El Mirasol, the achievement of his late work was Playa Riente, which Ida M. Tarbell called "one of the most perfect great houses in America." It was built in 1923 for Joshua and Nell Cosden. Cosden, once a Baltimore streetcar conductor, had made millions in Oklahoma oil. (He made and lost several fortunes over his lifetime.)[1] Finding Palm Beach hospitable to their somewhat *nouveau* origins, the Cosdens bought a site on the ocean ridge, the only piece of property on North Ocean Boulevard that did not have a road separating it from the ocean. This commission was a gift for Mizner, and as usual, he responded with relish.

"I worked all night on an old Gothic palace," he said about the house, "built out into the sea, with a great Gothic hallway, with a vista from the front door straight through to the ocean, and a stairway leading up to the main floor, which was to occupy the top of the ridge."

This overnight vision was realized almost perfectly; Addison asserted that the house was never changed from these original sketches. It was originally called Guardiola, but its fame rested on its second name, Playa Riente (a Spanish-Italian hybrid meaning "Laughing Beach"). Three times the size of El Mirasol, it was indeed a Gothic palace. At the north end of the sixty-foot entrance hall, a "flying" staircase reminiscent of Stanford White's at Rosecliff, richly ornamented with wrought iron, led to the *piano nobile*. One wing, facing east over the ocean and west onto a large patio, contained the main living room. It had biscuit-yellow walls and an ornately coffered, color-washed ceiling. Below antique Spanish ceiling brackets hung valances made of fifteenth-century red velvet. For this room Addison and Nell Cosden bought a huge yellow carpet with flower decorations, made in 1595 by nuns in a convent near Granada for the city's cathedral.

The opposite wing contained a dining room with ceiling and frescoed walls painted by Frederico and Achille Angeli, the artist-brothers whom Addison had imported from Florence after Nell Cosden admired their restoration work at the Davanzati Palace. The Angelis' frescoes also decorated Nell's bedroom and private loggia, where a "Juliet" balcony jutted out over the ocean. (The frescoes were so greatly admired that Achille Angeli was hired to paint a mural entitled *Defeat of the Spanish Armada* for the Everglades Club dining room, which he completed in 1925.)

The most dramatic room was the ballroom (also called the music room), which had wall panels painted by the well-known Spanish artist José María Sert. (Sert also designed a lantern that was 8 feet high and 2½ feet wide for the ballroom.) The long rectangular panels, depicting events in the life of Sinbad the Sailor, were painted over silver leaf, with trompe l'oeil draperies of crimson velvet lined with silver hanging down the sides. Through these open "curtains" were revealed scenes of people, animals, trees, and oceans all tumbling about, creating an almost cinematic effect.

The panels had first been exhibited to great acclaim at the Wildenstein Gallery in New York. During the show, Sert, no stranger to self-promotion, made the following remarks to the press: "Your self-made American, unlike the European profiteer and parvenu, has an extraordinary idea of what is in good taste. Now Mr. Cosden, for example, he is a self-made man, and therefore has made his money through his own intelligence. I wouldn't say he was a connoisseur but he certainly has a sense of beauty."[2] Joshua Cosden was no doubt gratified by that modest compliment. He was certainly pleased with Sert's panels, which gave the house a cachet beyond any other in Palm Beach and were the topic of every dinner party.

Compared to the exhilarating interior, the gardens were striking in their restraint. The west-facing front of the house, with its two wings, cloisters (with gargoyles), and colonnaded veranda, looked out onto a rectangular ornamental pool, flanked by vast expanses of austere and expensive lawn. The ocean side featured a long stone terrace along the beachfront, with two graceful staircases rising up the seawall to the main patio.

Perhaps the most inspired idea that came to Addison the night he designed the house was to install a tunnel running from the west front to the other side of the building (similar to the floor-through hall of an English Georgian country house), leading out to the bathhouses and beach. The house's entryway was on the level of the ocean ridge, so that from the Moorish-style front door, one had a clear view of the sea through this ground-level tunnel. (Mizner liked the tunnel and designed another one in 1924 for Paul Moore's house, Collado Hueco. Moore's son, Bishop Paul Moore, remembered spending winters there: "We had an elaborate place, complete with tennis court, swimming pool [and] a tunnel under the road to our own beach.")[3]

For many connoisseurs, Playa Riente was the consummation of Addison's art. But its extravagant beauty was also its undoing. The Cosdens, who had so lovingly and meticulously put the house together with their architect, were able to enjoy it for only three short years. Then Joshua Cosden suffered serious financial reverses and was forced to sell the house in 1926. The buyer was Mrs. Horace E. Dodge, widow of the car manufacturer, who paid $2.8 million. Hugh Dillman, who represented Mrs. Dodge at the sale, married her three weeks later. Dillman was twenty years younger than his bride, but that kind of statistic raised few eyebrows in Palm Beach circles. The Dillmans immediately hired Addison to add a servants' wing and a patio at a cost of $160,000.*

With the completion of Playa Riente, Palm Beach was recognized as the residential capital of Florida's Gold Coast, with Addison Mizner its presiding genius. "As Florida has much the same climate as Santa Barbara and Pasadena," wrote a critic in *Architectural Forum*, "although lacking the romantic background of the Spanish mission, the architec-

---

*The couple divorced after quite a long run, in 1947.[4] In 1957 Mrs. Dodge (having reverted to her former name) put all the contents of the house up for auction, and ordered the house to be razed to the ground. There was much local anguish over this ruthless destruction of an unrivaled piece of architecture. The sale was emotional—more than 1,150 items went, including rare Flemish tapestries, an Aeolian pipe organ, several masterpieces of Venetian furniture, and a portrait attributed to Velázquez. The nine Sert panels were also sold (and are now in the Detroit Art Museum); the Angeli frescoes went the way of the sledgehammer.

ture of Southern Europe is equally suitable here."[5] Others concurred. "Like the far-famed gardens of Seville, with the architectural embellishments which distinguish the Sevillian type from those of Cordova and Grenada, the patios of Palm Beach are invested with comparable charm. . . . Addison Mizner . . . is the wizard who has created this illusion of Andalusian splendor."[6]

The only sour note was sounded by the young architect Howard Major.* Architects are notoriously competitive, and perhaps jealousy of Mizner's seemingly unassailable position caused Major to write an article slamming Spanish architecture in Florida (although avoiding mentioning Mizner by name): "Personally I consider the houses, and particularly the small, so-called Spanish and Italian buildings, nothing more than aberrations." Amusingly, while denigrating the Spanish/Italian idioms, Major clung to an equally historicist taste, promoting what he called "our national style. . . . The houses of 18th century Charleston, with verandas and balconies for each floor, are most fittingly suited for Florida's climate."[8]

Although the drumbeat of modernism was syncopating its way through the rest of the United States by this time, the severe lines of Gropius, Le Corbusier, and Mies van der Rohe were alarming to many Americans, who were reluctant to adopt anything so progressive. Initial reaction to the new streamlined look of European furniture and furnishings at the Paris Exhibition des Arts Décoratifs et Industriels Modernes in 1925 was muted. Richardson Wright, the influential editor of *House & Garden,* said of the furniture, "The pieces look elephantine and out of proportion. . . . They appear to have been made for people who are very much overweight." And in her seminal book *American Homes of Today,* Augusta Owen Patterson firmly asserted that "no especial disgrace attaches to Americans in being unable to invent anything architectural in the one hundred and forty-nine years of our natural existence, when

---

*Major had come to find work in Palm Beach and was originally given jobs on Mizner's projects. When Gurnee Munn, for instance, was having work done on his house, he realized that Addison was overextended and asked whether the architect might delegate someone to supervise the painting of the walls, woodwork, and so forth. "How about Mr. Major?" he asked. "Mrs. O'Brien spoke most highly of his taste and ability when she was here last week."[7] Mrs. Stotesbury also used Howard Major when Addison was unavailable.

we consider that in the two thousand five hundred years since the building of the Parthenon, there have only been four outstanding codifications of the orders."[9]

So it appeared that Addison Mizner would not be toppled. Fashion writers joined the fan club. "Next to white in favor for millinery, as well as other wearing apparel, is the 'Mizner yellow,' " trilled a reporter in the *Palm Beach Daily News*. "It is a shade between the mimosa and the apricot and has found favor because of its almost universal becomingness."[10] Mizner's name was so influential that at least one client thought that by claiming him as her architect, she could get into the Everglades Club.

Addison was also getting rich. The price of his houses was escalating daily. El Sarimento, built for A. J. Drexel Biddle, Jr.; El Solano, the house Harold Vanderbilt bought from Addison, with its new additions; and Edward Moore's Sin Cuidado were all million-dollar projects in today's currency. For all these houses, the architect's special building materials were required—bricks, tiles, pecky cypress, wrought iron. The interiors had to be fully furnished with antiques (or reproduction antiques), damasks, velvets, and tapestries. In a virtual monopoly, Addison Mizner, through Mizner Industries and Los Manos Potteries, supplied the lot. Mizner mania was at its height. Every winter visitor, it seemed, wanted his own piece of oceanfront land with a Mizner house on it, regardless of the price.

Some commentators began to be anxious about the rapid development. "It is with mixed emotions," wrote one columnist, "that those who know and love Palm Beach regard the entirely unprecedented building which has taken place since last year. . . . Many there are who wonder, frankly, that the place will not be spoiled . . . and that Palm Beach will become so eroded and congested as to make it an undesirable place to live."[11] But few listened. Addison was unstoppable—and so was Florida real estate.

In the mid-1920s the increasing demand for land in southern Florida sent a clear signal to real estate developers. Carl G. Fisher, a wealthy entrepreneur, constructed the Dixie Highway, a major arterial road that took tourists from the north down to Miami Beach, which he was turning into a popular vacation resort. Another developer, George E. Merrick, had the same idea for Coral Gables. State promoters encouraged this trend, urging tourists to invest in desirable Florida real estate.

Like old hunting dogs, Addison and Wilson Mizner heard the familiar gold rush call. They had grown up in the paradoxical logic of frontier fever, and it made perfect sense to them. But Florida offered profits that would have been unthinkable in 1900. In the Klondike, retrieving the gold had been an almost prohibitively slow and labor-intensive effort. But in southern Florida, all you had to do was put down stakes, as their father had done in Benicia, and come up with dollar bills.

In mid-1924 Addison and Wilson proposed to construct Mizner Mile, which was to be a strip of development in Boynton Beach, a few miles south of Palm Beach. Summoning up his trademark Spanish castles and a two-thousand-room hotel, Addison insisted that Mizner Mile would be a surefire financial and architectural success. He had seen the demand his houses had created in Palm Beach. Moreover, he had discovered a new talent with the planning of the streetscapes of Via Mizner and Via Parigi. Why not go further and plan a whole town?

The Mizner Mile proposal was Addison's greatest gamble so far, a foray into speculative real estate—about which he knew nothing. Wilson knew even less, but the idea fed directly into his talents as a fast-talking salesman and professional hustler. He threw himself enthusiastically into his brother's new scheme.

But these amateur developers immediately ran into trouble. Ocean Road happened to run along the beach where they planned to build Mizner Mile. But direct access to the beach was essential to the project. How do you move a highway? The Mizners' solution was to build a bypass, then dig up the slice of Ocean Road on which they wanted to build. Over the protests of the mostly Finnish farmers in the line of fire, they went ahead with the bypass. The next step was to dig up Ocean Road, which Wilson with a hired crew attempted to do in the middle of the night. But the bulldozers were stopped by angry Finns. Emilie Keyes, the local society reporter of the period, said that Wilson, presumably partying earlier that evening, had arrived to do his dastardly deed dressed in a silk hat, white tie, and tails.[12]

The outrageousness of this plan could only have originated with Wilson, and since he, as well as Addison, had invested heavily in the project, he was particularly enraged at this setback. For over a year, he kept Mizner Mile alive, fending off litigation, sending letters to the Boynton Beach city officials arguing for its reinstatement, and writing position papers pointing out its potential for their city. "In addition to this vast improvement, those interested in the Mizner Mile plan to fill in those swamps which extend its entire length along Lake Worth. These swamps are the breeding place of most of Boynton's mosquitoes . . ." etc., etc. But his pleas fell on deaf ears, and the project collapsed.*

In March 1925 Henry Flagler's flagship hotel, the Breakers, burned down for the second time, signaling the end of wooden hotels in the region. (The new fireproof hotel, designed by Schultze & Weaver, reopened in 1926.) Less than a month later, on April 21, 1925, Karl Riddle, a city engineer hired by Addison, opened a new office in Palm Beach with two draftsmen. On May 5 the news broke: A grand hotel, the Ritz-Carlton, was going to be built in Boca Ratone (sic) by a new company, the Mizner Development Corporation, under the leadership of Addison Mizner. The New York architect, Warren Whitmore, who had designed New York's Ritz-Carlton Hotel, was to be brought in as consultant.

Boca Ratone? Is that how it was spelled? Where exactly was it? People vaguely understood it to be a small farming community south of Palm Beach, where fruit and vegetables were shipped north on the Florida East Coast Railway. Was it intended to replace the Breakers? What was Addison Mizner up to?

On May 31 a huge double-page advertisement appeared in the local newspapers announcing an offering of residential lots in Boca Raton (now having lost the *e*) by the Mizner Development Corporation. The lots, readers were told, were the choicest on the east coast of Florida: "The landscaping and shrubbery planned will exceed in color and splendor any townside development ever conceived in Florida." The advertisement also promised, "Every building in this residential area will be architecturally supervised by Addison Mizner." Recognizing that Mizner had built houses for "men of large affairs," the advertisement promised readers that "the man with a small winter cottage can say that Addison Mizner, who has built the most exclusive homes in Palm Beach, is also the architect of his modest home, for every building, whether large or

---

*In 1925, in an effort at conciliation, Addison built a women's club in Boynton Beach at a cost of $50,000. It still stands today: it has a fine double-width vertical-beamed pecky cypress ceiling, fine light fixtures, and generously proportioned public rooms.

small, will have the attention and approval of Mr. Mizner." A map of the plats was published, showing the golf course, the access roads, and the development's situation vis-à-vis Lake Boca Raton and the Atlantic Ocean. Another helpful map showed Boca Raton's location in relation to Palm Beach and Miami.

At the bottom of the advertisement, to reassure the doubtful, was a list of approximately one hundred stockholders in the corporation, including most of Addison's Palm Beach clients, along with the duchess of Sutherland, Peggy Thayer, Paris Singer, two Vanderbilts, and T. Coleman du Pont, a real estate entrepreneur who had briefly been senator from Delaware, from 1921 to 1923.[13]

Boca Raton was going to be, as the publicity said, "The First Tailor-Made City in All The World." Following the appearance of this sensational piece of news, the newspapers were flooded with more advertisements, not only about Boca Raton and the Mizner Development Corporation but about other extraordinary land-investment opportunities, including George W. Harvey's copycat Villa Rica, which promised a train station and exclusively Spanish architecture (but without the Mizner name). So many other offers were advertised that the Mizner Development Corporation announced that it was "not associated in any way or responsible for the promises of any other development in or out of Boca Raton."

The excitement was palpable. Addison's announcement confirmed what many Americans had come to believe: that southern Florida was the new El Dorado. People were pouring into the state, it was calculated, at five times the rate of the nineteenth-century migration to California. Florida! Not the least of its charms in these Prohibition days was that Miami was near wet Havana, wet Bimini, and wet Nassau. Bootleggers disguised themselves as fishermen, and locals frequently saw limousines lining up at wharves supposedly to collect a great "catch." The Florida land boom became more and more frenetic.[14] Instant books enthusiastically described the advantages of living in Florida, where the climate was such that one could "save money on fruit and overcoats." It was the only frontier state left, and "the Floridian who fails to make money out of the state's growth should have his head examined for osseous formations."[15]

The Mizner brothers had no intention of growing osseous formations.

The Mizner Development Corporation opened offices in Miami, Lake Worth, Tampa, Jacksonville, and New York. Buses were hired to take prospective buyers to Boca Raton. A professional marketing and promotion expert, Harry Reichenbach, moved down to Palm Beach to write the increasingly fevered copy for the newspapers. (Wilson brought in an old Barbary Coast chum to be butler for Mrs. Reichenbach, but at an engagement party for Maurice Fatio and Eleanor Chase, the new help went into a trance on the floor, causing Wilson to say, "He's only had a little too much cut glass [dope]." The butler turned out to be a drug addict, recently out of jail for manslaughter.)[16]

The corporation sold the Boca Raton lots in a way that only accelerated the inflationary frenzy. Buyers had to put down only a small deposit, a "binder," which was provisional on establishing title. Meanwhile, the binder-holders could resell their lots at a higher price. As the boom escalated, lots changed hands twenty or more times, each time increasing in theoretical value until the paper fortunes were enormous. To allow the deals to take place even faster, legalities were finessed. The Mizner Development Corporation brazenly declared, "You may have this advertisement attached to and made a part of your contract or deed." Follow-up promotional material, mostly written by Reichenbach (who came up with "The Tailor-Made City"), proclaimed that the corporation's initial offering had broken all records, and that after the May 14 announcement, over $2 million worth of lots had been sold.

The offering was a triumph, and the credit went in large part to one portly architect, the darling of the media. Addison's name and picture were splashed all over the newspapers: "ADDISON MIZNER, who created the magnificent winter homes, regal clubs and resplendent casinos of Palm Beach . . ." "ADDISON MIZNER, the visionary creator of a city with Every Atom of Beauty that Human Ingenuity Can Add to a Land Endowed By Nature . . ." "ADDISON MIZNER, the Builder of a Dream City in the Western World . . ." "ADDISON MIZNER, the Genius of Planners, Poet of Architects, Foremost Thinker of the Future."

Wherever Addison appeared, the press and photographers flocked to get close to him. Surrounded by chows and monkeys, he was the Pied Piper of the land boom. His serene expression and baby face added to his mystique. He represented the dreams of thousands of Americans, who yearned to be recipients of his bounty, his promise to transform their drab and dreary lives into a flowery landscape of beauty and romance. (Mizner was not alone: his colleague and rival, Maurice Fatio, was infected by the frenzy, drawing up plans for "Olympia-Picture City," to be built in what is now Hobe Sound.)

Not even Palm Beach itself was immune. On Worth Avenue, a school was opened for "high pressure salesmen." Anyone who felt like it, licensed or not, could open an office to sell lots. Horace Chase said that the easiest way to commit suicide was to stand on a street corner and say, "I want to buy a lot," and be mobbed to death by eager realtors.

One noticeable absentee from the action was Paris Singer. Although listed in the original advertisement (his name obviously a useful lure), Singer had embarked on a separate development—his own never-never-land—and played no part in Boca Raton. He had bought a small island opposite Lake Worth, where he envisioned a development more glamorous and luxurious than even Mizner had come up with: a multimillion-dollar resort, with two huge hotels, a thirty-six-hole golf course, and very highly priced residential lots. Tunnels, aerial ferries, and drawbridges would connect his island to Lake Worth. The Blue Heron Hotel, with designs by Mizner, would be the most luxurious ever built. To appease resentful locals, he assured them there would be an ocean development with "a popularly-priced beach for all the people."[17]

Singer, who had spent a large part of his fortune on unprofitable building ventures, was banking on the sale of the island lots to fund the project. But while he was away, an overeager realtor sold all the lots for between $4,000 and $20,000. Singer could have sold them for a much higher price. On his return, he insisted on doubling the purchase price to the binder-holders. But they either could not or would not pay. Work on the Blue Heron soon came to a grinding halt and with it the whole project. The service wing of the hotel was the only part of the building ever completed. (In sad recognition of this crazy venture, the island on which he had built his hopes was later named Singer Island.)

While Singer struggled to keep his project warm, Mizner's development plans were becoming as overheated as the Florida summer. Announcements of the Ritz-Carlton Hotel continued to dazzle. A $6 million budget would produce the most elegant hostelry in the country. How could the plan not be fulfilled, with the backing of Mizner's tame millionaires along with Irving Berlin, Frances Alda, and other celebrities?

As if one hotel were not enough, a smaller version called the Cloister was already breaking ground, to be ready for the January 1926 season. Construction contracts for widening inlets, building jetties, and laying twenty miles of streets were announced. The Florida East Coast Railway approved plans for a charming Spanish-style railway station.

Taking a moment out of the frantic activity, Addison wrote to his brother Henry, urging him to come and share in the excitement of Boca Raton. In particular, Addison wanted to build a cathedral in memory of Mama Mizner, and he wanted Henry's advice. "I remember your difficulties with your Bishop," he said, "and I want to build one thing by my own pleasure without any interference from outside influences." Addison, deeply anticlerical, meant that he did not want the cathedral to have any religious affiliation. He would build a beautiful building with the very finest religious things in it, but it would belong to him, and if the Episcopal Church wanted to take it over after his death, well and good.[18]

Henry, his health declining, decided to take advantage of Addison's magnanimity and arrived, along with his wife and daughter, on his brother's doorstep. As plans for Boca Raton grew more and more ambitious, Addison came up with the idea of building Henry a church, as well as Mama Mizner's cathedral, providing God's work (and housing) for the whole family. Addison also produced plans for his own house in the Tailor-Made City—the most fanciful yet, a Spanish fortress on an island with a portcullis and moat, connected to the mainland by a drawbridge. Really.

But why stop there? Addison called on José María Sert to design a four-hundred-seat theater for the new city, which Sert visualized as "rather in the style of the unfinished Palace of Charles V near the Alhambra in Granada."[19] As well as being the new Alhambra, Boca Raton was also going to be the new Venice, with a Grand Canal and Byzantine palaces, even gondolas. The Venice angle became Wilson's project. "I found him one day in the Via Mizner," remembered Alex Waugh, "his huge frame pinning to a chair a little Italian, whose misfortune was either to manufacture gondolas or act as agent for those who did. He was describing to Wilson a state or ceremonial gondola. . . . But Wilson, his imagination fired, was bent on improving it with cocktail bars, food lockers and seats that would convert into beds." Waugh asked Wilson why this was necessary, since the Grand Canal was in fact only "a short stretch of ditch." "Why hell," Wilson answered, "with the miles of canals we plan to have, people could well be away for days."

The world's most magnificent road, El Camino Real—the King's Highway—two hundred feet wide with twenty traffic lanes, ran into the same problem as the proposed Grand Canal, however. It would actually run only half a mile, joining the scrub to the highway. But to Boca Raton's promoters, facts were becoming less and less important. For instance, there was a closed season for fishing in the fresh waters of Lake Okeechobee. But in order to promise fishermen year-round sport, the lake was suddenly pronounced salt water. Bad luck for the fish! Other miracles occurred. Pictures of glorious ranges of mountains appeared in sales brochures. *Mountains in Florida?*

But who cared? "Mizner and City Hold Love Feast at Boca Raton" ran a newspaper headline. Stories of million-dollar sales of land lit up the front pages. More ads were produced and articles written. "America's Moving to Florida!" the headlines shrieked. "The Coast of Heaven? Florida!" they cried. Celebrities poured in. The movie star Richard Barthelmess discussed plans to make a film in the new city. According to Alva Johnston, the still-notorious Evelyn Nesbit was brought down to sing "at a combination real-estate office and night club." (Did Wilson help arrange her visit?) Novelist Arthur Somers Roche, Addison's good friend, announced plans to start an artists' colony. Marie Dressler, transported from Palm Beach as hostess of the new venture, made confident noises to the press and was given the title "the Duchess of Boca Raton." Millionaire banker Otto Kahn added his name to the illustrious moguls enlisting in the cause. Even William Jennings Bryan, the famous presidential candidate and villain of the Scopes monkey trial, came to Coral Gables to give his support to the boom.

The Boca Raton project engineer, Karl Riddle, had his hands full. One of his earliest triumphs was to produce, with unusual speed, an aerial survey—the newest technology—of 18,000 acres of the undeveloped land.[20] A man of estimable efficiency, he hired numerous construction workers, dredgers, water experts, and electricians to keep up with the increasingly fanciful plans for Granada and Venice-on-the-Atlantic, as well as approximately seventy surveyors and other personnel. He sent sixty designers to Cuba for instruction in Spanish architecture, headed by Carlos Barragan-Dorcas, one of the chief architects on Mizner's team.[21] He obtained permits for the land and water improvements. He handled the interference of Addison's entourage, in particular Horace Chase, who had taken upon himself certain important responsibilities, such as assuring the quality of the grass for the golf course at the Cloister Inn. Addison tried to keep his hardworking engineer happy by building him a house in West Palm Beach. In his daily ledger, Riddle remained calm. "Work progressing nicely," the entries read.

Addison's own work schedule was unprecedented. He oversaw the layout of the city, which meant planning roads, parks, lot divisions and subdivisions, and so on. He drew up plans for the grand public buildings and private palaces that would lure the rich to the resort. Clients such as the Cosdens, for instance, asked him to design them a new mansion in Boca Raton that would rival in splendor their old one. He was also in charge of designing houses in a residential area of Boca Raton for the lesser mortals—executives, local residents, and high-level employees who would work in this imaginary paradise. He became an expert on human resources, which meant keeping Wilson and Horace from offending too many of his colleagues—no small matter. Even Baron Haussmann did not have such a weighty schedule when he transformed Paris in the 1860s. A man much younger than Addison, and in better health, would have flinched at the undertaking.

But the architect pushed on, unable and unwilling to stop. As master visionary, Addison had to keep on promoting Boca Raton, to keep everyone's confidence high, to keep those investors coming. In an address to one hundred salesmen in Palm Beach, he declared, "It is my plan to create a city that is direct and simple. . . . To leave out all that is ugly, to eliminate the unnecessary, and to give to Florida and the nation a resort city as perfect as study and ideals can make it." To a New York reporter, he asserted, "Boca Raton will be a city of sunshine and picturesque exclusion. It will fill a world need. . . . All of my life I have dreamed of building such a city. But the opportunity never presented itself until now. I am happier today than ever before in all of my life."[22]

In August 1925, as the final touches were being given to Addison's elegant design for the Mizner Development Corporation's administration building in Boca Raton, the company elected new officers: Anderson T. Herd as vice president and general manager, T. Coleman du Pont as chairman, and Jesse Livermore, a New York businessman, as head of the finance committee.

That same month a strange and ominous glitch occurred in the royal progress. To construct the huge number of buildings envisaged by Boca Raton's planners, an immense amount of building materials would have to be imported. In a startling announcement, the Florida East Coast Railway declared in August 1925 that freight congestion prevented any more deliveries into southern Florida except perishable goods. Spokesmen explained that there had been a catastrophic backlog in unloading the cars, which were stuck in the state's southern railyards and could not leave. Volunteers from Palm Beach rushed to try to unload the cars, but the embargo remained. A shortage of vegetables and ice, as well as overstressed utilities, made working through those late summer weeks almost unbearable.

In September Addison made a quick trip to New York to counteract northern skeptics, whose criticisms of the real estate hysteria in Florida were beginning to create a bad impression. "There is much talk about the Florida 'boom,'" Addison announced soothingly, "but so far as I can see there is no 'boom.' Land values are mounting steadily and large fortunes are being made exactly as they have been made in Los Angeles and New York. Property bought now will increase in value as improvements are made. There is nothing artificial about it."

But a note of unease was creeping into discussions of Florida real estate and Harry Reichenbach's escalating prose. On October 10, 1925, in a more urgent response, Florida Governor John W. Martin gave a speech at the Waldorf-Astoria in New York. In the presence of Baron Collier (a major developer of Florida's west coast), Coleman du Pont, and Jesse Livermore, he said that Florida wanted permanent residents, not speculators. His audience agreed, commenting on the damage done by the persistent advertising for Florida's "get-rich-quick schemes." Then Coleman du Pont got up to speak. "There are many people in Florida who are overstating things," he declared. "You have laws down there for that sort of thing and these people can be made amenable to them. I'd bag about four of them and give them the limit. That would discourage the rest."[23]

This was a direct hit at Reichenbach, but du Pont's remark was ignored. On November 6, 1925, the Mizner Development Corporation announced that October sales had reached $6.7 million, bringing the total to $26 million in twenty-four weeks! "Nowhere else in the history of big business has this accomplishment been paralleled!"[24] On November 8, hopeful participants were assured in further promotional advertisements that "Prosperity Will Be With Us For A Long, Long Time!"[25]

Then Coleman du Pont and Jesse Livermore resigned.

Du Pont's stated reason was "differences of opinion between him and the other directors about proper methods of business management and organization." What triggered his revolt was the fact that in the continuing flow of publicity stories, his name had been exploited without his permission, and he was furious. Reichenbach had gone too far.[26] Addison, while apologizing by wire, publicly shot back that "the differences between General du Pont and the directors are solely over the personnel of the directorate. He wanted some men on it and the directors wanted others." A few days later more directors resigned, complaining that the officers "refused to adopt the kind of management required to make the corporation a success."[27]

The most critical element to the success of any speculative venture is confidence. In public relations terms, these resignations were devastating. Reeling from the blow, Addison immediately announced a complete reorganization of the company, adding a distinguished new chairman, James F. Schapercotter, "a powerful figure in Northern financial circles who was largely responsible for the rise of the Lehigh Valley railroad," and the reassuring name of George D. Graham, chairman of the House Judiciary Committee and former justice of the supreme court of Pennsylvania. ("YOU MUST HAVE JUDGE GRAHAM HERE FOR MEETING MONDAY MATTER VERY GRAVE," Addison wired Wilson, who was in New York.)

In another effort at damage control, Addison threw a big Thanksgiving party in the newly completed administration building in Boca Raton, hosted by the company chairman's wife, Mrs. Anderson T. Herd. The new offices, located on the corner of the Dixie Highway and Camino Real, closely resembled El Greco's house in Toledo, Spain, with a small interior courtyard and a first-floor balcony. (Addison very much admired the artist's house and had collected several pictures of it in a scrapbook.) For the opening, the courtyard was decorated with massed containers of shrubs and palms, and some five hundred people partook of the buffet of turkey and other foods.

But that precious commodity, confidence, had been destroyed, and no Thanksgiving buffet amid the potted palms could restore it. From then on, it was a matter of stanching the wound that du Pont and his colleagues had inflicted upon the Mizner Development Corporation and its presiding genius. Thousands of investors were implicated, and the extent of the bloodbath was just beginning to emerge.

Amazingly, the whole wild ride had lasted only eight months.

CHAPTER 19

"WE SIMPLY DID NOT HAVE ENOUGH MONEY TO HOLD OUT."

For a while, it seemed that Boca Raton might yet have a chance. Reassuring statistics brought a brief flush to the pale faces of the financial analysts. For example, construction in Palm Beach County for the year 1925 had come to nearly $14 million, a figure unsurpassed in the county for forty years.[1] Karl Riddle continued to enter in his daybook, "Work progressing nicely." Clients continued to visit his office to check on their projects. Discussions were held about the location of roads, lights, and electrical wires.

The Cloister Inn opened as planned. (It was hastily renamed the Ritz-Carlton Cloister, and then back to the Cloister, as hopes that the actual Ritz-Carlton would ever materialize vanished into the Boca Raton dustbowl.) The directors of the Mizner Development Corporation gave their architect-hero a Rolls-Royce in gratitude for his work in completing the hotel in the face of the Florida embargo on materials. (He sold it two weeks later.)[2] "Addison Mizner is the Michelangelo of America," pronounced Alexander P. Moore, former ambassador to Spain, at the opening ceremony on February 1, 1926, attended by the usual suspects, including the Munns, the Cosdens, the Satterwhites, and the Claflins.

The inn had Mizner's signature layout—an enclosed interior courtyard, a tower, windows with *rejas,* and a cloister with unusual top-heavy columns that in the general chaos had been mistakenly installed upside down. (Addison insisted he liked them that way.) The entry was dominated by a huge Romanesque arch opening into a forty-foot-square lobby. There was a charming interior garden with a long rectangular canal reminiscent of the Generalife in Spain. Mizner used his usual design artillery: pecky cypress ceilings, a 40-by-84-foot vaulted dining

room with pastel-colored stained-glass windows whose light would flat-
ter the women, doorframes made of coral from the Florida Keys, "woodite" columns and balustrades, and antique Spanish furniture. The stair
risers were six inches high instead of the usual eight, to allow the ladies
to descend more easily and gracefully, a typical Mizner detail.

Another glamorous opening took place on February 6: a crew of new
faces were shipped in to join the old Palm Beach crowd in an attempt to
give last-minute ballast to Mizner's sinking vessel. One guest was a powerful echo from the past: Mrs. Stanford White. She announced to the
press afterward, "Since Stanford White there has been no one with such
exquisite sense of artistry. The building is superb." Maybe Addison
briefly found consolation in that accolade. His name had at last been
linked to the architect he so much admired.

In celebration of the opening and to keep up declining spirits, several
songs about Boca Raton were written. Irving Berlin reportedly wrote one,
but if he did, it did not survive. "Tango Cancion" by Murray and Mary
June Smith was dedicated to Addison and ran as follows:

> Spain, France and Italy, you are renowned,
> But here's one palace that I have found,
> Boca Raton, with a beauty all of your own,
> Boca Raton, in my dreams you stand all alone.
> Spanish delight, from your shore I never will roam,
> How I love you, I'm thinking of you, always my Boca Raton.[3]

Even if it had been a good song, it was not enough. The success of
the Cloister came too late. By the middle of 1926, the Boca Raton development project was a matter of saving face and waiting for the creditors.
Now not even Karl Riddle could keep the anxiety out of his diary: "Discussed possibility of laying off men. . . . McWare and others were in
about checks. . . . We notified all Boca Raton employees that after April
1st we could not guarantee payment of salaries." Recognizing the des-
perateness of the situation, Riddle even began exploring the possibility
of leasing the land for oil exploration.

Newspaper promotions continued to appear. The Mizner Development Corporation announced an entirely new scheme called Distrito de
Boca Raton, with fifty-eight ocean lots and a beach club between the

ocean and the intracoastal waterway, south of the Boca Raton inlet. The company promised that Mizner himself would approve all designs, and each oceanfront house would cost a minimum of $40,000 (worth almost nine times that in today's currency). In order to protect the beauty of the site, Mizner specified that the electrical wires would be buried underground, "an idea far ahead of its time for south Florida."[4] Plans for some of the luxury houses were drawn up, and Frances Alda, Irving Berlin, and Marie Dressler loyally put their names down for them.

In fact, the only Addison Mizner houses that ever actually got built in Boca Raton were a few he designed for the directors and employees of the company (and his brother Henry) in what is now Old Floresta. He produced ten different types of floor plans for these modest one- or two-story dwellings, with simple stucco facades and tile roofs, two or three bedrooms, loggias and decks, and large living rooms with grand stone chimneypieces—small versions, in effect, of his Palm Beach palaces. That El Mirasol, Playa Riente, and El Sarimento could be so successfully miniaturized shows once again how well Addison understood space and proportion.

But his design ideas were also remarkably progressive. He had grasped the aesthetic advantage of burying electrical wires underground. He also recognized the psychological consequences of designing an entire community—something that few planners saw as significant until after the Second World War. For instance, to avoid the homogenized, cookie-cutter effect of residential development, Addison made sure that similar floor plans were not sited on the same street. Prefiguring the New Urbanism of the late twentieth century, Old Floresta, with its tree-shaded streets and low-lying houses set back in nests of shrubbery, is the only extant example of Addison's town planning, and its charm and variety make one wonder what he would have achieved had the Boca Raton project ever come off.

Still, these small building projects could not mask the underlying instability of the situation. There were more resignations from the board. On April 30, 1926, Addison put his name to a balance sheet of the Mizner Development Corporation. It did not convince. Mizner Industries was almost closed down. "We simply did not have enough money to hold out, moral effect or not," said Addison's personal business manager, C. R. Crandall.

In May, Addison left for Europe on his usual buying trip. Perhaps he should not have gone. The list of his purchases from antiques dealers in Madrid, Granada, Seville, and Córdoba is staggering—antique embroideries, iron chandeliers, Gothic cupboards, refectory tables, jars, plates, *rejas,* fountains—the inventory of objects runs into the thousands. It was as though he had completely repressed the disaster back home. Roaring through the ancient Spanish cities, he thought only of having to furnish 650 rooms in the Cloister Inn and the houses of several clients for whom he still worked. The quality of the antiques was high; many of his merchants gave him certificates of authenticity. The bills were also high— antiquity is expensive.

The trip was cut short. The message finally reached him that there was no more money to pay for his hotel rooms or purchases. And in an alarming development back in Florida, various contractors who had not received payment were now beginning litigation against the company. The beleaguered architect hastened home.

In June 1926 a suit was filed in federal court by Guy C. Reed, a New York carpet manufacturer and minority stockholder, demanding that the Mizner Development Corporation be placed in receivership. "The affairs of the company are in such condition that they are not financially able to meet past obligations nor to fulfill promises made to purchasers of the Boca Raton development." Reed also claimed false advertising. Federal Judge Rhydon M. Call threw out the suit, declaring that the claim of mismanagement was not proven; but the negative publicity was lethal.[5]

Admitting defeat, in July the stockholders of the Mizner Development Corporation voted to hand over the company's financial and business management to Central Equities, a Chicago corporation. Negotiations had already been under way for six months. (On December 13, 1925, Karl Riddle wrote his last, terse diary entry: "Appointment with Central Equities.") Under the agreement, Addison Mizner was retained as president, as was the name of the corporation. Central Equities agreed to provide capital, collect money from the sale of lots supposedly amounting to some $6 million, and receive a percentage of the net profits. For many bankers and realtors, this transaction came as a major relief, not only to Boca Raton but to the entire east coast of Florida. Mizner officials observed that the deal should be regarded as conclusive evidence of the present soundness and future worth of "America's Riviera."

The Central Equities deal turned out to be a fiasco. The corporation

was secretly run by two former vice presidents of the Mizner Development Corporation, who applied all lot sales to their own account, put a
meager $100,000 into the corporation, and from then on abandoned
their responsibilities.[6] Sales of Boca Raton lots came to a standstill.
Installments on binders never got paid. Disenchanted contract-holders
cut their losses and left town. Others went to court. Banks folded.

Boca Raton was not the only place affected. People had speculated
in real estate all over Florida, and by the summer of 1926, forty banks in
Florida and Georgia had failed.[7] The rising tide of lawsuits threatened to
swamp the state's courts.

After studying Florida bank records of the period, which were not
unsealed until over sixty years later, author Raymond B. Vickers revealed
that a vast bank fraud conspiracy across Florida and Georgia had
financed the real estate extravaganza with depositors' money, and that
the partners of the Palm Beach National Bank, who were also on the
board of the Mizner Development Corporation, consistently and crimi-
nally embezzled customers' money to finance the failing land deals. (He
also says that although various observers knew the extent of the fraud,
the U.S. Justice Department was reluctant to investigate, since one of
the key players was Congressman George D. Graham, who had been so
urgently recruited to the Mizner Development Corporation's board.)
Vickers lays the blame for the sleazy business squarely on Mizner's
shoulders, declaring that he "provoked a banking crash of historic proportions."[8]

Mizner certainly went along with the bankers and their speculative
borrowing and lending schemes, but to accuse him personally of provoking the crash is absurd. Addison was interested in the money only
insofar as it allowed him license to build his architectural utopia. His
history of precarious solvency proves that business acumen had never
been his strong point. (His partners recognized this fact. In most of the
Mizner Development Corporation documents, his title as president is
repeatedly justified on the grounds of his "artistic ability and architectural genius," rather than any financial expertise.)[9] The fact that the
activities of the Mizner Development Corporation executives and their
banking confreres were illegal would have horrified him. He was drawing up blueprints, not promissory notes. It is true that in the summer of
1926, when the Palm Beach National Bank asked the directors of the

corporation to write notes to shore up the finances of the company, Mizner wrote one for $30,000, which he did not have, to apply against houses that, it turned out, he would never build. This was naïve, but not criminal. It was the act of a man who still believed in miracles. Today it would be called denial.

But then something happened that confirmed there would be no miracle but rather a malediction. In September 1926, a ferocious hurricane swept southern Florida. It tore up the coast from Miami to Palm Beach, leaving devastation and floods. Estimates of the damage reached hundreds of millions of dollars. Hundreds of lives were lost and houses destroyed. The disaster horrified the country. (Reading about it in New York, Louise Darry once again wrote to Addison, expressing her anxiety about his safety.)[10] This time there was no recovery. The physical and psychological wreckage was terminal. Boca Raton, the dream city, was returned to what it had always been; a sandy desert, laid about with a few sticks of wood and wind-blasted palmettos. The proposal to carve an artificial landscape out of the coastal swamps of southern Florida was finally, in Wilson Mizner's lingo, nixed by Nature.

By the end of 1926, no more proud sales announcements were forthcoming from the Mizner Development Corporation, no more news of fabulous Mizner castles arising from the Atlantic Ocean was reported. The silence was deafening. The newspapers were filled now with advertisements from insurance agents.

Addison was never religious (although he might have been tempted to pray during these tribulations). But oddly the one building he completed that terrible year was a church. In early 1926 members of the Riverside Baptist Church in Jacksonville asked him to design them a new building. The invitation could hardly have come at a worse time, and Addison turned it down on the grounds of overwork and ill health. But when the pastor responded that the congregation would pray for him, Addison relented.

Perhaps he saw it as an opportunity to fulfill the promise he had made to his mother before she died, which he later repeated to Henry and a group of potential Boca Raton investors: "I intend to construct a cathedral in honor and in memory of my mother as fine as anything in the United States. It is one of my fondest hopes, and I can think of no place in the world more fitting than Boca Raton for this structure." Jacksonville replaced Boca Raton as the site of Addison's dream. "We are happy," the Jacksonville parish replied, "that Mr. Mizner should have chosen our church for the realization of his mother's request."

It was indeed a cathedral. Huge and Romanesque, with an arcaded cornice, a rose window, an octagonal nave, and other Byzantine touches, it must have given the Baptists pause as they passed through the Chartres-like interior and knelt before the elaborate wrought-iron grill-work of the altar screen to greet a surprised God.

In February 1927 newspapers announced that Addison Mizner was ill with pneumonia, and that little hope was held out for his recovery. Wilson, Henry, and Ysabel were reportedly at his side. The stories appeared in both the local and the New York press, indicating the extent of Addison's fame (or infamy). Almost immediately Dr. Hobart Warren, Addison's physician, put out a statement denying that his patient had pneumonia and declaring that his only problem was phlebitis, a flare-up of his leg condition. The statement was issued at the request of the Mizner Development Corporation. Perilous as the company's status was, rumors of the demise of its only valuable asset were not to be tolerated.

Addison was indeed ill through the spring and summer of 1927. His sickness at this time was more than physical. He was bruised beyond measure by the appalling losses in his business and private life. His world of work, friends, and family was in rubble, and he stood like Ozymandias, vast and legless in the desert of his colossal dream. Nothing more wretchedly defined this *annus horribilis* for him than the death of his beloved monkey, Johnnie Brown. Addison buried his faithful companion in the Via Mizner, a stone's throw from the villa where Johnnie and Nettie, the kinkajou, had so often cavorted. Unlike Addison's parents, the little creature was honored with a small stone marking his grave that can still be seen today:

JOHNNIE BROWN
THE HUMAN MONKEY
DIED APRIL 30, 1927.

Wilson was another deserter. Mama's Angel Birdie had amused himself with his fantastic schemes of gondolas on Boca Raton's "Grand Canal" and other publicity stunts, such as hiring actors dressed up as matadors and picadors to give authenticity to the Spanish "realm." But in August 1925, he decided to take on a writing assignment that required his presence in New York. He was hired as script doctor to a musical comedy called *Naughty Cinderella,* starring a current Broadway favorite, Irene Bordoni. Putting on hold his work on Boca Raton's Venetian night life, he breezed out of Florida and set up shop at the Ritz-Carlton in New York. Before he left, he committed the ultimate betrayal of his brother by covering in white paint the lovely frescoed walls with which Addison had decorated his house. When asked about this act of vandalism, Wilson replied that it was "so as to see the mosquitoes."[11]

Over the next two months, Addison repeatedly wired Wilson for advice on the rapidly disintegrating situation in Boca Raton. Wilson responded that he was busy working on the show, which was "improving but not good." He had another reason to stall. A pretty young actress from Kenton, Tennessee, one Pauline Armitage, had a role in *Naughty Cinderella,* and she had taken a shine to the aging reprobate. Things developed so fast that in early September Wilson announced to his big brother that they were getting married. "I never felt so well," he exclaimed. Addison, who had telegraphed his friend Arthur Somers Roche that Wilson was "CHASING CHIPPY IN BORDONI SHOW," sent a guarded note of congratulations.

Sometime in late September, Pauline Armitage was taken out of the show and sent to the hospital with a nervous breakdown. Wilson kept in touch with her by telephone. He wired Addison that she was "willing to do anything I demand so everything is fine."[12] Wilson came down alone to Palm Beach in the middle of December 1925. He stayed just long enough to attempt to set up a separate corporation for himself, to avoid paying a note for $15,000 he owed the bank, and to lend $6,000 to his brother, before returning to New York and his unhappy fiancée.

In February 1926, while *Naughty Cinderella* was running at the Lyceum Theater, Pauline Armitage jumped from a fourteenth-story hotel window to her death. In her possession was a clutch of letters from Wilson Mizner. The press noted that Wilson had been engaged to the actress and that the engagement had been broken off. While it was clear that Armitage was unstable, hostile comments by her maid and other friends caused many to believe that Wilson was implicated in her death. Certainly the actress's mother thought so. She wrote the most pathetic letter to him, recalling to him her daughter's bright and responsive nature, and how Pauline had "begged me to share with her her new found happiness—in her love for you."[13]

Wilson, hoping to avoid the scandal, returned to Palm Beach and denied that he had ever been engaged to Pauline Armitage. "Miss Armitage was a friend of mine. . . . We are all deeply shocked." He did, however, send money (through an agent) for Pauline's funeral. A friend of the Armitage family terminated any further investigation, saying that he saw no advantage to Pauline in visiting further disaster upon the man she loved.[14] The Palm Beach press remained tactfully silent on the matter. Only in New York was Pauline Armitage seen as a casualty of Wilson's treacherous life.[15]

This kind of publicity was hardly what Addison needed. The tragedy took place at the height of the social season, and the colony was abuzz with the scandal. In a rather tasteless aside, a woman friend wrote to Addison that she loved him more than ever—"However, I *do* promise *not* to jump out of the window from the fourteenth story!"[16]

Wilson blithely reappeared in Palm Beach off and on through 1926 and early 1927, but for him, Florida was over. He may have smelled failure as the Boca Raton project began to unravel, but he also smelled the even more dangerous fragrance of creditors. "I never open my door but a writ blows in," he complained. His only asset was the house (with apartments) that Addison had built for him, and he put it on the market. But it was mortgaged to the hilt and therefore unsalable. He also attempted to get his Packard roadster shipped to California. The obstacle here was that it was not clear he was the legitimate owner. (The man who sold it to him wrote in January 1926, pleading for payment, saying that he himself had invested in the Mizner Development Corporation and was now broke.)[17]

The machinations with which Wilson avoided paying bills and postponed litigation were always creative. He even sent a wire to Anderson Herd, the general manager of the Mizner Development Corporation in New York, saying, "LOSING MY HOUSE ON ACCOUNT OF NOTE COMMERCIAL BANK WHAT CAN YOU DO ANSWER." Of course, he sent the wire collect. (Wilson was barking up the wrong tree this time. Herd was arrested in New York later that year for obtaining $100,000 from a Palm Beach realtor under false pretenses.) Wilson had survived worse setbacks. By June

1927, thanks to his theatrical reputation, he was set up in Hollywood as a screenwriter for the Famous Players/Lasky Corporation. "I knew Mizner could write the sharpest dialogue in the business," Jack Warner said.[18]

The year 1927 also saw the departure of their brother Henry. Swept up in Addison's enthusiasm, he had requested a transfer from his St. Louis congregation in hope of receiving a parish in Boca Raton, but the bishop of South Florida refused, because Henry did not have a "definite parochial charge." (The canny bishop saw what many foolish investors didn't: there would be no parish in Boca Raton.)[19] Henry's house was also tied up in a second mortgage that he could not pay. With no church, no house, and no future, in October 1927 Henry took his family to Paris where they could live cheaply and complete their daughter's education. Addison never saw his brother again. A year later Henry had a crippling stroke. He died in Paris in July 1930.

Like most astute observers, Addison's longtime colleague Alex Waugh had also read the writing on the wall by 1927. Resigning his position as head of the failing Mizner Industries showroom, he took a job with a local antiques shop, which did not last long. He then took off for Europe with Horace Chase and spent the two summers before the Wall Street crash in European watering holes with a group of wild young men, mostly American. One night they bumped into Scott and Zelda Fitzgerald in Montmartre and managed to get the famous couple, both drunk, back to their apartment on the rue Tilsit.

These were reckless times, and two of Waugh's closest friends died young. Gay Bullen, with whom Waugh rented a house in Morocco, died of a blow from the rudder of his speedboat on the Riviera, a loss from which Waugh never fully recovered. Horace Chase was also marked for an early death. A keen aviator, in June 1928 he was flying his worn-out plane to Baltimore, where he planned to take delivery of a new one. The plane crashed, and Horace and his copilot were killed. Horace was not yet thirty. He had enlivened his uncle's life with his escapades, and it was a sad loss for Addison, already reeling from so many. "He was a rash and humorous daredevil, just disbelieving in the whole idea of fear," Alice DeLamar said, one of many people who loved him. In a revealing epitaph, Addison's friend George Osborn recalled poor Horace, "so desperately in love with desperate life."[20] Waugh was sobered by these tragedies and returned to England to work for Warford's, ancient-building restorers, the ideal position after his years with Addison Mizner.

There were other casualties of the Boca Raton fiasco: perhaps the most painful of all was the friendship between Addison and Paris Singer. Singer had been far too preoccupied with his own project to support Addison's Boca Raton adventure, and (perhaps fortunately) he had not invested in his friend's scheme. Moreover, Singer had never approved of Wilson and did not like Wilson's increasing involvement in Addison's life and work. But the root of the problem was, as usual, money. To finance his Blue Heron development, Singer had sold bonds worth $2 million to H. C. Rorick and the Spitzer-Rorick Trust and Savings Bank of Toledo, Ohio. The bond was secured by Everglades Club Properties. When Singer's project collapsed, the Everglades Club found itself responsible for this debt and by 1928 was in receivership.

Singer owed Addison approximately $75,000 for the architect's work on the project, which Singer, disputing the sum, refused to pay. In early 1927 the friends stopped speaking. Enter the lawyers. That the two giants of Palm Beach's history should be throwing writs at each other was almost inconceivable. Their friendship had been one of the great stories of the time, surviving crises of confidence, geographical absence, low moments, and unimaginable success. Local observers were appalled by the breach, ascribing it to all sorts of rumors, even pointing the finger at Isadora Duncan, who was now struggling to survive on the French Riviera, and with whom Singer, living nearby and still partly in love, remained in touch. (Later that year came the further blow of her tragic death, when she was accidentally strangled by her scarf in the back seat of a Bugatti.)

The truth is that both men were under tremendous financial pressure and could hardly see beyond the creditors' letters piled up on their desks. The disaster of Singer's Blue Heron development had left him so broke that he was trying to sell his home on St. Jean Cap Ferrat. But Addison was in similar trouble. He was sick and weary, and he felt hurt and angry at his friend's refusal to pay a bill that would certainly have eased, if only temporarily, Addison's situation. In a fit of pique, he even removed his name from membership in Singer's greatest creation, the Everglades Club.

In a shocking aftermath, in April 1927 Paris Singer was arrested at his beloved Everglades Club on the charge of defrauding real estate investors to the tune of $1.5 million. Less than two weeks later, the case was thrown out for lack of evidence. But Paris's pride had been irrevocably damaged by his public humiliation in his most private of playgrounds.[21] Immediately after the acquittal, he left Palm Beach for New York.

Addison knew how much his old friend must have suffered from this brutal experience. Although the money issue still rankled, his naturally generous nature won out, and he broke the silence by writing Singer a letter of sympathy. Paris was deeply touched and immediately responded, thanking him for his "kind thought." He then went on to outline his plan for a new golf course and homes on Everglades Club land. Including a wonderful two-color sketch, he described the idea with all the old enthusiasm and energy, just as though nothing had happened between them. Singer said that Addison should design houses on this land "as you alone in all the world can" and that many people would want them. "You see old chap," Singer wrote, "Palm B. will be the first thing to revive and then the newer places will come along." He signed the letter "Your old friend, the enemy, Paris."[22]

Later that year, he wrote again. "My dear old Addison," he said. "This summer while in Europe I have naturally thought a great deal of all our troubles and have pondered over all that has happened since you and I went down to Palm Beach together ten years ago for our health, and of the warm friendship which came of it and the pleasure we both had from working together in building up the place. I have also meditated on the mistake we made of each starting our own different developments. While we cannot wipe out our mistakes it seems to me it would be better for us both to forget the past and start again in cooperation with a clean slate."

He pointed out that both their lawyers believed they had valid claims, and that neither he nor Mizner would profit from the litigation—"but the lawyers will." He then added the prescient observation, "Neither of us has many years still to live and it seems rather foolish for us to spend them fighting each other. . . . I hope that our old warm friendship could be restored. Won't you please write me and if you are coming to New York soon let us meet and dine together and talk it over."[23]

Who could resist such an appeal? Certainly not warm-hearted Addison. He told Paris that the "feud" had arisen because Addison felt that if all of Singer's holdings were with Rorick, "I would have much rather had the money than let Mr. Rorick have it." He said that they should forget the matter and wait until Singer came to Palm Beach, "where," Addison added, "I am still endeavouring to stall off creditors and smile through." In the increasingly affectionate terms both men now addressed each other, Addison confessed, "I am looking forward to seeing you more than anything else in the world."[24]

Paris was delighted by the reconciliation. "My dearest old Addison," he immediately wrote back from New York, and explained that, thanks to negotiations between the lawyers, "I understand our mutual claims are wiped out." He urged Addison to allow his name to figure in the list of members in the Everglades Club book for 1928. "It is the one name that has any real right to be there, and when you took it off you gave me one 'right in the jaw'!" Of all the horrible blows that had happened to him that year, he added, Addison's removal of his name was the one that hurt the most![25]

These letters vividly reveal the deep feeling the two men had toward each other. Although enormously different in background and disposition, they shared a sense of adventure and, perhaps even more important, a passionate love of architecture. While Paris Singer never practiced the profession, his abiding interest in it and admiration of Addison's talent created a powerful bond between the two men. Singer's competitiveness and moodiness sometimes caused friction, and Addison sometimes felt the pressure of being put in the middle of his friend's marital problems with Joan over the years. But the underlying strength of their affection proved triumphant in these last testing days of their broken dreams.

Addison was fifty-five and Paris sixty-one at the time of these epistolary exchanges, and for both of them, time was running out. While Addison continued to struggle with his failing health and career, Paris's life took another downward turn. His mistaken effort to secure the bonds sold to Rorick with Everglades land spelled disaster for the club, and although he remained as president through 1930, he had irretrievably injured his reputation and his glamour, and after 1927 his tower apartments there remained mostly empty. The 1929 stock market crash further depleted his funds, and he spent his last years with Joan quietly in his austere Moorish house, Les Rochers, in St. Jean Cap Ferrat. (It has since been demolished.)

Paris Singer, this "strange silent man," as the newspapers described him, died in London in June 1932. "Up north of the inlet," a Palm Beach obituary read, "the hulk of the unfinished Blue Heron hotel is silhouetted against the sky looking down on desertlike sand dunes, a monument to [this] mad genius."[26] Singer died just seven months before the man with whom he had shared his greatest achievements, his dearest friend, Addison Mizner.

CHAPTER 20

"STOP DYING AM TRYING
TO WRITE A COMEDY."

In March 1927 three creditors of the Mizner Development Corporation filed involuntary bankruptcy proceedings against the company in federal court in Jacksonville, where not long before Mizner's great Romanesque church had been consecrated by the faithful.[1] Later that summer, the Mizner Development Corporation, including the Cloister Inn and the little that existed of Boca Raton, was put on the auction block. The ensuing months saw the rapid dismantling of the Mizner empire into the hands of the hovering sharks. Furniture and furnishings from the Cloister Inn were auctioned off at prices far below their actual worth.

In October 1927 Jerome D. Gedney, a New York attorney representing the real estate developer and former Mizner backer Clarence Geist, bid $5,000 at auction for the company, plus assumption of all outstanding obligations, which were estimated at $10 to $15 million. He was the only bidder. After the bankruptcy judge delayed a decision, commenting that the purchase price seemed very low, Geist ultimately paid $71,000 for the Boca Raton properties.[2] He declared that all Boca Raton contract-holders would be protected and would be able to obtain clear title to their properties. He also said that the Cloister Inn would be reopened in January 1928 as a private men's club.[3] (Geist hired Schultze & Weaver, who had rebuilt the Breakers, to redesign the inn, and it opened in 1930. It is now the Boca Raton Hotel and Club.)

Other million-dollar lawsuits were filed against the corporation and its directors. A Lot Purchasers Association in Miami was formed to sue them. Income tax officials began to lurk. The second mortgages on Henry's houses in Palm Beach and Boca Raton were foreclosed. Suppliers continued to write pleading letters. Witnessing the inevitable demise of his company, the architect said, was "like the death of a diseased child, as it had to come ultimately."[4]

A few commissions trickled in. In 1927 John R. Bradley, brother of the Palm Beach casino owner Edward Bradley, asked Addison to build a house in Colorado Springs, Colorado. This was a very different type of location, and after visiting the site, he responded with his usual sensitivity to the new environment. His plan was inspired by the flat prairie landscape of Colorado Springs, which rolls eastward from the Rocky Mountains. Stripped of all fancy decoration, Casa Serena has an Indian Pueblo feel, suited to the southwestern plains. It has a U-shaped floor plan, built up on three levels, with an enclosed patio and cloister, a Moorish tower, and small *rejas*-enclosed windows. (The house, with several additions, became the Fountain Valley School in 1930.)[5]

While ideally suited to the topography, Addison's sober, stripped-down design also exposes the architect's state of mind at this comfortless time. He had very little to cheer about. He finished a project for Mrs. Glen Hodges on Worth Avenue. He started making sketches for a house for Woolworth heir James P. Donahue. But in October Addison became ill after a trip to check on the Bradley house in Colorado Springs. Nell Cosden and Peggy Thayer took him to the doctor. After a battery of tests, they diagnosed some sort of tubercular trouble and insisted on rest, adding that another hot summer in Palm Beach would not be a good idea. They also instigated a series of treatments to "burn out my tonsils with X-Ray."[6]

Addison's old friends and clients watched with increasing dismay as the architect fended off his predators and struggled to keep up appearances. A few were bitter at being taken in by the Boca Raton ballyhoo. Marie Dressler, who had helped sell lots and quickly retreated back to New York after the crash, wrote later, "I had sold a good deal of [land] before I realized that not only was I a sucker, but that I was making suckers of those who bought through me."[7] But most of the Palm Beach colony did not blame the misguided architect for the disaster.

In a show of solidarity, several of his friends got together under the leadership (and financial backing) of Alice DeLamar to assemble a book about Addison's work. One of the most important contributors to the project was Frank E. Geisler, a well-known photographer whose pictures of Mizner's houses had appeared in many magazines. Geisler agreed to donate some of his early photographs and also to photograph Addison's later work for the book. (Alice DeLamar believed that photographs of houses should be taken from a certain height, and she provided a truck with a special platform to make sure the camera was correctly positioned.) The book featured 185 of Geisler's photographs. Paris Singer was also contacted, and he wrote a passionately admiring introduction to his old friend.

Ida M. Tarbell, the well-known journalist who in 1904 had published a scathing exposé of the Standard Oil Company monopoly, was the unlikely writer chosen for the book's text. Tarbell's muckraking instincts had taken a rest during a visit to boomtime Florida. "Florida represents the most ambitious, chaotic, spectacular, pioneering adventure in history," she had declared. There was no bursting bubble in Florida, she concluded, but a pot of gold at the end of a rainbow. Ignoring Florida's disappointing failure to support her prediction, Tarbell now wrote an admiring text for Addison's book, mostly retelling his familiar stories about his childhood, travels, and architectural principles.

Florida Architecture of Addison Mizner was published by William Hellburn in 1928, at twenty dollars a copy. A hundred specially bound leather presentation copies were produced as gifts and signed by the author. When the book appeared, Addison wrote a deeply touching letter to Alice, whom he called "My Lorenzo the Magnificent." "I have been so ill since The Book took shape that I have never made it quite clear how much I appreciated the greatest compliment ever paid a living architect," he wrote from California. "I should be very conceited about it; but it has had just the opposite effect, for now I will have to do something to justify myself." He added that he was doing work that he hoped wouldn't "shame" her.[8]

Florida Architecture of Addison Mizner had a significance beyond promoting the architect. When Addison became obsessed with planning Boca Raton, he lost his longtime monopoly on building palaces for the rich in Palm Beach. A new generation of architects were anxious to prove that the era of his domination was over. Marion Sims Wyeth, a Princeton and Beaux-Arts graduate, had first arrived in 1919 to witness the dramatic opening of the Everglades Club and over the next few years built Spanish- and Italian-style houses for E. F. Hutton, Clarence Geist, and Jay F. Carlisle. Wyeth's social connections were even better than

Mizner's, and he competed for many major commissions, his biggest being the design of Cielito Lindo for Jimmy Donahue in 1927, where the rich playboy later entertained the Duke and Duchess of Windsor. (This was the commission that Addison had hoped to win.) Wyeth also worked with Joseph Urban, the theatrical designer, on Mar-a-Lago, Urban's flamboyant project for Marjorie Merriweather Post.

Bruce Paxton Kitchell followed Wyeth to Palm Beach, and John L. Volk arrived in 1926, but perhaps Mizner's greatest rival was Maurice Fatio, who opened an office in partnership with William A. Treanor in 1925. Fatio was even more successful than Wyeth at charming the wealthy colonists, and the number of his commissions soon began to compete with Mizner's. Emblematic of the two men's changing positions in the architectural firmament was Joseph P. Widener's decision, after Mizner did sketches for his house on South Ocean Boulevard, to give the commission to Fatio. Later, Fatio again seized a commission from Mizner after the senior architect had done a great deal of work, this time for Alexander Camp in Texas.

Although these rejections were painful, Addison never held a grudge against Fatio, and they became friends. During Addison's lonely summer in 1927, while his company was being sold from under him, he and Fatio would occasionally go to the movies together.[9] Even in this cutthroat world, Addison seemed incapable of making enemies. Marion Sims Wyeth, who had taken many commissions from Addison, later said, "We talked about architecture. We were never rivals."[10]

It is a tribute to Addison that these architects continued to produce mostly Spanish or Italianate houses for their Palm Beach clients. But as the fallout from Boca Raton continued, these by-now-familiar designs conveyed a sense of unease. The Mizner "look" assumed a suspicious shadow, the shadow of failure. This sense was abetted by the continued attacks on historicism by a group of younger critics who were fervent supporters of the Bauhaus and the "less is more" school of architecture. "There is nothing modern or genuinely creative in [Mizner's] style," wrote Michael Ross in *Home & Field*. "He harks back to the Gothic with a vengeance, and some of his effects are grandiose rather than grand. Possibly building a Gothic chapel and calling it a dining-room smacks of the nouveau riche. Possibly making the entrance hall like the nave of a cathedral is altogether inappropriate."

The new wave of architects in Palm Beach responded to these negative vibrations and began to propose different styles—Norman and English, in wood and brick. Maurice Fatio produced a Louisiana-style house with wood board siding and louvered windows, and a Tudor cottage with a steeply pitched roof and half-timbers. Howard Major, the architect who had first come out in print against the Spanish invasion, designed Major Alley, a group of small houses clustered together like a London mews, with Georgian front doors and Caribbean-style roofs and shutters. There was no question that these new architectural styles and materials, while still historicist, were a refreshing change from stucco cloisters and wrought-iron balconies.

Yet even the critic Michael Ross had to admit that Addison Mizner's original vision took a lot of beating. Referring to Mizner's exuberant nature, delighting in color and ornament, Ross asked his readers, "Have you ever looked at the dramatic ocean front of the Cosden house and discovered his dramatic capacities? They have run like a thread over what was once the flat Florida landscape."[11]

The publication of *Florida Architecture of Addison Mizner* did not persuade the modernists, and it received little national attention, but Curtis Patterson, the reviewer in *International Studio,* an affiliate of *The Connoisseur,* ventured to estimate Addison's influence with that of Pericles and the building of the Acropolis, and with the Renaissance popes, who entrusted the new St. Peter's to Bramante and Michelangelo. Patterson asserted that Mizner's work "stands out with a definiteness which, to an almost justifiable degree, is comparable with that of the Acropolis and St. Peter's against their background."[12]

Pericles! St. Peter's! Bramante! Michelangelo! Palm Beach reverberated with approving noises. Newly energized, in 1928 Addison was back at his drafting table. He produced a house for Jerome D. Gedney, Clarence Geist's attorney, in Manalapan, which turned out to be one of his most attractive. Less grandiose in size than some, it had a long horizontal design, hugging the line of the beachfront. With roofs at several levels and a simple stucco exterior reminiscent of his Colorado Springs work, it revealed its glories, like most of Mizner's houses, only when the visitor passed through the public rooms and into the cloistered interior courtyard with the fountain at its center. The interiors were equally pleasing. The hall had a high vaulted ceiling and circular oculus, casting a soft light. On the second floor, reached by a spiral staircase, two bedroom wings were connected by an open loggia. The rooms were enriched by his signature pecky cypress ceilings and colorful tile floors. Other commissions at this time were a brokerage office and apartment for John H. Harris in Miami Beach, and a nurses' lodge in the Good Samaritan Hospital in West Palm Beach. He also did additions to Playa Riente (now owned by the Dillmans), and to the Phipps house, Casa Bendita.

Addison's most prominent assignment was to design another Cloister Inn, this time in Sea Island, Georgia. It was commissioned by automobile millionaire Howard E. Coffin, who wanted to create a small resort community there.[13] (When Coffin and his cousin, Alfred W. Jones, called on Addison, they felt sure the famous architect would not have time for them, little knowing the true state of affairs since the Boca Raton collapse.) The 460-room hotel was a virtuoso Mizner performance, with cloistered walls, tile roofs, cathedral ceilings, towered stairways, and plant-filled patios. Its popularity was such that an annex had to be built (by Francis D. Abreu). Alfred Jones so liked the results, he asked Mizner to design a house for him and his new wife nearby. (Addison had not lost his outspokenness. When Jones's wife asked Addison about a mantel, the architect replied that he planned no mantel, "as some son-of-a-bitch will just put a clock on it.")[14]

Increasingly losing local commissions to his competitors in Florida, Addison was forced to look for work farther afield. In Bryn Mawr, Pennsylvania, he designed La Ronda, a vast suburban mansion for leather millionaire Percival E. Foerderer. The design harks back to the architect's El Mirasol days. Its massive proportions, vaulted and coffered ceilings, Gothic stone chimneypieces, elaborate fifteenth- and sixteenth-century furnishings, frescoes, and tile floors were in the classic Mizner idiom described by a visiting reporter as "romantic revival."[15]

Critics might say that by this time Addison was on automatic pilot, his creativity subsumed by the trauma of Boca Raton. But that year he also produced some brilliant work for his old client Alfred E. Dieterich, who had moved from Millbrook to Montecito, California. Admittedly, the exterior and interior of the 18,000-square-foot Casa Bienvenita had all the familiar Mizner flourishes (including a Prohibition-inspired secret door into the wine cellar, a detail he had first designed for the Sloanes' Concha Marina), but the gardens on this project exhibit once again the architect's multiple talents. He laid out a formal Elizabethan-style flower

garden alongside the terrace, while the main garden, in modest obei-
sance to the Villa Lante in Italy, consisted of a long flight of steps on an
axis with the house's central flagstone patio, leading to a circular fountain, and on up a steep incline, lined with terra-cotta pots and ever-
greens, to a small classical pavilion at the top.[16] (A later owner, Mrs. Van
Rensselaer Wilbur, said of the house, "We find it rather charming for a
small country place.")

This burst of creative energy was not simply the exertions of an old
warhorse back in the traces. The familiar elixir of love was once more
working its magic on his weary bones. The object of his affections this
time was Jerry Giradolle, a gorgeous twenty-two-year-old whose father
was a French restaurateur in New York. Addison brought Jerry, his latest
treasure, down to Palm Beach. Giradolle had long eyelashes, was full of
fun, and generally charmed the natives, including a reluctant Alice
DeLamar. Once more she watched her old friend shed his years with this
"Autumn Crocus infatuation," as she called it. "He had cast off the list-
lessness that had befallen him since his health began to fail. He had
pried himself out of that large out-size armchair that he spent far too
many hours vegetating in. I can see that humorous twinkle in Addison's
eye, how it came to life again, and that benign and beatific expression he
so often had."[17]

As usual, Addison put his new pocket Adonis in charge of the office
and furniture factory and bought the boy a Cadillac, which he could ill
afford. Jerry soon found ways to escape his benefactor and get into a lot
of trouble, aided by large amounts of alcohol. On one famous occasion,
Jerry and a group of friends drove around Worth Avenue after dark,
singing and laughing at the tops of their voices, finally paying a raucous
midnight visit to the darkened estates of the Stotesburys, Guests, and
Cosdens. This was more than even indulgent Addison could allow. Not
for the first time, he asked Alice to help him keep Jerry under control.

Jerry, like most of Addison's infatuations, was equally attractive to and
attracted by women, and he finally landed a little widow of uncertain
age, as Alice put it, with a small but cozy income, with whom he
absconded. The couple returned once to Palm Beach and behaved very
badly, leaving bills and angry residents behind. Addison's hopes again
were dashed.

On September 16, 1928, another hurricane hit the southern coast of

Florida, even worse than the one two years earlier, with damage estimated at $10 million. Addison's commissions dwindled to a trickle. In 1929 he received only one big assignment: Colonel Bradley asked him to design a new club, the Florida Embassy Club, to be built on Royal Park Way. But as a sign of Addison's frailty, it was announced as a joint project with Lester W. Geisler. (Geisler, no relation to the photographer, and another of Addison's associates, Byron Simonson, were to take ever more prominent roles in the firm.) The $175,000 club was planned as an exclusive dining and dancing venue, modeled on the club with the same name in New York. The one-story building had a central tower with an octagonal window and a tile roof. A cloister opened onto a dancing patio, which was lit with colored lights. The Embassy Club opened on January 30, 1930, to the usual fanfare.

The Embassy Club is an example of Addison's architecture in its last phase. Just as many artists, from Michelangelo to Matisse, tended to produce simplified and plainer work in their later years, Addison brought to his late designs a sort of minimalism. The facade of the Embassy Club is almost without ornamentation. In his sketch, once again using his skills as a garden designer, he offset the plainness of the architecture with a wonderful variety of trees and shrubs. (The club building, which was later redesigned by Marion Sims Wyeth as the Society of the Four Arts, has lost most of its original landscaping, although a beautiful garden created by the Garden Club of Palm Beach has since replaced it.)

Just as in his first years in New York, at this time gardens, more than houses, gave Addison a creative outlet. In 1929 the members of the Palm Beach Garden Club decided to beautify their town by creating a memorial park and fountain (in honor of Henry Flagler and the town's founder, Elisha Dimick) on South County Road. The list of contributors to the Fountain Fund (which raised over $25,000) included many of Addison's old friends and clients, such as Hugh Dillman, Willey Kingsley, the Phipps family, Mrs. Henry Rea, and Edward Stotesbury. Addison, waiving a fee, drew up plans for the garden. A little flurry occurred when Harold Vanderbilt, chairman of the fountain commission, decided to invite other local architects to submit plans, but Maurice Fatio, showing the depth of his respect for the older architect, sent a letter to the *Palm Beach Daily News*, saying, "In view of the fact that Mr. Addison Mizner is the originator of this beautification proposal and has himself submitted a fountain design to adequately meet the requirements, which to my mind could not be improved upon, I feel that the matter is already in able hands and do not care to make a competing entry."[18]

Fatio's judgment was correct. The park is one of the most elegant of all Addison's garden designs. A long, rectangular ornamental pool, an echo of the Generalife in Spain, is framed with a border of stone and two rectangular beds of turf. (The beds were originally planted with shrubs.) Four pairs of royal palms stand like sentinels alongside the dark water of the canal. At the south end, a spectacular fountain with four rearing horses rises from a wide flight of steps, with a narrow rill allowing water to trickle down into a shallow bowl like the one in the Court of the Myrtles in the Alhambra.

Addison also made a spectacular new garden for Mrs. Henry Rea, who had bought a Mizner house, Lagomar, from John Magee in 1924 and had since become a close friend. (Addison kept a framed picture of her in his bathroom.)[19] These projects injected new life into Mizner Industries, whose products were used exclusively. Further work for Mizner included a row of shops at the Phipps Plaza on County Road, also in conjunction with Geisler.

Throughout the 1931 season, Addison gave a series of parties and dinners. There was a grand New Year's Day Open House at the Villa Mizner between two and four in the afternoon, with the names of the faithful listed in the gossip columns, proving that the old architect could still pull them in: Cosden, Cromwell, DeLamar, Dillman, Donahue, Fatio (now married to Eleanor Chase, Wilson's old flame), Gedney, Geist, Hutton, Munn, Rea, Shearson, Stotesbury, Vanderbilt, Warburton, Widener, Wyeth, Ziegfeld. Later that month Mizner entertained a figure from his glory days, Achille Angeli, the Florentine muralist who had painted the panels for Playa Riente. A prized guest was Syrie Maugham, a friend from his days in New York fourteen years earlier. In another Mizner coup, he hosted a dinner at the Everglades Club for the archbishop of San Domingo, who it is said particularly appreciated the Spanish decor.

All these showy events concealed the truth: Addison was broke.

He was not alone. The 1929 stock market crash had bankrupted many of the people who once frequented Palm Beach. Addison's bravura act was similar to that of Condé Nast, the magazine publisher who had owned a huge empire throughout the period Addison was building houses in Palm Beach and who lost control of it after the crash. (The two had met—Addison was entertained in Palm Beach by Condé Nast in 1927.)[20] Like Mizner in Palm Beach, Nast depended on celebrity-studded parties in his Fifth Avenue duplex for his public image; he continued to live in the apartment and entertain lavishly throughout the 1930s, while only a select few knew that he was mortgaged, in hock, "a ghost at his famous parties, a stylish facade."[21]

The new owners of Nast's magazines secretly paid his expenses. Addison's friends also secretly found ways to help him keep afloat. Back in April 1927, Irving Berlin had lent him $25,000 for six months, at 6 percent interest. (Addison managed to pay off two interest installments before he died.)[22] Edith Rea often paid his household and servants' bills. Edward Moore, who had bought Addison's house, Sin Cuidado, found ways to help.

The Mizner family was less supportive. Wilson tossed off encouraging telegrams from time to time, telling his brother of his Hollywood writing contracts. Meanwhile, Mama's Angel Birdie continued to sustain huge debts in Palm Beach, which he failed to pay. During the glory days, he had cunningly opened up a joint account with his brother, which left Addison responsible for the bills. Finally, even long-suffering Addison began to lose his equanimity. He wrote a letter to Wilson, saying, "I am enclosing a list of the bills you owe locally and which throw you into a very unpleasant light and naturally come back on me. . . . If it is possible for you to pay off an account a certain monthly proportion of the bills, I think it would be very advisable. . . . I hate to have this sound like a 'letter from home' but I have about all I can carry."[23] Wilson wrote back with his usual bravado, suggesting that they build houses in a new place— California. Exasperated, Addison said, "You speak of some day of our having houses in California—just who is going to buy them?"

Addison also missed the intimacy he had once enjoyed with Ysabel. In June 1930 she married McKim Hollins, brother of Marion, the golfer. The wedding was in Pebble Beach, and Wilson gave the bride away. Ysabel had become fond of the bottle, and McKim was a well-known drunk (it was rumored that the marriage had taken place on a bet), but Wilson assured Addison that at the wedding both bride and groom were perfectly sober. Wilson was even happier to report that Kim Hollins had become seriously wealthy after the payment of a real estate option by the Standard Oil Company, and that Ysabel was going to be a beneficiary, quite apart from acquiring a large monetary gift from her new sister-in-law, Marion. "Taking it all together, the little girl has done quite well by herself," Wilson said.

There was one other bright spot during these times. In April 1928 a young woman called Madena Galloway had come to work for Addison as his secretary, and she kept his world together with fortitude and humor for the last years of his life. She had arrived in Palm Beach to work for North Carolina Power and Light but heard Addison was looking for help, and within a few weeks, she would have laid down her life for him.[24]

Her job was enormous. Addison's business affairs were a mess. Quite apart from keeping his correspondence and papers in order, she took on the onerous burden of trying to help him pay his debts. She saw to the renting of the Via Mizner shops (which had been vacated and were standing empty). She bought Wendell Weed (who remained on Addison's payroll till the end) a new suit of clothes for twenty dollars. She tried to protect Addison from "chiselers": "It makes me furious the way people try to take advantage of you, when not a one of them could ever do anything worthwhile for you. Be practicing 'NO' all the way home so you will be prepared."

Like all the others who had worked for Addison, Madena Galloway adored him. She fretted over him like a nanny. An effective businesswoman, she followed up on every detail of his personal and professional life, worrying over his health and attempting to create order out of chaos. He was hopelessly inefficient at answering her questions, so she would make up little questionnaires, such as:

1. *Do you want to accept Mr. Michaelyan's offer to take the shop on a percentage basis for this season?*
YES_____ NO_____
2. *Is it all right to buy the suit for Mr. Weed?*
YES_____ NO_____

Addison clearly enjoyed these tricks and (usually) obediently filled in the blanks. They were always "Miss Galloway" (when he wasn't spelling it "Galaway") and "Mr. Mizner" to each other, but their affection and mutual dependence were powerful boosts to the architect's waning energies.

The year 1931 produced one last major commission, a large Spanish-style house for Mr. and Mrs. William J. Williams in St. Petersburg, with a budget of approximately $90,000, "one of the largest and most expensive mansions in St. Petersburg." Casa Coe da Sol was situated on Boca Diega Bay. It had a balustraded central staircase at the entrance, a second-floor cloistered gallery, and a Moorish coffee room with a triple-domed ceiling and very elaborate tile work. Addison also used art deco for the first time, in a guest room and bathroom, "perhaps in recognition of changing styles," Donald Curl suggested, adding that Casa Coe da Sol was "one of his most dramatic houses."[25] The travel involved in the job was less arduous than most, but Mrs. Williams was slow in paying her bills, and her tardiness did not help the financially pressed firm.

In April of that year, Addison went to Washington to discuss plans for a new federal building and post office for Palm Beach, a highly desirable commission and one that would have major consequences for Mizner's firm. By this time, his colleague Byron Simonson was doing most of the drafting and office business, but Addison, recognizing its importance, threw himself into the project. It dragged on, subject to Washington's bureaucratic whims, well into 1932.

With business slow, Mizner returned to his first love, writing. With the help of the invaluable Madena Galloway, he began to dictate his memoirs. News of this project acted like a shot of testosterone on Wilson, who was trying to get screenplays produced in Hollywood. How dare Addison upstage his little brother? Wasn't Wilson the famous writer in the family? Within a few days of the announcement of Addison's book, gossip columns revealed that Wilson, too, was writing a memoir. He had a collaborator in the person of Anita Loos, whose fame and writing skills would no doubt overshadow anything Addison might produce. The book was to be called *A Child's Life of Wilson Mizner.* It never saw print.

The first part of Addison's autobiography, *The Many Mizners,* was published by Sears Publishing Company in New York in September 1932. Addison's literary style had not improved much over those early efforts at short-story writing in his early twenties. But he completed the manuscript in a remarkably short time, relating the story of his family, his experiences in Alaska, and his early years in New York until the death of Mama

Mizner in lively if unmellifluous prose. On the whole it received good notices. Critics called it "cockeyed," "rollicking," "racy," "Rabelaisian."

Alice DeLamar, with her usual candor, thought a far better job could have resulted with the collaboration of a competent ghostwriter. "Anecdotes that came off wonderfully when they were told orally in Addison's inimitable style of talking, often fell flat in print when jotted down verbatim. All the flavor was lacking. The real picture of the warm personality of the man was just not there in the book."[26]

One of the most poignant consequences of the publication of *The Many Mizners* was the reappearance of a figure from Addison's Alaska days, Louis Jonke, the former waiter they called Och Gott Louie, who had accompanied Addison to Dawson after the other brothers had disappeared. Now confined to a wheelchair in a nursing home in San Francisco, Jonke wrote to Wilson (addressing the envelope simply "Mr. Wilson Meizner [sic], Hollywood, Calif."), saying he had heard about the book and asking for a copy, as he could not afford to buy one. Addison instantly mailed him a copy, and Och Gott Louie, thanking him, said he remembered the old times in Alaska and "got a good laugh out of it."[27]

In January 1932 Addison gave his usual New Year's Day party. On March 10, he gave a speech at Rollins College in Winter Park, explaining to the students that Spanish architecture was not indigenous to the region and had to be adapted to the Florida climate. Reiterating the theme he had first expressed thirteen years earlier to the ladies of the West Palm Beach Women's Club, he lamented that in developing this kind of architecture, "home builders have stepped over the bounds of good taste in their effort to make their homes 'beautiful.' " They have disregarded the beauty in *simplicity,* he said, adding, "After all, simplicity and good taste are essential in architecture." He concluded by affirming his faith in the American people "to make progress in developing good taste, not only in architecture but in all forms of art."[28]

Such public appearances, however, were rare. Addison no longer traveled to Europe in the summer. Instead he had to endure the heat of Palm Beach in June, July, and August, which is not recommended for a man with a heart condition. He had no money. He was alone much of the time, for all the winter residents had gone back north. His last maid, Ozie Bella Brown, who came to work for him in 1929, remembered that most of the time he ate (still too much) by himself on a tray. Like Addison's other employees, Ozie adored her boss, saying he was enormously generous, which she believed was his downfall, freely giving his money and possessions away. He also loved her hot-chocolate cake.[29]

The crash of 1929 had drained the country of its optimism, and money was no longer available or appropriate to be spent on building fantasy palaces. "I am afraid building will be the last thing to pick up, and God alone knows when anything else will," Mizner wrote gloomily to a friend in 1932.[30] The grand old man of Florida architecture, now slow-moving, weak, and badly overweight, stayed atop his beautiful Spanish eyrie, while younger architects, more energetic in seeking clients, passed by the elegant wrought-iron gate of Villa Mizner without looking up.

Byron Simonson, Addison's associate, was eager to get more business, including the commission for another post office, this time in West Palm Beach. Aware of the difficulties with Washington, he promised that he would do all the work under the Mizner name and share the profits. Addison, however, depressed at the lack of progress with the current post office deal, refused to bid for the project.[31]

As early as 1928, perhaps for the first time sensing that he might ultimately leave Florida, Addison had bought 57,000 acres with a small ranch house near Carmel, California, for $15,000. (The land was bought with a loan in the name of Addison Mizner Incorporated.) In 1930 he made the unusual move of applying for registration as an architect to the board of architecture for the State of Florida. Up to then, his status had been "registered by exemption" in New York, but in July 1930 he took the Florida examinations—Addison, who had barely passed an examination in his life. (Byron Simonson said he was terrified.) He did well enough to be granted a special license, "registered by Senior Examination." The point of acquiring this certificate was that it would allow him to practice architecture in California.[32]

Since the Boca Raton fiasco, he had made several trips to Pebble Beach, with side trips to the ranch, where he was making additions to the farm buildings and landscaping the property. In 1932, besides the acquisition of an architectural license, there were other indications that he was planning to return permanently to California. Writing about the beauties of the Monterey Peninsula, he recalled his background with nostalgia: "Having been born in California I was seized at an early age with wanderlust and have lived for many years all over the world. It was nearly thirty years before I returned to my home state. I had seen so many things in the interim that I thought nothing could ever rival the gardens of England, the strange beautiful barrenness of Spain, some of the great mountains and rivers [and] rice fields in China, the tiny gardens and temples of Japan or the jungles of South America."

But he went on to say that he had now fallen in love with California all over again, especially the Monterey Peninsula, and "like an old fool with a young bride," the other landscapes fell away in an unflattering comparison.[33] In a last bid for a fresh, debt-free life, this Californian optimist once more prepared to pick up his belongings and try a new frontier. The "old fool" had done it enough times before. Why not reinvent himself one more time?

He had another, personal reason to spend more time in California. Ysabel, "lightly spawning," as she put it, had a baby in June 1932, called Kim Mizner Hollins, and Addison could hardly wait to see this latest addition to the family. Failing in health though he was, he thought nothing of making the six-thousand-mile drive across the country to see his beloved niece and the latest Mizner. Shortly after the announcement arrived, Arthur Somers Roche watched fondly as Addison settled his three-hundred-pound form into the seat of his roadster, accompanied by his favorite chow, Ching (who always traveled with him), and, after spraying himself with a Flit gun as a last defiant gesture to the mosquitoes, stepped on the starter: "He was off to San Francisco to greet the child who would carry on the fun-loving tradition of the clan."[34]

Addison and Wilson were reunited for the occasion, and Addison stayed on with Ysabel through July. Evidently starved for intellectual stimulus, he had Madena Galloway send him a box of books, including *Brave New World* by Aldous Huxley and *Mr. and Mrs. Pennington* by Francis Brett Young (a popular English novelist of middle-class life). A photograph of him was taken at the races at Del Monte, with the caption "Mr. Mizner is a brother of Wilson Mizner, the wit." "This should put you in your place," Wilson wrote on it.

During this time, more bad news arrived from Palm Beach. Mizner Industries, the last surviving fragment of Addison's business career, had declared bankruptcy. Thanks to one of Addison's more complex partnership arrangements, Mizner Industries owed Addison Mizner, Inc., something over $36,000. Since Addison Mizner, Inc., had about $700 in the bank, this failure to pay sank both companies. Facing this loss, Addison had no resources with which to pay the interest, mortgage, or running expenses on his California ranch, and in a gesture of despair, he signed it over to his niece. With this failure, another door closed. In a bitter note to Madena Galloway from Pebble Beach, he said that he was now "living on Ysabel."

In late August 1932 Wilson was stricken with pneumonia and spent several weeks in the hospital. By this time, he had parlayed his ephemeral career as a wit into something more substantial. He had become part owner of a restaurant called the Brown Derby, which became a legendary Hollywood hangout. Every night Wilson would be there at his table, handing out drinks and delivering epigrams, surrounded by his faithful admirers, including Florence Atkinson and Anita Loos. He was also writing screenplays for Warner Brothers. After recovering from this bout of pneumonia, he returned to the Ambassador Hotel, where he lived, making a few wisecracks to the press (who continued to slavishly report on his sayings), such as "I haven't breathed since '86 anyhow, so what difference did pneumonia make to me?"

Addison traveled from Pebble Beach several times to Los Angeles, anxious about the health of his little brother, whose pneumonia was connected to a heart problem as serious as his own. Thus Addison and Wilson, the last survivors of all those promising Mizner boys who had charmed San Francisco with their witty, swashbuckling ways, now greeted each other like two broken-down boxers against the ropes, slugging it out for a few more rounds for old times' sake.

On a visit to the Ambassador Hotel at the beginning of December, Addison himself collapsed (more competitiveness?) and, as he said, "took the spotlight" off Wilson for a while. He told Ysabel he had "culinary (or kitchen) thrombosis—at least that's what it sounds like." The doctor who examined him in Los Angeles found considerable myocardial damage, probably recent coronary thrombosis, and pronounced the prognosis to be "guarded." In spite of these health problems and financial worries, Addison, as always, tried to remain sanguine. His letters to Madena Galloway reflect his effort not to lose heart. "I think you had better pay the Jacksonville interest," he wrote her, "for fear some bank snaps shut." Then in the same breath, he added, "Ching looks like a different dog and spends hours chasing rabbits and deer."

Addison planned to visit Mineral Springs, Texas, for a few days to take a cure and then drive back to Palm Beach. This was an impossibly grueling journey to attempt alone, in the middle of December, so soon after his heart attack. "The trip was very rough from Los Angeles to El Paso," he admitted to Wilson on December 23. "I woke up in El Paso with a pouring rain, and from there on it was about as rotten a trip as can be imagined. It soon turned to snow and sleet and the temperature dropped from ten degrees to ten below zero." Arriving at the springs, he was considered too sick to take the water. The doctor examining him instead supplied him, as Addison said with typical humor, "with an identification card as to where to ship the corpse." Addison got back in the car. "I felt a little groggy when I reached Houston so rested up for a day and felt fine. In Alabama I struck stretches of road from five to twenty miles long of red clay—like we used at the pottery—and the cold lasted into northern Florida."[35]

Somehow, showing almost superhuman grit and courage, he managed to complete the terrible drive. Back in Palm Beach, he collapsed. On January 12 he had a series of heart attacks, combined with difficulty in breathing. In this seriously weakened condition, he received yet another blow. The wrangling with Washington over the budget for the Palm Beach federal building and post office had forced Addison to come up with cheaper materials—stucco instead of limestone facing for the facade, for instance, and plaster instead of marble for the walls of the lobby—and to delete plans for fountains in the courtyard. (Enormous numbers of revised sketches were produced, far more than the project merited.) But in spite of all these accommodations, the government finally canceled the project. Byron Simonson and Addison's office had accumulated huge fees for engineering, drafting, travel, blueprints, and the like, as well as hours spent by Addison, Madena Galloway, and their attorney. Much of this was never billed to the government, which already owed them over $2,000. These losses would never be recouped.

Furious and disappointed, Addison dictated a memo to Madena Galloway in which he said, "It seems so strange that when seven hundred millions of dollars have been appropriated for the building of post offices all over the country, that the $180,000 appropriated for the Palm Beach post office, that would give employment to a starving community, should be the one and only one stopped."[36]

This is not the voice of the cheerful Addison Mizner, but the disconsolate note of a sick man, desperately worried about money and his future. Sadness closed in with the news on January 26 that his old friend and sparring partner, Alva Belmont, had died in Paris. Addison had not been in touch with her since she started devoting her energies to her French estate, but the feisty suffragist had played a major role in his career, and she was greatly mourned.

Addison continued to work on the second volume of his autobiography, struggling against time to complete the manuscript that so many of his friends hoped would be even more amusing and revelatory than the first. On January 30, 1933, another heart seizure overtook him, an attack serious enough for Wilson to send several anxious telegrams, including the much-quoted wire "STOP DYING AM TRYING TO WRITE A COMEDY." Ysabel paid a flying visit, during which time Addison gave her a ring that had belonged to his mother. In making this gift, Addison was finally coming to terms with his mortality. "What have I to live for?" he reportedly asked worried visitors. "I've seen everything, been everywhere, and done everything. Now I can wait for the door to open."

On February 2, at the insistence of Wilson, whose concern at this time was exemplary, a Miami cardiologist visited Addison and, noting the patient's serious overweight, warned that his coronary sclerosis was advanced, and that at any time he might suffer a recurrence of his cardiac failure "with probable fatal results." The doctor prescribed absolute rest in an attempt to restore the damaged heart, but he added, "Mr. Mizner's restlessness under restraint constitutes a definite hazard."

Friends knew that the end was near. People telephoned and sent flowers. Marjorie Hutton sent a note of distress and asked if she could visit. Irving Berlin, who had cooled on the Mizners after the Boca Raton foolishness (aggravated by the nonpayment of Addison's loan), now returned to the bedside and kept Wilson apprised by telegram. Edward Moore, one of Addison's most faithful friends and clients, came by and interrogated Madena about the true facts of the architect's situation. On leaving, he took a check out of his pocket and made out the sum of $10,000 to cash and said, "Give that to Addison and tell him that it is a present from me." In response, Addison wrote on a slip of paper, "MARY BAKER EDDY MOORE YOUR PILLS ARE THE ONLY ONES THAT HAVE DONE ME ANY GOOD," and told Madena to give it to Moore, which she did.[37]

Although grateful for this gesture, Addison did not want charity or sympathy, and Madena was instructed to convey messages of confidence to the many inquiries from friends. So convincing was she that on February 3, Ysabel and McKim wired from California: "BOTH HYSTERICAL WITH JOY OVER YOUR IMPROVEMENT . . . PLEASE HURRY AND GET WELL ENOUGH TO COME OUT TO US RIGHT AWAY." On February 4, Wilson's companion and former "wife," Florence Atkinson, equally unaware of the seriousness of Addison's condition, sent a telegram telling him that Wilson had been made an honorary captain of the Los Angeles Police Department. "THANK GOD MAMA IS DEAD," Addison wired back.

A day later on Sunday afternoon, February 5, at 5:45 pm, Addison Mizner died.

CHAPTER 21

"THE KINDEST OF MEN, A LOYAL AND GENEROUS FRIEND, AND A HARD WORKER."

Addison had made a firm statement to Madena Galloway that he did not want a funeral service of any kind, religious or otherwise; that he wanted to be cremated without any fuss; and that the expenses of his burial were to be as reasonable as possible. He also told Madena that he wanted his ashes put in a certain Mizner-blue jar and sent to California.

But as often happens, the dead person's desires were not entirely followed. First of all, a plan by friends to have him lie in state in the mortuary had to be forcefully canceled by Madena. She could not, however, prevent the memorial service that was held on Thursday, February 9, at Villa Mizner, with Bishop Nathaniel Seymour Thomas officiating. The clergyman gave only a brief prayer, then moved into the secular realm, reading portions of Shelley's "Hymn to Intellectual Beauty," "Prometheus Bound," "Adonais, an Elegy on the Death of John Keats," and "Ozymandias," each poem reflecting different aspects of Addison's life. The reading ended with Tennyson's "Crossing the Bar." The tenor John Charles Thomas sang Stevenson's *Requiem*, set to music and played by Sidney Homer on the piano that had accompanied so many artists during Addison's soirées.

Villa Mizner looked particularly splendid that day. The rooms, with the pale-colored light from the stained-glass windows washing over Addison's fine Spanish furniture and furnishings, tile floors, wrought iron-work, paintings, tapestries, and reliquaries, powerfully evoked the departed architect. The flowers were spectacular, sent by friends from all over, including many of those who had followed Addison's Palm Beach journey since its inception fourteen years earlier—a short time for so much history. Yellow roses from the Huttons, pink gladioli, irises, daffodil, tulips, and carnations from the Dillmans, Easter lilies and red gladioli from Edith Rea, and, in a very personal tribute, a small bunch of orange blossoms pinned to Addison's chair from Eva Stotesbury.

The crush of guests was made up not only of the top echelons of the Palm Beach colony whom "darling Addie" had so long worked for and entertained. As well as clients and friends, an astonishing number of townspeople showed up. As an eyewitness described it, "Workmen who had helped create his visions in stone and tile, artisans who had copied the old wrought ironwork which he brought back from Spain . . . all met on common ground to pay tribute to a departed friend."[1]

The reporter Emilie Keyes was very moved by the occasion: "Without his ecclesiastical robes, Bishop Nathaniel Seymour Thomas . . . stood behind a huge mass of golden roses to conduct the memorial. Before him were gathered several hundred persons, crowding the room and thronging the hall outside. . . . Unable to obtain a place in the crowded room, in the hall stood Mr. and Mrs. Edward T. Stotesbury, the first to commission the noted architect in his Palm Beach career that was to transform the community into a dreamland of lovely homes. And outside the window, a tiny monkey walked restlessly up and down during the services, as though Nettie were inwardly chattering a farewell to the master, whose inseparable companion she had been."[2]

The only notable absences were family. Wilson, now very sick himself, remained in Hollywood. Margot and Alice Mizner were in Paris. The one who might have been expected to attend, Ysabel Chase Hollins, did not make the trip. She sent roses and gardenias. (After her uncle's death, Ysabel's life moved into the shadows. She showed enough talent to become a writer, but such hopes faded as her marriage dissolved into alcoholism. She died alone in 1967 in a cottage on the Pebble Beach estate not far from the charming house her uncle had so fondly built for her).[3]

Three other tributes to Addison were announced shortly after the memorial service. The Painters Local No. 452, of which Addison was an honorary life member, published a resolution expressing its deep regret for the death of "our departed brother." A few days later a special meeting was called at the Chamber of Commerce in West Palm Beach for the adoption of a resolution signed by the building trades of Palm Beach County, mourning the passing of "a great worker, a great friend and a great architect." The town council voted to change the name of the plaza north of the town hall, where Addison's memorial fountain and park were located, to Mizner Plaza.

Addison's ashes were sent to Cypress Lawn Cemetery in San Mateo, California, not far from Pebble Beach. There, in the lonely presence of Ysabel Hollins, Addison was placed in the ground. Just as in the case of Lansing and Ella Mizner, neither then nor later was there ever a marker.

But there were better ways to memorialize Addison. Letters poured in, all of them recalling darling Addie's wit, open-heartedness, and hospitality. His valet, Arthur Bedford, wrote an elegy to his beloved employer, recalling his love of people and animals, and his "big, broad smile." Journalist Alan Howard, writing in *The Social Spectator*, entitled his obituary "The Passing of a Giant." In an anonymous review of *The Many Mizners,* a writer captured the essence of his character: "You can see if you read between the lines that Addison Mizner, known to the wide world as a playboy when he was not architect and decorator, was the kindest of men, a splendid son, a good brother, a loyal and generous friend, and a hard worker. Addison Mizner was one of those simple souls who believed it best to trust all and be deceived than to doubt one worthy soul."

After the outpourings of grief and love came the hard facts about Addison's estate. He had made two different wills in two years. His first will, dated April 26, 1926, divided his estate into thirds, with three beneficiaries, Wilson, Henry, and Ysabel. In a later will, dated June 1928, he left $10,000 to Wilson, with the remainder of the estate split among Ysabel and Henry and Margot. He left his valet, Arthur Bedford, $5,000, with an extra $1,000 for every year after 1928 that he was in his employer's service. He bequeathed to Mary Ellin Berlin, daughter of Ellin Mackay Berlin and Irving Berlin, all his personal silver except that marked "Mizner." (This was perhaps in compensation for Irving Berlin's unpaid loan.) Other portraits and miniatures went to Ysabel.

On June 3, 1932, Addison wrote to his attorney, E. Harris Drew, asking for the return of this will, which he wished to cancel: "Things have changed so materially in finances that I would like to re-arrange the matter." But after cutting out his signature from the document, he told Madena Galloway he did not wish to make a new will; that since he owned practically nothing and everything belonged to the corporation, he thought the best thing would be to divide the stock among Ysabel, Wilson, and Henry's widow, Margot. Added shares were given to Madena and to Arthur Bedford. He completed this transaction in June 1932, stating that they were to be transferred after his death. The residuary estate was to be divided three ways among Ysabel, Wilson, and Margot, with the silver, portraits, and miniatures going to Ysabel. Since he died intestate, these distributions became a question for the lawyers.

The appraisers appointed by the judge of Palm Beach County found a modest number of possessions in the deceased's estate, the largest assessment being for traveler's checks worth $618, and estimated royalties from *The Many Mizners,* worth $750. There was some jewelry—emerald cufflinks and studs, onyx and diamond cufflinks, a gold cigarette case, a platinum sapphire ring, and some good antique silver salvers and dishes, including a rare chalice. The incomplete manuscript of his second memoir was worthless. The total value of Addison's possessions came to $2,604.50. The most nostalgic document among his papers was the stock certificate for $10,000 in the long-defunct Golden Gate Mining Company that had once been the treasured possession of his father.

As to his personal debts, a bank in West Palm Beach had a judgment against him for $30,000, and he owed his attorney, E. Harris Drew, $2,500. Mizner Industries and Addison Mizner, Inc., both owed large sums to various creditors, who wasted no time sending in their claims. Madena had repaid some of Edward Moore's cash gift but still owed him $4,000, and many small outstanding sums had been given by Mrs. Rea. Lawyers for Irving Berlin realized their quest for payment was hopeless. Madena hoped that everyone else would feel the same way, and that none of these debts would ever actually be called in.

Madena and Harris Drew were named coexecutors, and their sorry duty was somehow to absolve Addison's estate of its obligations. Madena furiously went to work. She wrote to his family and old friends, asking for loans to pay off mortgage interest and other outstanding debts. Ysabel did not respond, which annoyed Edward Moore, who complained he was "carrying the bag" when she was so much richer. (Indeed, Ysabel seems to have taken no further interest in her uncle, failing to answer letters or to sign documents that were sent to her. Harris Drew had to fly to California to get her signature.)[4]

Madena was determined to keep Addison Mizner, Inc., afloat; it still owned the Via Mizner shops and Addison's house. She was put in charge of the company in order to rent these properties, which was extremely difficult in such a depressed economy. She tried to put together a trust fund for Wendell Weed. Bills from suppliers continued to pour in, and Madena fended them off or paid them as best she could. She fired off letters to dealers and collectors who might be interested in buying Addison's furniture, tapestries, and rare books. She had some hope for his collection of fifteen crucifixes, dating from the eleventh through the seventeenth century, which had been on exhibit at the Boston Museum of Fine Arts, thanks to Frank G. Macomber, a winter resident and curator of the museum's department of decorative art. But in such an economic slump, nobody was interested. (The crucifixes are now in the Norton Museum of Art in West Palm Beach.) Alice DeLamar and Edith Rea bought a small number of antiques, but there were few other takers. There was a humiliating public sale. (Madena asked the newspapers running the advertisement to make the print as small as possible.) She put the rest in storage. (Madena's extraordinary efforts on behalf of her beloved Mr. Mizner did not go unnoticed. In April 1933, two months after Addison's death, Arthur Somers Roche, one of the architect's closest friends, inscribed a copy of *The Many Mizners* "to Madena Galloway, who ought to have been one of the Many Mizners.")

Madena wrote to Wilson almost every day after Addison's death, updating him on the financial situation. Wilson was now completely bedridden himself. Refusing to go to the hospital, he stayed in his room in the Ambassador Hotel, where Anita Loos anxiously monitored his decline.* With Addison gone, Mama's Angel Birdie was the last Mizner. He did not linger long. In an odd freak of timing, he died two months almost to the day after his brother, on March 4, 1933. He was fifty-eight years old.

---

*Her feelings for Wilson were genuine and deep. Every year after he died, she marked the date in black on her calendar.[5]

Perhaps it was no freak. The two brothers had an almost symbiotic relationship. It is tempting to describe them as the "good" and the "bad" brother, and that is how many people saw them. Both supertall, one portly, the other rail-thin, one fair, one dark, the "day" Mizner and the "night" Mizner—in a novel it would seem too neat. Their similarities were as striking as their differences. Both were quick-witted and verbal, and both loved racy humor. They were both Californians at heart, easterners by ambition. Neither ever had a lasting relationship with anybody.

They had been shackled together at birth by their mother, the omnipotent, adored, and adoring jailer. When she died, the chains came off, but not for long. Alice DeLamar, Alex Waugh, Madena Galloway, and a few other close friends knew the depth of the two brothers' connection to each other. When Wilson abandoned Florida, Addison was bereft. Addison openly admitted that Wilson was "my chief weakness and dreaded menace." Yet he also candidly declared that his brother was "the only one I knew and loved in the world." Sadly, the truth, in all its complex paradoxes, did not set him free.

Wilson left the whole of his estate, including copyrights, manuscripts, and the nonexistent $10,000 he inherited from Addison, to Florence Atkinson, the woman who had played his wife in Palm Beach and remained a stalwart companion. "He was the best and dearest friend I ever had," she said on hearing the news. "Only a few pierced that gay and cynical armor of brilliant wit and learned of the kindly understanding man beneath it." Like his brother, Wilson requested no funeral service or memorial. His cremated remains were taken to Cypress Lawn Cemetery in San Mateo. Ysabel, who had seen Addison's ashes interred there only two months earlier, was the sole member of the family to see Wilson's ashes laid in the unmarked ground beside his brother's.

Wilson Mizner was fortunate to escape the opprobrium that Addison received after his death. Journalists wrote the usual commentary about Wilson's colorful life and the passing of this decadent, irreverent, profligate Broadway legend, "Hollywood's Bad Boy." Although his witty sayings have not lasted, posterity has given Wilson the benefit of the doubt, and he appears as an audacious and intriguing roué in many theatrical memoirs. Writing about the two brothers, Alva Johnston (in 1953) and John Weidman (in 1999) conceded that the character of Wilson dominated their material.

Addison's career, on the other hand, while far more substantive, came under attack almost immediately. The architectural establishment rose up with one voice against him. He was an outsider. He came from California. He didn't have a Beaux-Arts degree. He didn't belong to the right clubs, like the American Institute of Architects, or sit on the right boards, like the Municipal Art Society. (He didn't sit on any boards.) His architecture was scorned for its reactionary style, and his Palm Beach mansions were regarded as absurd white elephants, totally unsuited to the times. Many of his houses were later "modernized," stripped of their elaborate decoration, and ravaged by air conditioning. Others were simply too large to maintain in a tight economy and abandoned; five houses, including three of his greatest ones—El Mirasol, Playa Riente, and Casa Bendita—were demolished.

Alva Johnston, in *The Legendary Mizners,* published in 1953, transformed the myth of the architect's lack of training and playboy lifestyle into fact. When Alice DeLamar discovered Johnston's intentions, she wrote him a long letter in an effort to persuade him of Addison's true character. After the book was published, she said, "When I met [Johnston] I knew right away that he would never understand anything about Addison and I knew I would dislike his book. I did."[6]

The damage went even further than she feared. Reviewer Frank G. Lopez took Johnston's libels and embroidered them. He described Addison as a "shady 'architect'" (his quotation marks) and "a pompous pseudo-esthete who, repugnant though he was, found women to climb into bed with." This vicious picture of the immoral, "never-legitimately-frocked 'architect'" was published where it would hurt the most: in the magazine of Addison's peers, *Architectural Record.*[7] Much later, the slanders were still being trotted out. Raymond B. Vickers, in his book on the Florida bank scandals of 1926, mocked the idea that Mizner might have had any architectural ability, referring to him as a con man, "seducing the elite of society with his fantasy."[8]

Now, of course, it's a different story. While Wilson Mizner has become a faded caricature of a distant age, the name Addison Mizner is today worth far more than the gold dust he retrieved from the Klondike. It is worth more than the fees he received from the Stotesburys and the Cosdens, and far more than all the antiques he purchased from Europe over the years. It is worth more than Boca Raton ever promised its eager speculators. Postmodernism, revisionism, and that old warhorse, customer demand, have forgiven Addison's architectural crimes.

To a hungry real estate group assembled in 1925 in Miami, Addison gave an oddly prophetic message: "Boca Raton is my life's work to which I shall give my all," he declared. "With me the name of Mizner ends and I intend to leave Boca Raton as my last monument." In a delightful irony, Boca Raton, like its neighbor, Palm Beach, is indebted to Addison Mizner's name today to such an extent that real estate promoters use it in sales pitches, not only to identify the houses that he built (or that they claim he built) but also to identify new developments and properties that have little or nothing to do with the late architect. He would be amused to see what is offered in his name—condominiums, shopping plazas, gated communities are proudly called Mizner Lake Estates, Addison's Reserve, Mizner Country Club, Mizner Park, and so on. The power of the Mizner mystique is such that one of his last and most charming houses, Villa Encantada, built for Jerome Gedney in 1928, was recently sliced into three parts at a cost of many millions of dollars and shipped sixty miles north up the intracoastal waterway from Manalapan, rather than be demolished. Even Mizner Industries has been resuscitated, selling pottery, wrought iron, and ornamental quarry stone. His name has become an icon, radiating romance and luxury.

Perhaps the most ironic twist of all should be credited to Philip Johnson, promoter in his early career of the International Style and enemy of everything Mizner stood for. In 1977 Johnson was invited by the governing commission of Miami to build them an office building. Hoping for one of Johnson's trademark modernist glass boxes, instead they were presented with a Mediterranean building in the style of Addison Mizner, with arcades, a terra-cotta-tile barrel roof, and cream-colored stucco walls.[9]

At the height of the Boca Raton boom, Addison made an unusually impassioned plea. "Merely to build is not enough," he said. "We must build beautifully, with constant thoughts for ocular balance, fine proportion and symmetrical ensemble. Erecting a structure that is ugly will, of course, serve as a housing domicile but so will a cow shed. All human beings yearn for beauty, and by careful study of environment an architect can use all of nature's gifts, the roll of the land or its plainness, the streams, plant life, shrubbery, trees and adjacent lakes and erect his structures so that they are in harmony with nature's bestowal and not a discord and jangle for the human eye to behold."[10]

Architects often use arcane and obscurantist language when discussing issues of architecture. In contrast, this simple, earthy disclosure of an irreproachable architectural aesthetic stands as the ultimate expression of Addison Mizner's life and work.

NOTES

ABBREVIATIONS

ACM—Addison Cairns Mizner

ALSWC—Avery Architectural and Fine Arts Library, Columbia University, Stanford White Correspondence

BRHS—Boca Raton Historical Society

EWM—Ella Watson Mizner

HSPBC—Historical Society of Palm Beach County

HWM—Henry Watson Mizner

LBM—Lansing Bond Mizner

LM—Lansing Mizner

MGN—Madena Galloway Nelrich archive

MM—Addison Mizner, *The Many Mizners* (New York: Sears Publishing Co., 1932)

OMC—Oakland Museum of California, Mizner Collection

PS—Paris Singer

PSNC—Preservation Society of Newport County

SFAPB—Society of the Four Arts, Palm Beach

WGM—William Garrison Mizner

WM—Wilson Mizner

§ PREFACE

1 A great many other Mizner papers are in the collections of the Historical Society of Palm Beach County, the Boca Raton Historical Society, the Society of the Four Arts, the Oakland Museum of California, and other archives.

2 Geoffrey Perrett, *America in the Twenties: Days of Sadness, Years of Triumph* (New York: Simon & Schuster, 1982), p. 359.

∮ CHAPTER I

Unless otherwise specified, all of Addison Mizner's quotes in this and subsequent chapters come from his autobiography, *The Many Mizners.*

1 Family file. MGN.
2 Ibid.
3 MM, p. 3.
4 Jacqueline McCart Woodruff, *Benicia: The Promise of California* (Benicia Centennial Committee, 1947).
5 Peter Thomas Conmy, *Benicia— Intended Metropolis* (San Francisco: Native Sons of the Golden West, 1958).

6 *Solano Republican,* June 15, 1866.
7 *Journal of Illinois State Historical Society* (October 1914), p. 265. MGN.
8 Ibid., pp. 264–66.
9 EWM, letter to Franklin Reynolds, April 3, 1853. OMC.
10 A. F. Rodgers, letter to HWM, 1907. MGN.
11 Family file. MGN.
12 LBM, letter to EWM, February 12, 1856. OMC.
13 Obituary of EWM in *St. Stephen's Chimes,* St. Louis, Mo., May 1915. MGN.

∮ CHAPTER 2

1 Elsie Robinson, *I Wanted Out* (New York: Farrar & Rinehart, 1934), p. 5.
2 *Solano Historian,* May 1989.
3 Ibid., December 1985.
4 George E. Hyde, letter to *Benicia New Era,* August 15, 1888.
5 Mizner file. OMC.

6 William Kip, letter to EWM, October 1, 1866. MGN.
7 According to Lucy Gray, a childhood friend of the Mizners, Henry climbed a tree to escape being kissed by Lucy and broke his collarbone falling out of it! (Lucy Gray, pencil note in her copy of MM).

∮ CHAPTER 3

1 EWM, letter to WGM, July 23, 1888. OMC.
2 Mizner children file. OMC.

3 Letter, EWM, ibid.
4 *Benicia New Era,* January 19, 1889.
5 Ibid., May 11, 1889.

∮ CHAPTER 4

1 Evelyn Wells, *Champagne Days of San Francisco* (New York: D. Appleton–Century, 1939), pp. 68ff.
2 Harry Ludlam, *Captain Scott: The Full Story* (Slough, Bucks, England: W. Foulsham & Co., 1965).
3 R. Huntford, Scott Polar Research Institute, London, letter to curators of *The Many Mizners* exhibition, OMC, September 1978. In his letter, which reveals the relationship, Huntford asked if the archives contained any other letters about or references to these encounters with Minnie Chase, explaining that Scott had acquired a black mark during his naval career that might stem from this incident. No other references were found, however.

4 *San Francisco Examiner,* June 14, 1891.
5 Arnold Genthe, *As I Remember* (New York: Reynal & Hitchcock, 1936), p. 46.
6 ACM's journal. MGN.
7 *Report of the Secretary of Foreign Relations of the Republic of Guatemala to the National Legislative Assembly Concerning the Capture and Death of General J. Martin Barrundia, March 31, 1891.*
8 Christina Orr, *Addison Mizner: Architect of Dreams and Realities (1872–1933)* (Palm Beach, Fla.: Norton Gallery and School of Art, 1977), p. 13, note 5.
9 Genthe, *As I Remember,* p. 54.
10 Frederick Platt, *America's Gilded Age: Its Architecture and Decoration* (New Jersey and New York: A. S. Barnes & Co., 1976), p. 17.

11 In MM, Addison says Martin was at Jamestown, but since Martin's brother Andrew went to Georgetown, it seems likely that Addison made a mistake—not his first.

CHAPTER 5

1 ACM journal. MGN.
2 Harold Kirker, *California's Architectural Frontier* (Salt Lake City: Peregrine Smith Books, 1986), p. 118.
3 Frederick Hamilton, "The Work of Willis Polk & Company," *Architect & Engineer*, vol. 24 (April 1911), p. 35.
4 *Architectural Record*, July 1916, p. 1.
5 Ibid., June 1909, p. 434.
6 *Wave*, April 15, 1898, p. 67.
7 *Architectural Record*, December 1913, pp. 556–83.
8 Richard Longstreth, *On the Edge of the*

CHAPTER 6

1 EWM, letter to ACM, November 10, 1897. OMC.
2 HWM, letter to ACM, July 23, 1898. OMC.
3 Wells, *Champagne Days,* p. 124.
4 F. La Roche, *En Route to the Klondike*

CHAPTER 7

1 ACM, letter to EWM, June 7, 1898. Unless otherwise indicated, ACM's quotes in this chapter come from MM and from his letters to his mother in 1898 and 1899.
2 Richard O'Connor, *Jack London: A Biography* (Boston: Little, Brown, 1964), p. 97.
3 Burke, *Rogue's Progress,* p. 25.
4 Pierre Berton, *The Klondike Fever: The Life and Death of the Last Great Gold Rush* (New York: Alfred A. Knopf, 1975), p. 401.

CHAPTER 8

1 Lanier McKee, *The Land of Nome* (New York: Grafton Press, 1902), p. 33.
2 Richard O'Connor, *High Jinks on the Klondike* (Indianapolis and New York: Bobbs-Merrill, 1954), p. 220.
3 ACM spelled the dog's name "Scramble" Eggs in his memoir (another example of his careless spelling), which was then perpetuated in later references.

12 EWM, letter to ACM, November 20, 1897. OMC.
13 LBM, letter to EWM, May 26, 1866. OMC.

World: Four Architects in San Francisco at the Turn of the Century (Cambridge, Mass.: MIT Press, 1989), passim.
9 Alva Johnston says Polk was *called* Whistler, "because of his genius for making enemies," indicating just one of many misunderstandings in Johnston's book about the Mizners: *The Legendary Mizners* (New York: Farrar, Straus & Young, 1953).
10 *Chicago American,* January 17, 1933, p. 19.
11 Mario Rosenthal, *Guatemala* (New York: Twayne, 1962). ACM's recollection is not entirely accurate as to dates.

(Chicago and New York: W. B. Conkey Co., 1898), passim.
5 ACM, letter to EWM, February 2, 1898. MGN.
6 John Burke, *Rogue's Progress* (New York: G. P. Putnam's Sons, 1975), p. 34.

5 Burke, *Rogue's Progress,* p. 36.
6 Berton, *Klondike Fever,* p. 387.
7 Ibid., p. 37.
8 According to Berton, *Klondike Fever,* p. 312, the sisters were called Gussie, Nellie, and Grace Lamore, not Pickering.
9 Jack "Doc" Kearns with Oscar Fraley, *The Million Dollar Gate* (New York: Macmillan, 1966), p. 27.
10 Ibid., p. 29.
11 HWM, letter to ACM, July 28, 1898.

4 A. J. Moore (Sunday editor of *San Francisco Call*), letter to ACM, October 30, 1901. MGN.
5 ACM, San Francisco driver's license, 1903.
6 *New York Times,* July 19, November 10 and 11, 1904.
7 *San Francisco Chronicle,* December 2, 1904.

ᕫ CHAPTER 9

1 Caroline Seebohm, *The Man Who Was Vogue: The Life and Times of Condé Nast* (New York: Viking Press, 1986), p. 41.

2 A. C. David, "The New Architecture," *Architectural Record,* December 1910.

3 Gerald Langford, *The Richard Harding Davis Years: A Biography of a Mother and Son* (New York: Holt, Rinehart & Winston, 1961), pp. 141, 153, 166.

4 Stanford White, letter to Richard Harding Davis, November 18, 1895, ALSWC, vol. 14, p. 306.

5 Helen Benedict, letter to Stanford White, January 12, 1899, ALSWC, vol. 21, p. 327.

6 Paul R. Baker, *Stanny: The Gilded Life of Stanford White* (New York: Free Press, 1989), pp. 346–49.

7 ACM scrapbook, SFAPB.

8 Architect Thomas Bollay, interviewed by author, May 11, 2000.

9 WGM, telegram to ACM. OMC. April 20, 1906.

10 Stanford White, letter to Daniel Burnham and Willis Polk, April 26, 1906, ALSWC, vol. 35, pp. 494 ff.

11 Stanford White, letter to James W. Morrissey, April 28, 1906, ALSWC, vol. 36, p. 16.

ᕫ CHAPTER 10

1 *San Francisco Call,* December 13, 14, 1905.

2 There are several spellings of Alice's name, and her signature often looks like "Alice De Lamar." But on one extant letterhead, her name is printed "Alice DeLamar," which presumably settles the matter.

3 Alice DeLamar, letter to Alva Johnston, March 14, 1948. HSPBC.

4 Fairfax Downey, *Portrait of an Era as Drawn by C. D. Gibson* (New York: Charles Scribner's Sons, 1936), p. 102.

5 Richard Harding Davis, in *Colliers,* August 4, 1906, p. 17. See also Langford, *Richard Harding Davis Years,* p. 255.

6 Evelyn Nesbit, *Prodigal Days: The Untold Story* (New York: Julian Messner, 1934), p. 227.

7 Addison joined the Lambs' Club in 1905; interestingly, his profession was entered as "writer and critic." He was not yet ready to call himself an architect. There is no record of who proposed him, but it was very likely his old friend Richard Harding Davis, who had joined in 1903.

8 Seebohm, *Man Who Was Vogue,* p. 146.

9 Mizner file. OMC.

10 Margaret Hayden Rector, *Alva, That Vanderbilt-Belmont Woman* (Los Angeles: Dutch Island Press, 1992), p. 235.

11 Allen Churchill, *The Upper Crust, an Informal History of New York's Highest Society* (Englewood Cliffs, N.J.: Prentice Hall, 1970), p. 201.

ᕫ CHAPTER 11

1 Robert B. Mackay, Anthony Baker, and Carol A. Traynor, *Long Island Country Houses and Their Architects, 1860–1940* (New York: Society for the Preservation of Long Island Antiquities, in association with W. W. Norton & Co., 1997), p. 19.

2 *Plain Talk,* December 23, 1911, pp. 117–18.

3 *Plain Talk,* November 1911, p. 72; December 9, 1911, p. 104.

4 EWM, letter to ACM, March 23, 1913. MGN.

5 EWM, letter to ACM, February 14, 1912. MGN.

6 EWM, letter to LM, August 16, 1890. OMC.

7 WGM, letter to HWM, September 2, 1920. MGN.

8 *San Francisco Examiner,* December 21, 1918, p. 11.

9 Mary Watson, letter to HWM, January 19, 1919. MGN.

10 EWM, letter to ACM, February 14, 1912. MGN.

11 Randall Bourscheidt, interviewed by author, August 16, 1999.

12 EWM, letter to HWM, September 2, 1914. MGN.

13 Johnston, *Legendary Mizners,* p. 139.

14 Jim Tully, *A Dozen and One* (Hollywood: Murray & Gee, 1943), pp. 115–16.

15 George Bronson-Howard, *Birds of Prey* (New York: W. J. Watt & Co., 1918), passim.

❧ CHAPTER 12

1 *House & Garden,* April 1916, p. 41; October 1916, p. 35; January 1917, p. 34.

2 *The Luxury Yachts* (Alexandria, Va.: Time-Life Books, 1981), p. 128.

3 *New York Times,* February 4, 1909, p. 9.

4 *Plain Talk,* September 16, 1911, p. 5.

5 Archibald S. White, letter to ACM, September 15, 1907. MGN.

6 *Plain Talk,* October 14, 1911, p. 37.

7 Ibid., pp. 37–38.

8 *Plain Talk,* November 25, 1911, pp. 85–86.

9 *Plain Talk,* February 17, 1912, p. 59.

10 Donald W. Curl, *Mizner's Florida: American Resort Architecture* (Cambridge, Mass.: MIT Press, 1984), p. 36.

11 *House & Garden,* October 1921, p. 33.

12 Mary Jane Poole, Caroline Seebohm, and Miki Denhof, *20th Century Decorating, Architecture, and Gardens* (New York: Holt, Rinehart & Winston, 1980), pp. 74–75.

❧ CHAPTER 13

1 Most of the material not otherwise identified in this and the following chapters comes from ACM's unpublished typescript of the second volume of his memoir. BRHS.

2 Claude Bragdon, "Architecture in the United States," *Architectural Record,* June 1909, pp. 426–34.

3 Ruth Brandon, *A Capitalist Romance* (Philadelphia and New York: J. B. Lippincott, 1977), p. 197.

4 Genthe, *As I Remember,* p. 183.

❧ CHAPTER 14

1 *Palm Beach Post,* August 8, 1918.

2 Ida Tarbell, *Florida Architecture of*

16 Walter Winchell, in *Daily Mirror,* September 14, 1932.

17 *Plain Talk,* April 13, 1912, p. 120.

18 EWM, letter to HWM, March 23, 1913. MGN.

19 ACM manuscript, p. 66. HSPBC.

20 HWM, letter to ACM, October 6, 1921. OMC. Courtesy of Sally Hollins.

13 Mackay, *Long Island Country Houses,* p. 268.

14 Ibid., p. 437.

15 Harold Bush-Brown, *Beaux Arts to Bauhaus and Beyond* (New York: Whitney Library of Design/Watson-Guptill Publications, 1976), p. 24.

16 *New York Times,* March 5, 1911, sec. 7, p. 5.

17 Alva Murray Vanderbilt Belmont, *Memoirs* (typescript), p. 166, Rare Book, Manuscript and Special Collections Library, Duke University, Durham, N.C.

18 *New York Times,* May 14, 1911, sec. 5, p. 5.

19 Donald W. Curl suggests this assignment was a consolation prize for losing the Beacon Hill commission; *Mizner's Florida,* p. 36.

20 *San Francisco Call,* January 26, 1916.

21 Betty Lee, *Marie Dressler, The Unlikeliest Star* (Lexington: University Press of Kentucky, 1997), pp. 117–18.

5 Alice DeLamar, letter to Mrs. John G. Hupfel, 1975. HSPBC.

6 In his memoir, ACM spells her name Joan Bates. Alfred and Elizabeth Kay, who knew her well, spell it Balsh. The author, for obvious reasons, prefers the latter version.

7 Stephen Birmingham, *The Last Resorts* (New York: Harper & Brothers, 1948), p. 329.

8 *Palm Beach Post,* July 26, 1918.

9 ACM, letter to HWM, 1918. MGN.

Addison Mizner (New York: Dover Publications, 1992), p. xxxi.

3 *Palm Beach Post,* September 5, 1918, p. 2.

Chapter 14 (cont.)
4 Edward C. Michener, *The Everglades Club: A Retrospective, 1919–1985* (Palm Beach, Fla.: Everglades Club, 1985), p. 16.
5 *Palm Beach Post,* September 14, 1918, p. 1.
6 Michener, *Everglades Club,* p. 19.
7 *Tropical Sun,* February 21, 1919, p. 8. HSPBC.

⑤ CHAPTER 15
1 *Palm Beach Daily News,* March 30, 1924. HSPBC.
2 Johnston, *Legendary Mizners,* p. 231.
3 Tarbell, *Florida Architecture of Addison Mizner,* p. xxxix.
4 Mary Fanton Roberts, "Exotic Beauty of

⑤ CHAPTER 16
1 Alex Waugh, unpublished manuscript, chap. 7, pp. 13–14. BRHS.
2 Ibid., p. 13.
3 Christina Orr, *Addison Mizner: Architect of Dreams and Realities (1872–1933)* (Palm Beach, Fla.: Norton Gallery and School of Art, 1977), pp. 24–25.
4 Alice DeLamar, letter to Alva Johnston, March 14, 1948. HSPBC, p. 15.

⑤ CHAPTER 17
1 Waugh manuscript, chap. 8, p. 22.
2 *Palm Beach Daily News,* January 8, 1925.
3 Edith Eglin, letter to author, December 4, 1999.
4 Agnes Munn, letter to ACM, September 16, 1925. MGN.
5 Eva Stotesbury, cable to ACM, November 24, 1926. MGN.
6 Oelrichs scrapbooks. PSNC.
7 Gerald Bordman, *Jerome Kern, His Life and Music* (New York: Oxford University Press, 1980), pp. 203, 304.
8 Laurence Bergreen, *As Thousands Cheer* (New York: Viking Penguin, 1990), p. 215.
9 Mary Ellin Barrett, *Irving Berlin: A Daughter's Memoir* (New York: Simon & Schuster, 1994), p. 63.
10 Alexander Woollcott, *The Story of Irving*

8 Gilbert M. Thompson, *El Mirasol* (New Jersey: Thompson, 1919), p. 7.
9 Alfred and Elizabeth Kay, *Reminiscences of Paris Singer, Addison Mizner, and Everglades Club* (fiftieth-anniversary keepsake for members, 1969). HSPBC.
10 Mrs. Merriweather Post, memo to Alfred J. Brannon, Jr., *El Mirasol,* p. 27.

Palm Beach Homes," *Arts & Decoration,* December 1923, p. 22.
5 Mackay, *Long Island Country Houses,* p. 228.
6 Orr, *Addison Mizner,* pp. 24–25.
7 Eva Stotesbury, letter to Bertha Berdel, October 1926. HSPBC.

5 Waugh manuscript, p. 13.
6 Interview in *Fort Lauderdale News,* November 26, 1983.
7 Donald W. Curl, "The Florida Architecture of F. Burrall Hoffman Jr.," *The Florida Historical Quarterly* (spring 1998), p. 408.
8 Waugh manuscript, p. 10.
9 WM, letter to WGM, May 26, 1922. MGN.

Berlin (New York: G. P. Putnam's Sons, 1925), p. 99.
11 Anita Loos, *Kiss Hollywood Goodbye* (New York: Viking Press, 1974), p. 99.
12 Waugh manuscript, chap. 4, p. 8.
13 A. Louise Darry, letter to ACM, undated. MGN.
14 Helen Sheehy, *Eva Le Gallienne* (New York: Alfred A. Knopf, 1996), p. 449.
15 DeLamar to Johnston, March 14, 1948, p. 19.
16 Anita Loos, letter to Camille Showalter, June 5, 1978. OMC.
17 Loos, *Kiss Hollywood Goodbye,* p. 98.
18 Jim Tully, "California Playboy," *Esquire,* July 1938.
19 DeLamar to Johnston, March 14, 1948, pp. 39–40.

❧ CHAPTER 18

1 Curl, *Mizner's Florida,* p. 111.
2 *New York Times,* February 7, 1924, p. 2.
3 Paul Moore, *Presences: A Bishop's Life in the City* (New York: Farrar, Straus & Giroux, 1997), p. 22.
4 Donald W. Curl, *Palm Beach County: An Illustrated History* (Northridge, Calif.: Windsor Publications, 1999), p. 68.
5 *Architectural Forum,* vol. 41, August 1924, pp. 73–76.
6 Harriet Sisson Gillespie, "Florida's Patios Rival Those of Seville," in *Arts & Decoration,* January 1926, p. 50.
7 Gurnee Munn, letter to ACM, September 9, 1925. MGN.
8 Howard Major, "A Theory Relating to Spanish and Italian Houses in Florida," in *Architectural Forum,* August 1926, pp. 97–104.
9 Augusta Owen Patterson, *American Homes of Today* (New York: Macmillan & Co., 1924), p. 23.
10 *Palm Beach Daily News,* January 8, 1925, p. 3. HSPBC.
11 *Palm Beach Post,* December 12, 1924.
12 Johnston, *Legendary Mizners,* p. 267.

13 *Palm Beach Post,* May 31, 1925.
14 Perrett, *America in the Twenties,* p. 358.
15 Kenneth L. Roberts, *Florida Loafing* (Indianapolis: Bobbs-Merrill, 1924), p. 42.
16 Johnston, *Legendary Mizners,* p. 214.
17 *Palm Beach Post,* June 6, 1925.
18 ACM, letter to HWM, August 15, 1925. HSPBC.
19 José María Sert, letter to ACM, June 10, 1925. MGN.
20 Karl Riddle, in *Engineering News-Record,* December 30, 1926.
21 Karl Riddle, interview with Sanford Smith, March 4, 1980. BRHS.
22 *National Magazine,* December 1925, p. 205.
23 *New York Times,* October 10, 1925, p. 4.
24 *Palm Beach Post,* November 6, 1925.
25 *Palm Beach Post,* November 8, 1925.
26 Johnston, *Legendary Mizners,* p. 281. Although Johnston provided no sources in his book, it seems clear he interviewed du Pont about the Boca Raton affair.
27 *New York Times,* November 25, 29, 1925, p. 25.

❧ CHAPTER 19

1 *Palm Beach Life,* December 1981, p. 132. HSPBC.
2 Riddle, interview with Smith.
3 Sheet music document. MGN.
4 Curl, *Mizner's Florida,* p. 156.
5 *New York Times,* June 22, 1926, p. 3; June 30, 1926, p. 1.
6 ACM, letter to WM, July 1, 1927. MGN.
7 ACM, letter to Pomposa de Escandon, August 17, 1926. MGN.
8 Raymond B. Vickers, *Panic in Paradise: Florida's Banking Crash of 1926* (Tuscaloosa, Ala.: University of Alabama Press, 1994), pp. 5–31.
9 James R. Nicholson (president of Central Equities Corporation), letter to WM, July 1926.
10 Louise Darry, letter to ACM, September 1926. MGN.
11 Johnston, *Legendary Mizners,* p. 294.

12 ACM and WM, telegrams, September 30, October 9, October 21, 1925. MGN.
13 Mrs. E. C. Elder, letter to WM, March 9, 1926. MGN.
14 J. M. Siebert, letter to WM, February 23, 1926. MGN.
15 *New York Times,* February 17, 1926, p. 23; February 18, p. 2.
16 Adele Robinson, letter to ACM, undated. MGN.
17 N. J. Hess, letter to WM, January 6, 1926. MGN.
18 Burke, *Rogue's Progress,* p. 262.
19 Bishop Cameron Mann, letter to HWM, November 16, 1926. BRHS.
20 George M. Osborn, letter to ACM, September 30, 1932. MGN.
21 *New York Times,* April 10, April 30, 1927.
22 PS, letter to ACM, May 27, 1927. MGN.

Chapter 19 (cont.)
23 PS, letter to ACM, November 19, 1927. MGN.
24 ACM, letter to PS, November 22, 1927. MGN.

❦ CHAPTER 20
1 *New York Times,* March 10, 1927, p. 7.
2 ACM, letter to WM, December 1, 1927. MGN.
3 *New York Times,* November 7, 1927, p. 21.
4 ACM, letter to WM, July 6, 1927. MGN.
5 Hunter S. Frost, *Art, Artifacts, Architecture: Fountain Valley School* (Colorado Springs, Colo.: Tiverton Press, 1979).
6 ACM, letter to WM, November 10, 1927. MGN.
7 Marie Dressler, *My Own Story* (Boston: Little, Brown, 1934), p. 213.
8 ACM, letter to Alice DeLamar, undated. HSPBC.
9 ACM, letter to WM, July 6, 1927. MGN.
10 Marion Sims Wyeth, interview with Christina Orr-Cahall, February 28, 1975, in J. Camille Showalter, ed., *The Many Mizners, California Clan Extraordinary,* p. 52 (1978). OMC.
11 Michael Ross, "Palm Beach Architecture at Its Best," in *Home & Field,* January 1930, pp. 11–13.
12 Curtis Patterson, "A Shelf of New Books: Addison Mizner and Florida," in *International Studio,* August 1928, p. 72.
13 Harold H. Martin, *This Happy Isle: The Story of Sea Island and The Cloister* (Sea Island, Ga.: Sea Island Co., 1978), p. 42.
14 Curl, *Mizner's Florida,* p. 186.
15 Matlack Price, "Returning to Romanticism," *Arts & Decoration,* October 1930, pp. 49–53.
16 Tim Street-Porter, *The Los Angeles House* (New York: Clarkson Potter, 1995), pp. 60–65.

25 PS, letter to ACM, November 28, 1927. MGN.
26 *Palm Beach Daily News,* June 25, 1932, p. 1. HSPBC.

17 DeLamar to Johnston, March 14, 1948, p. 46.
18 Maurice Fatio, letter to Oscar G. Davies (publisher of *Palm Beach Daily News*), March 9, 1929.
19 Madena Galloway note. MGN.
20 ACM, letter to WM, October 11, 1927. MGN.
21 Seebohm, *Man Who Was Vogue,* p. 14.
22 MGN, letter to Irving Berlin, March 8, 1929. MGN.
23 ACM, letter to WM, July 1, 1927. MGN.
24 MGN, letter to WM, February 28, 1933. MGN.
25 Curl, *Mizner's Florida,* pp. 194–95.
26 DeLamar to Johnston, March 14, 1948, p. 18.
27 L. Jonke, letters to WM and ACM, September 21 and November 2, 1932. MGN.
28 *Palm Beach Post,* March 10, 1932.
29 Ozie Bella Brown, interview, 1992. HSPBC.
30 ACM, letter to A. D. Butler, June 21, 1932. MGN.
31 MGN, letter to AM, September 20, 1932. MGN.
32 Curl, *Mizner's Florida,* p. 191.
33 Addison Mizner, "A Mecca for Artists," *California Arts & Architecture,* January 1932, pp. 27–28.
34 Arthur Somers Roche, foreword to MM.
35 ACM, letter to WM, December 23, 1932. MGN.
36 ACM, undated memo. MGN.
37 MGN, letter to WM, February 28, 1933. MGN.

❦ CHAPTER 21
1 *Palm Beach Daily News,* February 10, 1933.

2 *Palm Beach Post,* February 10, 1933.
3 Sally Hollins, interview by author, December 4, 1999.

Chapter 21 (cont.)

4 DeLamar to Johnston, March 14, 1948, p. 44.

5 Cari Beauchamp, *Without Lying Down,* A Lisa Drew Book (New York: Scribner, 1997), p. 305.

6 DeLamar to Johnston, March 14, 1948, note on letter. OMC.

7 Frank G. Lopez, "We Were Having Some People In for Cocktails," in *Architectural Record,* July 1953, p. 46.

8 Vickers, *Panic in Paradise,* p. 22.

9 Franz Schultze, *Philip Johnson: Life and Work* (New York: Alfred A. Knopf, 1994), p. 352.

10 *Miami Town Talk,* February 7, 1926, p. 98.

INDEX

Mizner, Addison Cairns (*cont'd*):
  in Florida, *see* Boca Raton; Palm Beach
  in Guatemala, 36–39, 63, 90, 95–97, 98, 187
  in Hawaii, 90–93
  ill health of, 49, 51, 157, 159, 183, 200, 228, 234, 237, 242, 248–49, 251–54
  influence of, 262–63
  interior decoration by, 124–25, 134–35, 138, 139, 164, 167, 168–69, 178, 179, 184, 187, 191–93, 210, 240–41
  landscape and garden designs by, 135–36, 138, 163–64, 187, 241–42, 243–44
  leg injury of, 31–33, 151–52, 154, 159, 171, 183
  lucky life of, 63, 72, 90, 93, 94, 105, 159, 184
  marriage prospects for, 85–86
  memoirs of, 84, 105, 116, 247–48, 253, 257, 258, 259
  money worries of, 59, 60–63, 64, 90, 92–93, 145, 226–27, 228, 232, 234, 244–47, 248, 253
  in New York, *see* New York City
  and parents' deaths, 52, 132–33
  personality traits of, 4, 47, 61, 79, 105, 120, 121, 145, 154, 162, 195, 200
  pets of, 36, 54, 125, 141, 142, 187, 188, 192, 195, 214, 228
  physical appearance of, 5, 29, 59–60, 68, 156–57, 195, 201, 260
  as public speaker, 165–66, 248, 262
  role models for, 57–58, 109, 149
  scrapbooks of, 109, 110–11, 118, 125, 134, 176
  sexual reserve of, 62, 115–17, 121–22
  sexual taste of, 122, 201–203
  teen years of, 29, 31–39, 40–41
  town planning projects of, 73, 191, 211, 214, 218, 224
  wealth of, 210
  writing as interest of, 54–55, 60–61, 62, 82, 84, 88, 91, 247–48
Mizner, Alice, 186, 256
Mizner, Edgar Ames:
  in Alaska, 65–68, 73, 74–75, 76, 79
  birth of, 23
  childhood of, 28–29, 34
  death of, 128
  and father's death, 52
  in Guatemala, 35, 36
  mother's hopes for, 85, 126, 128
  physical appearance of, 43
  in San Francisco, 42–43, 64–65
Mizner, Ella Watson (mother):
  Addison's support of, 111, 126–27, 141
  birth and background of, 14–17
  cathedral in memory of, 216, 227–28
  children of, 12, 22–23, 24, 27, 85
  community projects of, 23–24
  death of, 131–33
  Guatemala home of, 36–39, 45
  marriage of Lansing and, 17–19, 47
  and Minnie's marriage, 31–32
  money worries of, 53, 64, 85, 114, 126, 127
  personal traits of, 23, 132
  and San Francisco earthquake, 113–14
  shipwreck experience of, 15–17, 36, 113
Mizner, Frances Marion Taylor, 128
Mizner, Henry Caldwell (uncle), 12–13
Mizner, Henry Watson (brother), 12, 15, 186, 257
  in Boca Raton, 216, 224, 227, 228, 231, 236
  childhood of, 25, 28–29
  death of, 231
  religious career of, 64, 114, 129
  and Spanish-American War, 88
  as student, 35, 38, 51
  on Wilson's dishonesty, 77–78
Mizner, Lansing Bond (father):
  as Benicia citizen, 20–22, 24, 34, 132
  birth and background of, 12–14
  decline and death of, 47, 49, 52–53, 65, 132
  government appointment of, 33–36
  in Guatemala, 34–39, 44–45
  law practice of, 20, 23
  in local politics, 20, 21, 26, 30
  marriage of Ella and, 17–19, 47
  in Mexican War, 13, 15
  name of, 12
  personal traits of, 27
  Spanish language skill of, 13, 33, 36
Mizner, Lansing "Lan" (brother):
  birth of, 22

ABOUT THE AUTHOR

CAROLINE SEEBOHM is the author of several biographies, including *No Regrets: The Life of Marietta Tree* and *The Man Who Was Vogue: The Life & Times of Condé Nast*, as well as several illustrated books on art and architecture.

grandee

insouciantly

sangfroid /

fin-de-siecle